Spring 2006   Vol. XXVI, no. 1
ISSN: 0276-0045   ISBN: 1-56478-446-0

THE REVIEW OF CONTEMPORARY FICTION

Editor
JOHN O'BRIEN
Illinois State University

Managing Editor
JEREMY M. DAVIES

Associate Editor
IRVING MALIN

Guest Editor
DANIELLE ALEXANDER

Production & Design
N. J. FURL

Editorial Assistant
BENJAMIN KUEBRICH

Proofreader
SARAH McHONE-CHASE

Cover Photograph
JERRY BAUER

The *Review of Contemporary Fiction* is published three times a year
(January, June, September) by the Center for Book Culture.
ISSN 0276-0045.
Subscription prices are as follows:

Single volume (three issues):
Individuals: $17.00; foreign, add $3.50;
Institutions: $26.00; foreign, add $3.50.

DISTRIBUTION. Bookstores should send orders to:

Review of Contemporary Fiction, ISU Campus Box 8905,
Normal, IL 61790-8905. Phone 309-438-7555; fax 309-438-7422.

This issue is partially supported by a grant from
the Illinois Arts Council, a state agency.

Indexed in *American Humanities Index, International Bibliography of
Periodical Literature, International Bibliography of Book
Reviews, MLA Bibliography*, and *Book Review Index*. Abstracted
in *Abstracts of English Studies*.

The *Review of Contemporary Fiction* is also available on 16mm
microfilm, 35mm microfilm, and 105mm microfiche from
University Microfilms International, 300 North Zeeb Road,
Ann Arbor, MI 48106-1346.

www.centerforbookculture.org

THE REVIEW OF CONTEMPORARY FICTION

BACK ISSUES AVAILABLE

Back issues are still available for the following numbers of the *Review of Contemporary Fiction* ($8 each unless otherwise noted):

DOUGLAS WOOLF / WALLACE MARKFIELD
WILLIAM EASTLAKE / AIDAN HIGGINS
CAMILO JOSÉ CELA
CHANDLER BROSSARD
SAMUEL BECKETT
CLAUDE OLLIER / CARLOS FUENTES
JOSEPH MCELROY
JOHN BARTH / DAVID MARKSON
DONALD BARTHELME / TOBY OLSON
WILLIAM H. GASS / MANUEL PUIG
ROBERT WALSER
JOSÉ DONOSO / JEROME CHARYN
WILLIAM T. VOLLMANN / SUSAN DAITCH /
 DAVID FOSTER WALLACE
DJUNA BARNES
ANGELA CARTER / TADEUSZ KONWICKI
STANLEY ELKIN / ALASDAIR GRAY
BRIGID BROPHY / ROBERT CREELEY /
 OSMAN LINS
EDMUND WHITE / SAMUEL R. DELANY
MARIO VARGAS LLOSA / JOSEF ŠKVORECKÝ
WILSON HARRIS / ALAN BURNS
RAYMOND QUENEAU / CAROLE MASO
RICHARD POWERS / RIKKI DUCORNET
EDWARD SANDERS
WRITERS ON WRITING: THE BEST OF *THE REVIEW*
 OF CONTEMPORARY FICTION
BRADFORD MORROW
JEAN RHYS / JOHN HAWKES /
 PAUL BOWLES / MARGUERITE YOUNG

HENRY GREEN / JAMES KELMAN /
 ARIEL DORFMAN
JANICE GALLOWAY / THOMAS BERNHARD /
 ROBERT STEINER / ELIZABETH BOWEN
GILBERT SORRENTINO / WILLIAM GADDIS /
 MARY CAPONEGRO / MARGERY LATIMER
ITALO CALVINO / URSULE MOLINARO /
 B. S. JOHNSON
LOUIS ZUKOFSKY / NICHOLAS MOSLEY /
 COLEMAN DOWELL
CASEBOOK STUDY OF GILBERT
 SORRENTINO'S *IMAGINATIVE QUALITIES OF*
 ACTUAL THINGS
RICK MOODY / ANN QUIN /
 SILAS FLANNERY
DIANE WILLIAMS / AIDAN HIGGINS /
 PATRICIA EAKINS
DOUGLAS GLOVER / BLAISE CENDRARS /
 SEVERO SARDUY
ROBERT CREELEY / LOUIS-FERDINAND
 CÉLINE / JANET FRAME
WILLIAM H. GASS
GERT JONKE / KAZUO ISHIGURO /
 EMILY HOLMES COLEMAN
WILLIAM H. GASS / ROBERT LOWRY /
 ROSS FELD
FLANN O'BRIEN / GUY DAVENPORT /
 ALDOUS HUXLEY

NOVELIST AS CRITIC: Essays by Garrett, Barth, Sorrentino, Wallace, Ollier, Brooke-Rose, Creeley, Mathews, Kelly, Abbott, West, McCourt, McGonigle, and McCarthy

NEW FINNISH FICTION: Fiction by Eskelinen, Jäntti, Kontio, Krohn, Paltto, Sairanen, Selo, Siekkinen, Sund, and Valkeapää

NEW ITALIAN FICTION: Interviews and fiction by Malerba, Tabucchi, Zanotto, Ferrucci, Busi, Corti, Rasy, Cherchi, Balduino, Ceresa, Capriolo, Carrera, Valesio, and Gramigna

GROVE PRESS NUMBER: Contributions by Allen, Beckett, Corso, Ferlinghetti, Jordan, McClure, Rechy, Rosset, Selby, Sorrentino, and others

NEW DANISH FICTION: Fiction by Brøgger, Høeg, Andersen, Grøndahl, Holst, Jensen, Thorup, Michael, Sibast, Ryum, Lynggaard, Grønfeldt, Willumsen, and Holm

NEW LATVIAN FICTION: Fiction by Ikstena, Bankovskis, Berelis, Kolmanis, Neiburga, Ziedonis, and others

THE FUTURE OF FICTION: Essays by Birkerts, Caponegro, Franzen, Galloway, Maso, Morrow, Vollmann, White, and others ($15)

NEW JAPANESE FICTION: Interviews and fiction by Ohara, Shimada, Shono, Takahashi, Tsutsui, McCaffery, Gregory, Kotani, Tatsumi, Koshikawa, and others

Individuals receive a 10% discount on orders of one issue and a 20% discount on orders of two or more issues. To place an order, use the form on the last page of this issue.

Contents

Steven Millhauser _____ 7
Danielle Alexander, Pedro Ponce, Alicita Rodríguez

Cohabitation: On "Revenge," by Steven Millhauser _____ 77
Danielle Alexander

"a game we no longer understood": Theatrical Audiences
  in the Fiction of Steven Millhauser _____ 90
Pedro Ponce

Architecture and Structure in Steven Millhauser's
  Martin Dressler: The Tale of an American Dreamer _____ 110
Alicita Rodríguez

A Steven Millhauser Checklist _____ 127

Acknowledgments _____ 128

_____

Dear Editor _____ 129

Book Reviews _____ 141

Books Received _____ 155

Contributors _____ 159

Steven Millhauser

Danielle Alexander, Pedro Ponce, Alicita Rodríguez

Introduction

Since his debut in 1972, Steven Millhauser has published novels, short story collections, and novella collections to widespread critical acclaim and, until recently, little popular attention. When he earned the Pulitzer Prize in 1997 for his novel *Martin Dressler: The Tale of an American Dreamer*, many reviewers predicted a rise in his readership. A survey of Millhauser criticism shows a marked increase following this, though not nearly adequate to what he deserves. No book-length work on Millhauser or his craft, general or academic, exists in English. The French, however, have notably embraced Millhauser, producing two books on his work: an introductory overview of his oeuvre and a collection of essays presented at a 2004 conference at the University of Lille, which honored the addition of his story collection *The Knife Thrower and Other Stories* to the French national teacher examination program, which certifies secondary-school teachers in specialized areas—in this case, *lettres anglais* (literature in English). Besides a healthy amount of book reviews spanning his writing career, there are only five author interviews, approximately a dozen academic articles, a few book chapters, and two doctoral dissertations published in English that deal wholly or partly with Millhauser's fiction.

Part of the responsibility for the lack of notice lies with Millhauser himself, who generally refuses to publicize himself, a consequence of his strong belief that an author's work should speak for itself: "Unless a writer is a trained aesthetician, his opinion concerning the nature of fiction is of no more interest than his opinion concerning the nature of the economy" (qtd. in Schuessler 57). In an article entitled "Two Mandarin Stylists," J. D. O'Hara divides contemporary American fiction into two categories—Mandarin and Vernacular (complex and simple), placing Millhauser definitively in the first camp. O'Hara blames Millhauser's limited audience on poor readers: "readers nowadays tend to prefer Vernacular writers. This may be traced to the famous decline in American literacy, as a result of which linguistic and intellectual complexity baffles them. It may stem from our earnest moral confusion of simplicity with truth . . ." (250). That Millhauser has gained more readers in France certainly justifies O'Hara's claim. But American resistance to Millhauser is not entirely due to a lazy readership: his fiction also works against realism and minimalism, our most recent cultural and literary trends.

His tales, whether in the form of stories, novellas, or novels, manipulate reality, stretching it until it seeps into another realm—otherworldly, fantastic, and strange. They begin innocently enough in a recognizable setting, often the northeastern United States, usually Connecticut or New York, places where the author grew up or currently resides. Yet Millhauser's uncanny talent for meticulous description, rending from his individual and our collective memories the details of quotidian life, slowly, subtly transforms reality into dream. He favors places that defamiliarize and destabilize: museums, arcades, hotels, amusement parks, skyscrapers. Many of these settings house both the gigantic and the miniature, and size is an obsession of Millhauser's, because a shift in scale necessarily alters our perception of everyday things, granting them a magical quality that normally goes unnoticed:

> discrepancy of size is a form of distortion, and all forms of distortion shock us into attention: the inattentive and jaded eye, passing through a world without interest, helplessly perceives that something in a bland panorama is not as it should be. The eye is irritated into attention. It is compelled to perform an act of recognition. (Millhauser, "Fascination" 33)

Within these transgressive spaces, Millhauser displays his lists, catalogs of syntactical and allusive genius, "in which the dynamics of expectation/formation and surprise are carefully modulated" (Sheridan 12); in other words, a pattern, though initially detected, always unravels—"the sunny tall grass" and "milkweed pods and pink thistles" become "the far sound of a hand mower, like distant scissors" (*The Knife Thrower* 81). These enumerations also work toward betraying reality, because though they may seem exhaustive, they underscore the limitations of language: "The art of the list is that although it sustains and systematizes the world's mortal hoard, it confesses, without succumbing to, its own insufficiencies" (Saltzman, "Archives"). Lists imply a beyond, for there are always forgotten items, unstated and hovering in the margins. Millhauser's narrators also serve to break the illusion of realism. Their voices mimic a great spectrum of literary styles, undermining any initial certitude regarding our geographical and historical location. With narrators recalling writers as diverse as Byron, Nabokov, Swift, and Chaucer, Millhauser's milieus become contaminated by anachronism. Additionally, these narrators are often disaffected, despairing, and dissolving. Readers cannot always place them in relation to the narrative, most notably when they are first-person plural narrators, as in many of the stories in *The Knife Thrower*, a ghostly royal "we" who use distance to grant themselves false innocence.

Millhauser is a storyteller of the *Arabian Nights* variety, weaving tale after tale in order to keep himself alive, for the role of the artist is to survive his art. We see this preoccupation with creation throughout his work: from automaton-makers to painters, magicians to biographers, his characters use art to try to survive life. But therein lies the danger, for at times their art subsumes their reality, paradoxically destroying them. The artist's dilemma is analogous to Millhauser's, for both begin in reality and end somewhere less definable. The shift from real to dream, tangible to intangible, is barely perceptible—Millhauser's eerily crafted objects at once resemble reality and transcend it. His penchant for dreamlike spaces, relentless attention to minutiae, reliance on literary allusion, and use of unreliable and archaic narrators all work against facile generic classification, though it is clear that he shuns realism. And this, no doubt, contributes to his limited American audience:

> This predilection for the fabulous and self-delightedly artificial stands in sharp contrast to the lion's share of American stories and novels published in the last ten to fifteen years, for current fiction is almost always at pains to present itself as naturalistic in subject matter and plainspoken in technique, and it will almost never admit to an originating impulse deriving from literature itself. But it would be difficult to name a writer more exotic, fey, perversely playful, allusive, literary, structurally elaborate, and philosophically speculative than Millhauser. (Fowler, "Miniaturist" 5)

—A. R.

Biography

Because Steven Millhauser places such an emphasis on form, providing biographical information seems a sort of betrayal. In an interview with Marc Chénetier conducted in 2003, Millhauser stated: "By training and temperament I believe that the text is primary, that the reader must not bring to the text anything that isn't actually there." And yet the temptation to associate details from Millhauser's personal life with the motifs of his fiction lurks, especially given the relationship between his childhood in Connecticut and the quotidian details of his twelve-year-old narrator Jeffrey Cartwright in the novel *Edwin Mullhouse: The Life and Death of an American Writer, 1943-1954*: "Not to wax biographical . . . but surely Mullhouse is Millhauser's childhood self" (Postlethwaite 69). Even Millhauser cannot deny this relationship: "Everything I had to say about Stratford is in my first novel, though in a fractured, meticulously distorted way" (qtd. in Interview, *Bomb*). If the information that follows betrays the author, so be it. Betrayal, after all, is one of Millhauser's favorite themes, perhaps best explored in the novellas "Revenge" and "An Adventure of Don Juan."

"Shy Author Likes to Live and Work in Obscurity," the title of Dinitia Smith's 1997 article for the *New York Times*, justly reflects both the assessment of Millhauser's interviewers and the few critical essays published on Millhauser over his career. The sources fortunate enough to have corresponded with, spoken to, or actually seen him have established a number of facts. Steven Millhauser was born Steven Lewis Millhauser on 3 August 1943 in New York, though he grew up in Connecticut, where his father worked as an English professor at the University of Bridgeport. His mother is peculiarly absent from sources such as *Dictionary of Literary Biography*, though Millhauser himself has testified to her existence on at least two occasions, identifying her as a first-grade teacher (Interview, *Bomb*) and as a reader: "It's good to know that my ninety-year-old mother isn't my only reader" (Millhauser, "Re: Hello").

Many sources point out that Millhauser earned a B.A. from Columbia University in 1965, though few specify his major. Most peculiar is the treatment of his mysterious academic career, which is consistently minimized in statements such as "did graduate work at Brown University for three years" ("Steven Millhouser," *DLB*); or "A three-year period as a graduate student at Brown University followed" (Smith). The jacket of his first novel, *Edwin Mullhouse: The Life and Death of an American Writer, 1943-1954, by Jeffrey Cartwright*, tells us that "he entered the graduate school of Brown University, from which he is currently on leave." We know little of the period between his departure from graduate school and the publication in 1972 of *Edwin Mullhouse*. After two additional novels and one story collection, Millhauser began a professorial career as a visiting associate professor at Williams College from 1986 to 1988, then as an associate professor and later professor at Skidmore College from 1988 to the present. His wife, Cathy, we learn only from Smith, "creates crossword puzzles." Since the late 1980s, Millhauser has lived in Saratoga Springs in upstate New York (Schuessler 56), a fact that might account for his "east-coast regionalism" (Kasper 89).

According to Jeffrey Cartwright, the narrator/biographer of *Edwin Mullhouse*, the biographer's job consists of order and inclusion: "Calmly and methodically, in one fell swoop, in a way impossible for the harried novelist who is always trying to do a hundred things at once, he can simply say what he has to say, ticking off each item with his right hand on the successively raised fingers of his left" (54). In this regard, the short biography of Steven Millhauser is now complete.

But Jeffrey Cartwright consistently and progressively shatters biographical objectivity by intruding into the story he tells, eventually changing the course of his subject's life by ending it, for his subject must be dead in order for his biography to attain closure: "The three-part division of his life had already established itself in my mind" (281). Undoubtedly, Steven Millhauser must periodically impose himself onto his fiction, as he himself admits: "many details of setting are based on my memory of particular streets and houses and rooms—and because memory itself is a form of history, these stories too may be said to have an historical basis" ("An Interview"). From this point forward, we will focus on Millhauser's work, keeping in mind that his ghostly presence may in fact be haunting it.

—A. R.

Novels

Edwin Mullhouse: The Life and Death of an American Writer, 1943-1954, by Jeffrey Cartwright (1972)

Steven Millhauser's first novel, published in 1972 by Knopf, won France's Prix Medicis Etranger and earned the author "rave reviews" (Schuessler 57); it did not, however, catapult Millhauser into the literary consciousness of America. Like much of Millhauser's work, *Edwin Mullhouse* is difficult to categorize, which may help to account for its popular and scholarly marginalization. The novel is a mock biography of Edwin Mullhouse, the narrator's childhood friend and author of *Cartoons*, a novel completed just before his eleventh birthday. Jeffrey Cartwright meticulously documents Edwin's life and times, organizing the biography into three major sections: "THE EARLY YEARS (Aug. 1, 1943-Aug. 1, 1949)," "THE MIDDLE YEARS (Aug. 2, 1949-Aug. 1, 1952)," and "THE LATE YEARS (Aug. 2, 1952-Aug. 1, 1954)." But Jeffrey increasingly becomes the center of his own story, a tendency that questions the claim of biographical objectivity and, by extension, the relationship between fact and fiction: "Jeffrey Cartwright is a classic unreliable narrator who constantly intrudes into his autobiography by calling attention to himself, his own wondrous memory, and his devotion to biography" (Adams 208).

Edwin Mullhouse is most often labeled a parody of literary biography (Smith; "Steven Millhauser," *DLB*; "Steven Millhauser," *CLC*; Boyd 35; Simson 74). Jeffrey's ironic voice and elevated language justify this interpretation, for he seems bent on lampooning "biography's conventions . . . in revisionist fashion" (Herreiro-Olaizola 78). In fact, his egoism and quirkiness grant him comparison to high literary stock: "Jeffrey is a Nabokovian child" (Rev. of *Edwin Mullhouse* 30); "Created out of literary DNA cloned from Nabokov's nutty, charming, sinister narrators" (Fowler, "Postmodern Promise" 78); "Not since Vladimir Nabokov set Dr. Charles Kinbote loose to wreak havoc on poet John Shade's heroic couplets in *Pale Fire* has there been a more deliciously loony literary critic than Jeffrey Cartwright" (Postlethwaite 68). At least one critic disagrees with the Nabokovian analogy, finding *Edwin Mullhouse* more akin to Thomas Mann's *Doctor Faustus: The Life of the German Composer Adrian Leverkühn, as Told by a Friend* (Rieckmann 62). Regardless of Jeffery's literary ancestry, his role as biographer is suspect. There is no doubt that Jeffrey cannot be trusted; he looms in the shadows like a cancer in remission: "Fortunately it has been my policy in this work to huddle modestly in the background except when my presence is absolutely necessary for the illumination of some facet of Edwin's life" (236). But Jeffrey interferes again and again until he finally drives Edwin to suicide; when Edwin loses his nerve, Jeffrey pulls the trigger for him, so that Edwin will have died at the height of his literary career, making his novel the "immortal masterpiece" required by the biographer (260). A less than subtle hint underscores Jeffrey's part in Edwin's death, as he admits in his preface that he did "all the dirty work."

The comparison to Nabokov is strengthened by the book's "Introductory Note," penned by Walter Logan White, one of Jeffrey's former classmates—now a professor who resurrects the biography, "proclaiming [it] to be a modern classic" (viii); and the "Preface to the First Edition," signed J. C., a condescending rant written in elevated language: "Let me say at once that in this instance there are none to thank besides myself" (xi). Millhauser piles on layer after layer of voices: the stilted formalism of nineteenth-century literary biography, the sly unreliability of a postmodern narrator, the inflated rhetoric of academic criticism. In *Beyond Suspicion*, Marc Chénetier discusses how the novel's allusive multiplicity rescues it from "mere cuteness": "It is these other voices, as much as the remarkable, uncompromising representation of an overly mythologized universe, that save the world of childhood from the clichés of popular culture, from the mush of preconceptions, and from the stereotypes of psychology and sociology" (247). The verbal tiers also contribute to the novel's comedy, for "much of the humor consists of the literary method as it contrasts with the trivial or mundane situation being described" (Pearson 146). With utmost seriousness, Jeffrey recounts Edwin's first years, his drooling and pointing, and his senseless exclamations, such as his early memorization of Dickens: "It wuzza besta time, it wuzza wussa time, it wuzza age a whiz, it wuzza age a foo!" (37). Moments like these should negate the idea that *Edwin Mullhouse* is an earnest study of the romantic splendors and unspoiled innocence of childhood.

However, it cannot be denied that the novel is, in some measure, an acute study of childhood. Accomplished through exceptional detail, this evocation of the formative years tempts many reviewers into categorizing *Edwin Mullhouse* as realism, a false comfort at best, for Millhauser uses quotidian reality to achieve the fantastic. Millhauser's details are not only incredibly specific, but also overwhelmingly abundant. Jeffrey describes the minutiae of Edwin's room, from its wallpaper—"The matte wallpaper, pebbled to the touch, contained a series of six vertical maroon lines crossed by a repeated series of four horizontal maroon lines on a silver-gray background"—to its wall map—"a map of the United States in full color, showing fish and steamships in the dark blue oceans, a palm tree in Florida, a skyscraper in New York, an ear of corn in Iowa, an Indian in Arizona, a log in Oregon, and nothing in Connecticut" (69). Every contour and accoutrement of their first-grade classroom is accounted for; every book Edwin ever read; every girl Edwin ever loved.

Millhauser's cataloging in *Edwin Mullhouse* has led some reviewers to facile conclusions, such as calling the novel "a heartfelt evocation of childhood" (Simson 74). In his 1996 article in *Critique*, "Steven Millhauser, Miniaturist," Douglas Fowler addresses this misconception, outlining how Millhauser's powers of description ultimately reveal something deeper: "Just as with Nabokov, a story that seems at first merely a parody turns out to culminate in serious philosophic speculation—with Millhauser, literary parody is often the cradle of his inspiration." But where is *Edwin Mullhouse*'s philosophical dialogue? The answer lies in Jeffrey's theory of *"scrupulous distortion,"* by which he explains the appeal of *Cartoons*: "For by the method of scrupulous distortion, Edwin draws attention to things that have been rendered invisible to us by overmuch familiarity. . . . We are shocked by distortion into the sudden perception of the forgotten strangeness of things" (265-66).

If we expand Jeffrey's analysis of Edwin's novel into a metafictional instruction for how to read Millhauser's novel, then we realize that everyday objects, once refracted by an author's perception, become magical. Jeffrey's scrupulous distortion is not unlike Victor Shklovsky's "technique of defamiliarization," wherein "Art removes objects from the automatism of perception" (219); or Julio Cortázar's "Instruction Manual," which asks that the "indifferent vigor of a daily reflex" be replaced by renewed focus (3). Millhauser himself takes up these very critical ideas in an interview with Marc Chénetier where he desires for his readers "to grow more and more estranged from the familiar" in order to "see things usually obscured by habit." *Edwin Mullhouse* should not be confused with the simple tale of an American childhood. Millhauser's elaborate details exist to alter the reader's reality; the microscopic focus that they demand lends the objects an unfamiliar strangeness.

Portrait of a Romantic (1977)

Through the use of a first-person narrator suffering from depression, boredom, and intelligence, *Portrait of a Romantic* continues Millhauser's fascination with heightened states of consciousness. Arthur Grumm, the twenty-nine-year-old voice of the novel, reflects on his life between the ages of twelve to fifteen—a time in which he cheated death while his best friend (much like Edwin Mullhouse) succumbed to it. Once again, the temptation exists to equate Grumm with Millhauser, perpetuating the fallacy that fiction is thinly veiled memoir. More astute critics recognize the layering of voices that works to separate the author from his subject and Grumm from himself: Millhauser "avoids the vulgarities of sincerity in part by distancing himself from the voices of his fiction" (O'Hara, "Mandarin" 252). This is accomplished through dialogic allusion, recalling authors as disparate as Joyce and Poe, not to mention a prowling Nabokov. Another mistake critics make is to classify the novel as an American bildungsroman, meant to "tell you some grim truths about adulthood" (O'Hara, "Portrait" 1679). While the similarities between *Portrait of a Romantic* and a coming-of-age novel cannot be entirely discounted—Arthur faces "problems not unconnected to those experienced by Salinger's Holden Caulfield and Glass children"—*Portrait of a Romantic* effectively eliminates the viability of this comparison through its multiplicity of voices: "But the irony here is more integrated to the voice, the sarcasm and self-criticism make themselves heard beneath Arthur Grumm's 'romantic' sighs" (Chénetier, *Suspicion* 247). As in *Edwin Mullhouse*, Millhauser manipulates the stratified voices to effect parody.

   Arthur Grumm the narrator is not Arthur Grumm the character, for the narrator re-creates himself as a protagonist, thereby giving "a fictitious account" of his own life (Smith). In large part, Arthur accomplishes this refashioning through the use of an exaggerated, writerly voice that is immediately apparent in the novel's opening paragraph: "Mother of myself, myself I sing: lord of loners, duke of dreams, king of the clowns. Youth and death I sing, sunbeams and moonbeams, laws and breakers of laws. I, Arthur Grumm, lover and killer" (1). His voice serves two purposes: it parodies romanticism and underscores his unreliability. The "cloak of romanticism" ("Steven Millhauser," *DLB*) conceals—attempts to conceal—his culpability in the death of his best friend, William Mainwaring, with whom he makes a suicide pact. For pages, Arthur reminisces in paratactic images while William holds a gun in preparation:

And then, the first time I saw you, it was in the bus, you were sitting in back, I couldn't see you too well, but then, when I was standing on the sidewalk . . . then we became friends, mother always said you were a well-behaved boy, remember the time we, and that summer, the bush-house, we had some good times together, you were always my best, and I'll never, but you were always, you never . . . and you were always so reserved, William, you never . . . of course I'm not expressing myself well, I realize that. . . . (309-10)

Arthur's words serve only to call attention to the words he refuses to speak, which would prevent William's death.

Some critics have found this voice problematic in its self-indulgence: "His [Arthur's] clear fictive attraction to the saturated longueurs of E. A. Poe . . . is always derailed by Millhauser's impulse to parody the *ennui* without curtailing the techniques that produce it" (Kinzie 124). Other readers, however, find that Arthur's voice works in concert with Millhauser's, "recurrently reminding the reader to keep a safe distance" (O'Hara, "Mandarin" 252). We must remember that the narrative action and the narrative voice serve to illuminate the conflict between fact and fiction. As with *Edwin Mullhouse*, in which the subject must die for the biography to gain life, *Portrait of a Romantic* "crystallizes the sinister usurpation of life by art" (Fowler, "Postmodern" 79).

Millhauser further stresses this dichotomy through his use of the theme of the double. Arthur instantly recognizes William as his likeness: "I first saw my double in the seventh grade" (24). The two boys are henceforth continually conflated, notably through the motif of the shadow, which consequently foreshadows William's death, for the protagonist must kill his shadow, who threatens to overtake him. The night wanderings of Arthur and William exploit this theme. When Arthur first sees William return to his house, the garage door fragments him: ". . . I caught a last glimpse of him standing in the garage, disappearing from top to bottom as the big white door came down" (59). Later Arthur will sneak into and William will sneak out of that garage door, allowing Millhauser to cut and splice the boys and their shadows: "When I came to the glowing blue-white garage door at the side of the house, my shadow leaped up and towered over me" (74). Millhauser further complicates this theme by a "doubling-of-the-double," (Kinzie 119) as Arthur meets his triple, Phillip Schoolcraft, a morose boy addicted to Russian roulette. Of course, William hates Phillip, for Phillip then serves as William's double, who threatens his existence (for some time, Arthur stops being friends with William in order to befriend Phillip). Throughout the novel, Millhauser repeats sentences verbatim, further emphasizing the theme of the double.

Perhaps the best evocation of Millhauser's penchant for doubling and repetition occurs in the section of the novel dealing with Eleanor,

Arthur's love interest, a sickly girl who lives in her room at the top of two flights of stairs, amid a collection of dolls, which all serve as her doubles: "Imagine Emmeline Grangerford in a set by Poe as described by Robbe-Grillet, and you have Eleanor at home" (Stade 13). Eleanor emphasizes Millhauser's debt to the nineteenth-century uncanny, as all that is familiar soon turns strange. Her awesome collection of dolls, costumes, and toys creates a "confusion between the animate and inanimate" (Millhauser, "Questions"). Eleanor's house is also doubled by a secret room with a gabled dollhouse that she calls "The Childhood Museum," which is further doubled by another secret room that leads to a maze of passageways and rooms full of abandoned clothes and toys. All of this doubling serves to confuse the reader, so that every original that becomes doubled—Eleanor by dolls, her house by the dollhouse, her childhood self by her future adult self (who is lurking just beyond her present adolescence)—eventually seems a shadow. Millhauser uses toys particularly to evoke the uncanny:

> Every child knows that the bear is stuffed, the dollhouse fake; at the same time, the bear is completely alive, the dollhouse more real than the actual house, since both are animated in every particle of their being by the force of the child's imagination. A further development of the uncanny occurs when the child grows up—the old toys, dusty and dead, still give off a tremor of the life that once flowed through them. ("Questions")

In the section of the novel featuring Eleanor, Millhauser manipulates her toys as an expert puppeteer, using them to voice the most salient properties of all that we consider uncanny.

From the moment of her appearance, Eleanor is ghostly, always disappearing. She even seems to have phantom limbs: "And different parts of her would seem to go their own way, as if she failed to watch over all of them at the same time" (150). In his dealings with Eleanor, Arthur becomes her double, so that he becomes perpetually tired and ill, as if her mysterious sickness were contagious. This allows Eleanor to get better, and she must finally cast him away in order to remain healthy. Arthur then reunites with William, again his shadow, who must die in order for Arthur to survive.

On the surface, *Portrait of a Romantic* continues Millhauser's treatment of childhood into an examination of adolescence. More importantly, his second novel continues his fascination with layering allusion and voice, so that the two novels enter into dialogue with each other. This drives his own body of work into its own deconstruction. What George Stade of the *New York Times Book Review* says about *Portrait of a Romantic* is equally true about Millhauser's twin first novels: "Once you reread the book the particulars begin to look different. The foreshadowings become luminous with afterglow" (30).

From the Realm of Morpheus (1986)

Steven Millhauser's third novel, *From the Realm of Morpheus*, was rejected by Knopf because "the manuscript was over 1,000 pages long and Mr. Millhauser refused to cut it" (Smith). Millhauser now admits that "In its original form, the book was a long error"—an error that lured him toward "shorter forms," which avoided his "disenchantment with the aggression of length" ("Questions"). Once Millhauser shortened the novel, Morrow published it in 1986, the same year as his short story collection, *In the Penny Arcade*. To date, the novel has received little attention from reviewers and critics alike; in fact, not one full-length analysis of *From the Realm of Morpheus* has been published. The lack of scholarship seems odd, for the novel is a veritable collage of literary allusions and styles; Millhauser explains that "The novel itself is highly allusive because its presiding spirit is the god of dreams, who in my view is the source of all imaginative creation; the novel, among other things, is supposed to be a kind of *summa* of the imagination" ("Questions"). At the onset of the novel, Carl Hausman, a bored young man of unspecified age, follows a baseball into the underworld where he meets Morpheus, god of dreams, who serves as his guide. The underworld, for all its oddities, exists as a double and reflection of the real world (Porée 10); here again we witness Millhauser's hovering between two realms, his characteristic conflation of dream and reality. During the course of their wanderings, which serve as a narrative frame, Carl meets various denizens of the deep, so that his journey gets interrupted again and again by the interpolated tales that—"like Aeneas, like Dante"—he faithfully records (Dirda, "Journey").

Carl Hausman proves to be an exceedingly calm voyager, always able to provide the most exacting details even while unsure of the nature of his surroundings and whether he will ever return to the upper world. Take the very moment of his fall: "I had proceeded in this manner for about fifteen paces when the wall unexpectedly gave way to empty space and I nearly fell; for a moment I had the sensation of hovering at the edge of the abyss" (19). As his tour of the underworld progresses, Carl becomes more and more infected with the speech and manner of his guide Morpheus, whose voice cannot easily be classified though it's been called "pseudo-Falstaffian Elizabethan lingo" (Crowley). Morpheus sees himself as a logophile: "Lover of words and lecher of words, licking my tongue into the dark crannies of syllables, lapping up secret juices, rooting with my swine-snout in the warm moist furrows, guzzling and snorting, licking my chops" (42). The overt sexual wordplay reveals the second vital element of his character: Morpheus is a Don Juan, a rake, a "charming rogue" (38). Two of the interpolated stories are Morpheus's, "The Tale of

Morpheus and Volumnia," recounting his cuckolding by a virtuous maiden and the evils of marriage, and "The Tale of Morpheus and Vivayne," describing his sexual conquest of one mermaid and his spurning by another. These stories give Morpheus the chance to indulge in self-pity—exclaiming "'Sdeath" and "'Sblood"—and the opportunity to discuss his views on the female gender: "for though a woman be upright, yet at last she will lie down on her back, and wooing, wed, or wild, what matter" (197). In her review for the *New York Times*, Michiko Kakutani views this as a character flaw: "And Morpheus . . . is really little but a boring male chauvinist who likes to carry on at length about the physical attributes of women and the horrors of domesticity" (2). Of course, this type of assessment ignores the self-referential playfulness intended by Millhauser. Morpheus's chauvinism is ironic, for in fact he makes a poor Don Juan—in one scene he repeatedly capitulates to the desires of his capricious and unfaithful wife, and in another he safeguards the giantess Ekli's feelings by admonishing Carl, who has been ambiguous about his own romantic intentions for her. The stories-within-the-story soon challenge the initial characterizations of Morpheus and Carl.

The narrative conceit of *From the Realm of Morpheus* has been compared to that of "the *Arabian Nights* or the *Canterbury Tales*" (Dirda, "Journey"). And it is within these fanciful stories that Millhauser displays his literary ancestry and adaptability. The first tale, perhaps the best, is "The Tale of Ignotus," a melancholy artist who comes alive out of his portrait. Labeled "a tale worthy of E. T. A. Hoffman" (Dirda, "Journey") and "like something thought up by E. T. A. Hoffman" (Crowley 2), this story explores the relationship between art and life. In typical Millhauser style, the theme of doubling appears, as there is an artist who paints an artist, the Ignotus of the title, who looks real and then becomes real; in fact, he can shift among two to three dimensions at will. Unfortunately, Ignotus's ability to come to life is discovered, and he is blackmailed, forced by a mediocre magician to perform the trick of exiting from and reentering the painting on stage. Of course, from the moment of his conception, the artist is doomed, for the artist who created the artist infused him with his own soul-sighing. When Carl first sees the painting, he comments: "I was thinking that the very idea of suffering has about it a touch of boastfulness—of irritating self-display—of emotion a little too pleased with itself—not to mention an air of special pleading" (58). What makes this story so remarkable is Millhauser's ironic treatment of the theme, for Ignotus is "a stock character whose romantic agony it is to recognize himself as such" (Crowley). Recalling Byron, Wilde, and Mérimée, "The Tale of Ignotus" shows that artifice can ultimately reveal hidden meaning.

The remainder of the tales showcases a who's who of world literature. "The Library of Morpheus" is rather Borgesian, housing the endings of famous unfinished masterpieces, the writings of fictional characters, and all the books lost from all lost civilizations. There are flying books, books whose characters interact with each other, books to be eaten, and books that devour you. When Carl takes a bite from DICKENS, it tastes "like roast lamb, peas, and mashed potatoes with gravy" (134). In "Mirror Tales," we recognize more of Borges, as well as the story of Snow White. The title giants of "The Tale of Heklo and Ekli" come from fairy tales. Carl and Morpheus get swallowed by a whale in "The Tale of the City in the Sea," alluding to the Bible, but this chapter merges into the story of the lost civilization of Atlantis, where the palace artists reconstruct the entire kingdom in miniature; this seems a direct reference to Borges's short fiction "Parable of the Palace," in which the actual Chinese palace disappears once the poet has finished reconstructing it in all its detail (44-45). In the last story, "The Tale of a Voyage to the Moon," the cities of the moon put one in mind of Calvino's *Invisible Cities*: "On the plain itself I saw several upside-down cities. These cities appeared to rest on the tops of their tallest trees, whose roots passed into a thick upper layer of white soil" (359). There are references to classical and medieval texts, Renaissance and Restoration drama, Pope and Swift: "Mr. Millhauser is parodying a whole body of literature one would have thought it impossible to re-create" (Crowley).

From the Realm of Morpheus is a dialogue with the Western canon. Carl and Morpheus may take readers on a tour of the underworld, but what they show us is words—a history of the manipulation of words. There are those reviewers who find the novel's intertextual drive tedious: "The danger, which Mr. Millhauser skirts throughout and does not entirely escape, is of being taken over by one's own skill at pastiche, enjoying for its own sake the re-creation of bypassed modes, and thus creating what is in effect one more book of a kind that few care to read any longer, even in the original versions" (Crowley). However, others attribute the book's "clever invention" to its wealth of allusions (Dooley 216). In his article "Replicas," Steven Millhauser explains the nature of the replica: "To begin with, the replica is a haunted object. It is always accompanied by the thought of a second object, the original, to which it ceaselessly refers" (51). Because a replica recalls an original, it always implies a relationship between something familiar and its ghostly double. *From the Realm of Morpheus* can be seen as a replica wherein we see the magician's sleight of hand behind his meticulously detailed act—this revelation of duplicity elevates it to a creation in its own right.

Martin Dressler: The Tale of an American Dreamer (1996)

When Steven Millhauser received a note from his department chair informing him to call a reporter "re: Pulitzer," he informed his students that "a grotesque error had been committed" (Smith). But *Martin Dressler: The Tale of an American Dreamer* did earn the Pulitzer Prize in 1997, an honor that increased Millhauser's cultural collateral: "Millhauser is now beginning to receive public attention commensurate with the critical acclaim his short stories and two previous novels . . . have already garnered" (Saltzman, "Wilderness" 591). Published in 1996 by Crown, the novel recounts the rise (and fall) of Martin Dressler, an American entrepreneur in New York during the late nineteenth and early twentieth centuries. If that sounds like a rather mundane description for a Millhauser fiction, it's because it neglects to mention what business Martin Dressler is in, and how Steven Millhauser tells his story. By concentrating on the skeleton of its plot, critics and readers often simplify an otherwise complex novel. The narrative voice, an almost reportorial third person, also complicates the novel's reception by creating the illusion of realism. *Martin Dressler*'s chameleon-like multiplicity allows for various levels of reading and interpretation, so that its genre is always in question.

When we first meet Martin, he is working at his father's tobacco store, inventing window displays to lure customers inside, in tune at a young age to the marketing of desire. His industrious and polite character quickly secures him a job as a hotel clerk, where his love affair with "great, elaborate structure" begins (24). Martin uses his business savvy, which is largely based on deciphering people's subconscious wants, to open a cigar stand in the hotel lobby, then to start a chain of restaurants, but he tires of every venture as soon as it succeeds, eventually finding his niche as a hotelier. The complex "architectural erudition" (Mangaliman) grants the novel a new life; it is the vehicle for the fantastic, as Martin's hotels become more and more elaborate, labyrinthine, and dreamlike, providing an ideal opportunity for Millhauser to exhibit his cataloging skills. Martin's vision culminates in the Grand Cosmo, a "constantly shifting Borgesian structure" that seeks to replace the real world by encapsulating it (Bradfield 23). Running parallel to Martin's architectural construction is his romantic development, which begins with his seduction by an older hotel guest, continues with his visits to a brothel, and ends with his relationship with the Vernon women, a trio composed of a mother and two contrasting daughters, one of whom he marries. Like his hotels, with their contradictory impulses toward the technological and the nostalgic, the practical and the fanciful, the real and the unreal, his twin "wives"—one fair, one dark; one ethereal, one tangible; one sickly, one healthy—satisfy his drive for duality.

Despite Millhauser's own contention that the novel's "profoundest impulse" is its "push toward the fantastic, the impossible," many reviewers distill the novel into realism (Barrineau 36). *Martin Dressler* has been called a "historical novel" (McQuade 1343), as well as "Dreiserian realism" (Barrineau 36). The comparisons to Horatio Alger are too numerous to count, and one reviewer sees Martin as a fully developed character and product of his era: Millhauser "introduces the scenery and feeling of the times and provides a psychological portrait of an American dreamer named Martin Dressler" (Irvine 123). However, Martin's emotions are told to us in broad sweeps—"An excitement came over him" (2), "he felt that an understanding had been reached: they liked each other" (76), "But he was pleased" (209)—leading another reviewer to conclude that "The characters are intentionally rather shadowy" (Rifkind A12). There are at least as many alternative readings likening the novel to "a fairy tale" (Birkerts 145), "an urban fable" (Sheppard), and "a fable" and "subgenre of fairy tale" (Burroway). One look at Martin Dressler's opening supports the latter view: "There once lived a man named Martin Dressler, a shopkeeper's son, who rose from modest beginnings to a height of dreamlike good fortune" (1). One reason some critics classify the novel as realism is the voice, whose "third-person narrator retains a cool distance from his protagonist" (Charles). The narrator's detachment conceals the subtle shift into Millhauser's version of the fantastic, which is always a hovering, a wavering between the realms of substance and dream, a liminal state that one critic has likened to a Calder mobile (Roudeau 13-14). In one scene early in the novel, Martin spies actors in the Vanderlyn Hotel:

> In the elevator, which suddenly began to fall, so that Martin stumbled back against a bench, Charley explained that a troupe of actors and actresses had rented a row of rooms on the fifth floor. They liked to rehearse at strange hours, sometimes they didn't come in till four in the morning, you saw all kinds of queer things in this line of work, and as Martin stepped out into the hot sunlight of the street he recalled with sudden vividness a curious detail: through one of the half-open doors he had seen the corner of a bed with a pair of crossed feet on it, one of which was naked and white and one of which wore a shiny black button-up shoe. (12)

This scene encapsulates several of the novel's obsessions: performativity, voyeurism, and bodily fragmentation (as with *Portrait*). When asked about these themes, Millhauser explains how they work against realism:

If I rely on such themes elsewhere [in other books], it must be because a writer is always, like Martin, a kind of demiurge, creating worlds that are separate from the writer's self, while also using that self to nourish those worlds—hence performance, spying, the self-destruction at the heart of creation.

Realism, which I reject and revere, assumes a solidity of identity, a fixity of external appearances, that is actively undermined by the themes you mention. (Millhauser, "Questions")

Many of these themes are developed through Martin's hotels, which exist to contaminate reality with slippage—a subtle confrontation of the reality of fictional space.

In *Martin Dressler*, Millhauser uses architecture to fulfill the fantastic. His hotels grow larger and larger, both up toward the sky and down into the underground, as they increasingly showcase the ornamental and the strange. The hotels become all-inclusive, broadening into atypical spaces recalling museums, department stores, and amusement parks:

It was noted that among the public rooms of the first two floors . . . was a scattering of peculiar rooms that seemed to be there to amuse or instruct. Thus there was a circular theater in which a panorama of the entire Manhattan shoreline continually unwound; a room containing a wigwam, a wax squaw gathering sticks, a young brave hacking a rock with a sharpened stone tool, and a seated chief smoking a long pipe, set against a painted background depicting a riverbank; and a hall called the Pageant of Industry and Invention, which contained working scale models of an Otis elevator, a steam train on an Elevated track, a Broadway cable car, and a steam crane lifting an I-beam, as well as full-scale models of a steam turbine, an internal combustion engine, and an electric generator with a drive pulley. (207-08)

The progression of the hotels into odd self-contained worlds allows Millhauser to showcase his talent for description, often in the form of lists. Here again this technique leads to the problem of generic confusion: for every reader who sees this as realistic period detail, there is at least another who views it as fantastic imagism. But matter should not be confused with substance; naming objects does not make them tangible. We must remember that these objects are composed of words, which are no more substantive than the imagination from which they emerge: "Despite their apparent commitment to the real, lists are also well-suited to the atmosphere of dreams" (Saltzman, "Archives").

The focus on architecture is taken up often in reviews and critical articles, which most often interpret it metaphorically. In "Performing the Spectacle of Technology at the Beginning of the American

Century: Steven Millhauser's *Martin Dressler*," Udo J. Hebel argues that the novel's architecture corresponds to the American drive toward technological innovation and its performativity during the turn of the century: *Martin Dressler* "fictionalizes the historic moment when the spread of modern technology merged with the collective impulse to theatricalize American culture as an 'imperial spectacle'" (192). Hebel makes a good case, following America's skyscraper fever and world's fair construction boom, though the focus on technology is too narrow, wholly ignoring the fantastic elements of Martin's hotels: for example, how does one explain the existence of an entire "Victorian resort hotel" within a hotel (260)? Critic Arthur Saltzman takes Hebel's argument one step further, attributing the construction in the novel to an American impulse toward the sublime in which "size may be championed as a validation of American birthright and destiny" ("Wilderness" 590). Many reviews approximate this idea by treating the hotels as metaphors for the American Dream, thereby reading *Martin Dressler* as allegory. In such interpretations, there is a lesson to be learned in Martin's drive for the bigger and better—"What does the book say about the American dream?" (Cusac). Perhaps "that the glitter and glory don't finally matter that much" (Birkerts 148). An allegorical reading is reductive: "To call *Martin Dressler* a cautionary tale about the lures of American capitalism would be to misunderstand the book's intentions" (Rifkind A12).

One good look at the Grand Cosmo reveals a dissolving realism, for while it houses "a very efficient laundry service," it also features "the Palace of Wonders, in which were displayed a two-headed calf, a caged griffin, a mermaid in a dark pool, the Human Anvil, a school of trained goldfish fastened by fine wires to toy boats in order to enact naval battles" (261-62). Martin's last hotel fails because it tries to contain the entire world, replacing reality with the illusion of reality. But illusion only enchants when it serves as an antidote to reality. In the Grand Cosmo, all reality appears as illusion, so that "which world is real and which simulacrum ceases to matter" (McLaughlin 186)—"the artificial and the real have exchanged places" (Burroway). This conflation of reality and dream deceives some readers, so that they are blind to the novel's more uncanny elements. What sets Millhauser's novel "apart from the formula it complements . . . is the incursion of the supernatural, the fantastic, and the fabulous into the conventional success story, with its solid foundation upon real-world capital and a burgeoning portfolio" (Saltzman, "Wilderness" 593). In reading *Martin Dressler*, we cannot note the efficient laundry service at the cost of ignoring the caged griffin.

—A. R.

Short Stories

In Steven Millhauser's "The Dream of the Consortium," the first-person plural narrator describes not only the reopened department store of the title but, arguably, the reader's experience of Millhauser's short fiction collections:

> We who have grown up with the old department stores know that one of their secret pleasures is the sudden, violent transitions between departments, the startling juxtapositions, as in the kind of museum where a room full of old fire engines opens into a hall lined with glass cases containing owls, herons, and sandpipers. In the new department store we saw the art of juxtaposition raised to bold and unexpected heights. . . . (*The Knife Thrower* 129)

Patrons are intrigued by the striking conjunction of rolltop desks and leggy mannequins, refrigerators and women's underwear: "Such transitions and confusions seemed to invite us to lose our way . . . and we who wanted nothing better than to lose our way plunged deeper into the winding aisles, grateful for anything that increased our sense of the store's abundance, that satisfied our secret longing for an endless multiplication of departments" (130-31). This sense of abundance is explored by Arthur Saltzman, who refers to Millhauser as "one of contemporary fiction's most assiduous list makers" (*This Mad "Instead"* 50). The paradoxical quality of lists—"conspicuous interfaces where art and life, system and surge, the magical and mundane coalesce"—extends, Saltzman argues, to the varied settings of "Millhauser's arcades, museums, malls, exhibition halls, galleries, chambered bookshops and mansions, and other esoteric collectives of insidious geometry and infinite regress" (50).

In the Penny Arcade, The Barnum Museum, The Knife Thrower and Other Stories—each offers the reader an eclectic series of displays and spectacles. If, as Saltzman points out, Millhauser's settings are analogous to the structure and limits of the list, so are Millhauser's collections themselves, which work through evocative juxtaposition to present different permutations of related themes.

In the Penny Arcade (1986)

Readers familiar with the narrative play of *Edwin Mullhouse* or the epic scale of *Martin Dressler* might be surprised by the contents of *In the Penny Arcade*, Millhauser's first story collection, originally published by Knopf in 1986. Included between the fictional life story of automaton-maker August Eschenburg and the surreal aftermath of a winter storm in "Snowmen," three stories display a striking realist style. "A Protest Against the Sun" recounts a young girl's day at the beach with her parents. In "The Sledding Party," Catherine hears her longtime friend Peter declare his love, an overture that infuriates and paralyzes her. The rural retreat taken by Judith in "A Day in the Country" ends with her confronting a profound unhappiness. These stories prompted Bruce Allen, reviewing the collection in the *Saturday Review,* to describe Millhauser as a writer "interested in people overpowered by their intelligence and their emotional resources" and "a sensitive analyst of late-adolescent angst and self-consciousness" (74). Meanwhile, Thomas Lavoie cited Joyce and Updike in describing how the title story "shows us a young boy discovering adolescence" (104).

Millhauser himself sees the eclecticism of his debut collection as an intentional experiment: "I had written several stories in a certain style, to which I felt I was saying farewell, and I chose to isolate them, to surround them with stories of a different type, in order to throw their existence into question" ("Questions"). In this sense, the realistic pieces in *Penny Arcade* represent a significant turning point for Millhauser's evolving style:

> It was a kind of homage to a certain kind of fiction I knew I wasn't going to write. Having said that, I can't help noticing that I returned to it, in a way, quite recently in [the novella] "Revenge." In general I see myself moving further and further away from psychological realism—a technique I profoundly admire, but one that seems to me exhausted. ("Questions")

Of course, any surprise felt at Millhauser's experiments with realism says more about the limits of critical labels than about the distinct features of the author's work. If we are induced to marvel at the creations of August Eschenburg or the increasingly elaborate snow sculptures built by the characters in "Snowmen," it is due to their realistic texture on the page. David Leavitt observes of the collection's concluding story, "Millhauser's Vermeerian gift for the tableau-vivant rendering of detail is given full reign [sic] in the odd and beautiful 'Cathay,' less a story than a catalog of wonders from a mysterious kingdom dedicated to the creation of complex miniatures—to precision and order" (118). This paradoxical poetics, mingling precision and mystery, is arguably central to Millhauser's fiction, even in those works that display more realistic tendencies. As she ruminates on Peter's confession in "The Sledding Party," Catherine slides into reverie during a parodic performance of "Blueberry Hill":

> [The singer's] cheek glistened, and Catherine was shocked: she thought he was crying. But she saw that he was sweating in the close, warm air. All at once she saw a bright green hill, covered with tall trees, ripe

blueberry bushes, and winding paths. Sunlight streamed in through the leaves and fell in shafts onto the lovely paths; and all was still and peaceful in the blue summer air. It was as if the world were waiting for something, waiting and waiting with held breath for something that was bound to happen, but not yet, not yet. Suddenly, Catherine felt like bursting into tears. (94)

Catherine's precisely rendered vision—itself inspired by the intense observation of an otherwise ordinary situation—sharpens her experience of the sledding party while failing to reveal what "something" she ostensibly awaits. Light can produce shadow as well as illumination; Millhauser demonstrates this paradox in his meticulously descriptive sentences. As Marc Chénetier has observed, "through the simple sharing of a sustained exercise of concentration, the writings of Steven Millhauser alter one's vision. Is there a better definition, a better use, a higher responsibility for fiction?" (*La précision* 88).*

At the same time, *Penny Arcade* is by no means lacking in fantastic elements. Eschenburg is a master of intricate mechanisms, fashioning, among other figures, "two fashionable clockwork women strolling along [and] a miniature couturier, who at the bidding of the women took up a pair of little scissors, cut material from a bolt of cloth, and proceeded to make before their eyes a dress . . ." (24). Millhauser's Cathay is ruled by an emperor with "a passion for hourglasses; aside from his private collection there are innumerable hourglasses throughout the vast reaches of the Imperial Palace, including the gardens and parks, so that the Turner of Hourglasses and his many assistants are continually busy" (150). "A magical, fairy-tale-like quality infuses these short stories," noted a reviewer for *Booklist*, adding that "the juxtaposition of fantasy and reality is beautifully rendered" (658). K. N. Richwine called the collection "a fair cross-section of the contemporary fabulist tradition" (1679).

The collection's eclecticism is significant not only in terms of the variety of styles presented, but also in terms of the themes shared by the assembled fictions. The realistic stories that make up the book's second section all portray plausible yet traumatic breaks with reality—from a disturbance on the beach in "Protest," to the love confession in "Sledding Party," to Judith's negative epiphany in "Country." The breaks represented in these pieces are anticipated by the first section, the novella-length "August Eschenburg," which combines elements of the bildungsroman and the fantastic to narrate Eschenburg's development from idealistic artist to resigned iconoclast. The world of the titular character is weighed down by the

---

* All translations from the French throughout this issue are those of the respective essay's author.

pragmatism of Hausenstein, whose crudely sexualized automatons eventually supplant Eschenburg's, despite the latter having achieved "a realism surpassing the old art of waxwork, for his fanatically imitative figures seemed to live and breathe" (41). Nevertheless, just as Eschenburg aspires to higher standards in his art, the story itself occasionally breaks with the everyday world of commerce and the fickle public, demonstrating what art for its own sake can accomplish, however fleetingly. As part of the opening night performance at Das Zaubertheater, a performance space for automaton shows funded by Hausenstein, August includes *Undine*, a tale involving a water sprite and a knight: "Hausenstein had been concerned lest this well-worn darling of the romantic age should prove an embarrassment, but the enchanted landscape was extremely effective, and the Undine automaton had an expressivity of gesture that was unsurpassed" (45). The mingling of the realistic and fantastic in "Eschenburg" prepares readers for the intrusion of the fantastic into the realism of the volume's second section.

Similarly, juxtaposition works later in the collection to elaborate further on the tension between individual insight and the desires of the crowd. The narrator of "In the Penny Arcade," close to entering adolescence, visits an amusement park arcade, only to find that its current decrepit state pales next to his memories of the place. The fortune-teller encased in glass is cracked and dusty: "I remembered how I had once been afraid of looking into her eyes, unwilling to be caught in that deep, mystical gaze. Feeling betrayed and uneasy, I abandoned her and went off in search of richer adventures" (137). He finds such adventure, but only when he separates himself from the jaded crowd around him: "It appeared that one of those accidental hushes had fallen over things, as sometimes happens in a crowd. . . . In that hush, anything might happen. All my senses had burst wide open" (141). Soon, "The creatures of the penny arcade were waking from their wooden torpor" (141). The mechanical cowboy stares the narrator down "in the full splendor of his malevolence"; the woman in a peepshow "smiled at herself in the mirror, as if acknowledging that at last she had entered into her real existence" (142). The arcade's creatures regain their capacity to fascinate when freed of "the shrewd, oppressive eyes of countless visitors who looked at them without seeing their fertile inner nature" (144). But if the title story seems to criticize the masses exploited by the likes of Hausenstein, the collection's next and final story approaches the same problem from the other side. The emperor of Cathay has limitless resources to indulge all of his fancies. Yet the freedom to create is just another form of oppression; it is speculated, for example, that the emperor, sated with the perfection of the women in his court, seeks out the unattractive in order to "lead his soul away from the torpor of the familiar into a dark realm of strangeness and wonder" (157). The juxtaposition of different entertainments within the collection allows Millhauser to explore his subjects with thematic as well as stylistic variety.

If critics recognized Millhauser's dual artistic tendencies, they were not always convinced that they worked together in *Penny Arcade*. Michiko Kakutani noted that "Mr. Millhauser writes with assurance and skill, equally at ease with a variety of literary genres, equally adept at recording the chatty non sequiturs of teen-agers and the dense, metaphysical musings of a 19th-century con man" ("Perceptions" 12). Yet "There is a sameness to Mr. Millhauser's characters . . . and their emotional afflictions of nostalgia, irritation and extreme joy also begin to feel overly familiar" ("Perceptions" 12).

Other critics tended to interpret the stories as parables. Robert Dunn saw Eschenburg's loss of popularity to more sensational automaton-makers as "an overly obvious depiction of artistic debasement . . ." (9). But Maureen Howard, writing for the *Yale Review*, saw the story's parabolic qualities as a strength: "the artistic pressures upon August are recognizably those of today, and the story's theatrical recall of Mann's Germany, done in eerie, mesmerizing detail, is an inspired way to suggest that we take a look at what we are up to in the so-called arts" (257-58).

Since the publication of his first collection, Millhauser's short fiction has been increasingly scrutinized on its own narrative and linguistic terms—particularly in France. Such close reading has revealed a number of insights often overlooked by the genre and thematic expectations of earlier reviewers. Ullmo compares the structure of "Cathay" to haiku (*The Knife-Thrower* 99) while David Sheridan explores the story in terms of its structure as a list. "Like the list in Borges' 'The Aleph,'" Sheridan observes, "this list proceeds by controlled variation, both formal and thematic features" (14). Each descriptive vignette works by juxtaposition to evoke the marvelous (13), concluding in the narration of an imperial contest of magicians. Sheridan's thematic reading of the ending is rooted in close scrutiny of structure: "What makes a satisfying aesthetic experience? What makes a thing marvelous? Closure is achieved because the work seems to provide an ultimate or definitive answer to these questions, which, loosely paraphrased, is 'an intermingling of artifice and nature, of imagination and reality'" (15).

If some critics found an uneasy balance between the real and the fantastic in Millhauser's short fiction debut, his subsequent collections would attempt to eliminate this problem, not by choosing one style over another but, rather, by interrogating the boundary taken for granted between them.

The Barnum Museum (1990)

The Barnum Museum, originally published by Poseidon in 1990, is a more unified collection, both aesthetically and thematically. Arguably, the most realistic piece featured is "The Invention of Robert Herendeen," the unreliable first-person account of the eponymous genius's greatest creation: "I decided to invent a human being by means of the full and rigorous application of my powers of imagination" (189). Olivia soon lives up to the "perilous gift" that fashions her (183); her creation is followed by the appearance of Orville, a rival for Olivia's attention and her grotesque counterpart in Robert's increasingly fraught reality. At one point, relates the narrator, Orville "began to roll up a leg of his narrow jeans. At the top of his running shoe began a white sock and at the top of the sock I saw or seemed to see nothing—emptiness—nothing at all. 'Stop that!' I said angrily" (201).

Robert, at least for part of the story, has a clear sense of the real and imagined. Other characters on exhibit are less sure. "Behind the Blue Curtain" begins as an everyday trip to the movies, but the real show begins after the movie is over, as the narrator journeys into a realm of living cinematic characters, where "a jungle girl dressed in a leopardskin loincloth and a vineleaf halter [stood] with her hands on her hips and her head flung back haughtily as two gray-haired gentlemen in white dinner jackets bent forward to peer through monocles at a jewel in her navel" (66). The carnival atmosphere takes an unsettling and erotic turn as the narrator reaches for a woman's corset: "My hand fell through the whiteness of that cloth. My sinking hand struck the velvety hard rug—I felt myself losing my balance—suddenly I was falling through her, plunging through her corset, her breasts, her bones, her blood. For a fearful instant I was inside her" (69). The narrator survives this strange encounter and manages to return to his impatiently waiting father. But the return to the everyday is given a disturbing nuance as the narrator recognizes himself as an actor in the world beyond the movie theater: "Through the brilliant glass doors I saw my father frowning at his watch. His look of stern surprise, when he saw me burst through the door into the late-afternoon sun, struck me as wildly funny, and I forgot to chasten my features into repentance as I seized his warm hand" (71).

In "Rain," the dissolution of the protagonist, Mr. Porter, is similarly associated with going to the movies, but the dissolution itself is far more extreme. The story begins with Porter trying to wait out a rainstorm under a theater marquee. Tired of waiting, he walks into the downpour: "By the third step he felt as if he had stepped into a bathroom shower" (157). His discomfort only grows as he finds himself in the wrong car with "the odd sensation that the world was unraveling, rushing out of control, as when, in his childhood, descending a dark stairway, he had reached out his foot for that last, phantom stair even as the floor, one step too soon, leaped up to meet him" (157). This futility is only magnified as Porter abandons his stalled car and yields to the dissolution foreshadowed by his earlier entrance into the storm: "Everything was washing away. His cheeks were running, his eyeglasses were spilling down in bright crystal drops, flesh-colored streams fell from his shining fingertips, he was dissolving in the rain" (161).

Critics have tended to focus on the fantastic elements of the story. Douglas Balz describes it as a story "in which the elements conspire to make the world dissolve." Mark Bautz calls "Rain" "a surrealistic account of a man caught in a thunderstorm." The sense that Porter is literally dissolving is reinforced by the last sentence, which refers to "an empty parking lot" where "a bright puddle gleamed"—presumably what's left of Porter (161). This reading, however, overlooks much of the concluding paragraph and, indeed, much of the story itself, in which Porter's is the focal point of view; the story's clammy texture would not be as palpable without his perspective on the experience: "Everything was coming undone. Black drops fell from his watchband onto his hands, blue drops fell from his shirtsleeves onto his arms. Have I wasted my life? The telephone booth was far, far away" (161). Seen in this way, the conclusion of "Rain" can be read as a radical act of imagination. Porter is unfulfilled by his role as a spectator, whether in a movie theater or in life itself, where one of the few characters he interacts with besides his cat is "a large woman who seemed to have sprung from one of the colorful Coming Attractions" (156). Porter's dissolution collapses the boundaries of spectatorship; his annihilation, no less unsettling for its unreality, hints at a potential escape from dullness and inertia: "a bright puddle gleamed, but then the rain washed it away" (161).

If Millhauser's second collection challenged readers to see beyond the limits of ordinary experience, it also appropriated the act of reading as a model for accomplishing such discernment. Just as *Penny Arcade* uses juxtaposed narratives to explore art, audience, and the nature of the real and the wondrous, *Barnum Museum* uses juxtaposition to explore similar themes, including the uses and abuses of reading. In "The Eighth Voyage of Sinbad," Millhauser crafts a complex meditation on the art of storytelling by juxtaposing several aspects of Sinbad's creation and reception, including Sinbad's reflection on his voyages, the history of the text of *The Arabian Nights*, and the imagined experience of a boy reading Sinbad's story in southern Connecticut. Millhauser's multilayered version figures reading as a kind of voyage, where a boy in Connecticut can be with Sinbad "in the black cave, in the Valley of Diamonds, and at the same time he feels his arm pressing against the fuzzy blue blanket and smells the smoking hot dogs and the river" (139). "The Eighth Voyage" is followed by "Klassik Komix #1," in which the reader's experience of "The Love Song of J. Alfred Prufrock" takes the mass-produced form of a comic book. Eliot's original imagery—e.g., "I should have been a pair of ragged claws / Scuttling across the floors of silent seas" (5)—loses its suppleness as metaphor; images are rendered literally and become literally grotesque: "In the yellow sand a creature part crustacean and part man is lying on his stomach. . . . His face is that of a crab or lobster" (*Barnum Museum* 141).

The play of reality and fantasy consumes an entire city in the title story. Like "Cathay," "The Barnum Museum" is a story told in vignettes, this time listing different exhibits that entertain and fascinate visitors. These include a Hall of Mermaids, a caged griffin, a flying carpet, and a Chamber of False Things housing "museum guards made of wax, trompe l'oeil doorways, displays of false mustaches and false beards" and other fabrications (80). This is not the cultural institution studied by Tony Bennett, "located at the centre of cities where they stood as embodiments, both material and symbolic, of a power to 'show and tell' which, in being deployed in a newly constituted open and public space, sought rhetorically to incorporate the people within the processes of the state" (87). In contrast, Millhauser's fictional museum, also "located in the heart of our city" (*Barnum Museum* 73), is a disorienting experience for visitors tantalized by its vertiginous and constantly multiplying rooms. The disapproval it provokes within the community hints at the danger belied by its fanciful exhibits:

> The enemies of the Barnum Museum say that its exhibits are fraudulent; that its deceptions harm our children, who are turned away from the realm of the natural to a false realm of the monstrous and fantastic; that certain displays are provocative, erotic, and immoral; that this temple of so-called wonders draws us out of the sun, tempts us away from healthy pursuits, and renders us dissatisfied with our daily lives. . . . (75)

To add to the confusion, these objections themselves could be "supported and indeed invented by the directors of the museum, who understand that controversy increases attendance" (75-76). The story works much like a miniature version of the collection's juxtapositions as a whole; instead of the unitary character and plot development of conventional narrative, Millhauser entices the reader with an accumulation of striking exhibits. The ambiguous voice—which evokes a community's response to the museum—wavers from personal to impersonal, mesmerized to bored, as it navigates the eclectic collections. But the fickle voice is by no means aimless; "Barnum Museum" concludes with a meditation on aesthetic experience similar to that implied by David Sheridan's reading of "Cathay." If the audience is left unsatisfied at the end, it is at least aware of desiring something beyond the mundane, something that can never be grasped but is nevertheless pleasurable: "is it possible that the secret of the museum lies precisely here, in its knowledge that we can never be satisfied? And still the hurdy-gurdy plays, the jugglers' bright balls turn in the air, somewhere the griffin stirs in his sleep. Welcome to the Barnum Museum! For us it's enough, for us it is almost enough" (91).

Millhauser's second collection was an important text for critics in assessing his oeuvre as a whole and its place within contemporary American fiction. In the conflicting registers of a legendary Sinbad embarking on another voyage and the same Sinbad "brought down" to mundane reality, Mary Kinzie discerns "a clue to the mode of parody in which Millhauser excels—the spoof of contemporary realistic narration in fiction. He incorporates into his metafictional sublime parodic imitations of what has come to be called fictional minimalism" (115). For Kinzie, Millhauser is not striving for realism, but "in these new stories [he] has accomplished a remarkable compression of the realistic with the fantastic . . ." (116). Douglas Fowler writes that *The Barnum Museum* "contains ten stories that are an attempt to make what we hold to be plausibilities yield up their forgotten core of strangeness" (146). Fowler's concluding remarks in his essay from *Critique* offer some context both for Millhauser's previous work and his next collection of stories:

> His is not a narrative of the linear, mimetic, naturalistic mode, but a stereoscopic fiction, and the reader must be prepared to question along with the author the solidity of the proscenium arch and the smug assumptions of a centuries-old covenant that had presumed to have settled once and for all the relationship between an artist's most urgent concerns and the reader or audience invited to observe those concerns—a reader or audience that in Millhauser's presence finds itself called upon to study the spectacle set before it through a confusing array of prisms and even read a part or two from the typescript unceremoniously thrust into his or her hands. (147-48)

The Knife Thrower and Other Stories (1998)

Millhauser's most recent volume of short fiction, *The Knife Thrower and Other Stories*, was originally published by Crown in 1998. The pieces collected here are in some ways more grounded than in previous collections. While stories like "Snowmen" and "The Barnum Museum" could take place anywhere, several selections in *The Knife Thrower* feature recognizable times and places. In "Balloon Flight,

1870," the narrator takes to the air in order to escape the advance of Prussian troops on Paris. "Paradise Park" tracks the fortunes of Charles Sarabee, an American amusement park impresario, around the time of the First World War. In "Kaspar Hauser Speaks," Kaspar addresses the residents of Nuremberg, Germany, where he arrived in 1828 (Ward), a feral child "half idiot and half animal" (201). The real Kaspar Hauser was eventually murdered in 1833 (Ward).

For Patrick McGrath, "Balloon Flight" "marks out new territory for Millhauser." Where flight has previously been an image of liberating escape, in the latter story, "the ascent into higher regions is connected to ideas of sterility and death." The higher the narrator rises with his companion, the more desolate and disorienting the experience: "We have died, Vallard and I, we have entered the shadowless realm, region of erasures and absences, kingdom of dissolution" (*The Knife Thrower* 156). McGrath's observations can be usefully applied to all of the collection's historical fictions. This volume significantly expands the range of its characters' experiences. But this is by no means an instance of a writer simply trading one muse for another. Millhauser invokes history to submit it to the same scrutiny as any curiosity. His approach has not changed, but its scale has. So France at war is a site of dissolution, just as the Barnum Museum is. In "Balloon Flight," according to Nathalie Cochoy, "the line ahead buckles and the nauseating azure [of the sky] splits consciousness like an axe blow. . . . The straining eye sees these landmark lines vanish into nothingness. Signifying contours are effaced . . . leaving the substance and sense of language to slip into indifference" (471).

Anne Ullmo, in her 2003 study of *The Knife Thrower*, sees similar effects in Millhauser's re-creation of nineteenth-century Germany and the United States in the early twentieth century. Kaspar Hauser's fictional monologue, Ullmo writes, "thus recalls the problematic of the nature-culture antithesis stirred by the discovery of child savages in the forests of Europe during an epoch when questions of the innate and the acquired were being posed . . ." (*The Knife-Thrower* 56). Sarabee in "Paradise Park" is "yet another instance of that peculiarly American phenomenon, the self-made man" (*The Knife Thrower* 167). But his story, as told by Millhauser, renders Sarabee's life mundane instead of mythical. As his ambitions grow, so does a sense of disappointment, barely forestalled by anticipation of the next big thing. Ullmo observes how language is used to create this effect: "But curiously opposed to the vocabulary of excess and superlative originality is a repetitive syntax that paradoxically leads the reader toward regions of ennui; an ennui that transforms rapidly into astonishment before the writer's capacity to establish a subtle game between desire and its deferred fulfillment" (*The Knife-Thrower* 27).

But the theme of desire and fulfillment continues to interest Millhauser on a more intimate scale as well. In "A Visit," the narrator visits a friend from college, only to discover that his friend's new wife, Alice, is a giant frog. While recognizing its absurdity, his friend's interspecies romance also leaves him strangely wistful. "[A]s I sensed that hidden harmony, clear as the ringing of a distant bell," muses the narrator, "it came over me that what I lacked, in my life, was exactly that harmony" (34).

"The Sisterhood of Night" begins as one kind of mystery and ends as another. The young girls in a nondescript town are suspected of orgiastic rituals, part of an alleged cult of silence. As McGrath observes, one of the only conclusions reached about the truth of these allegations is that the unknown lurks even in those we are closest to: "What shall we do with our daughters? In the night we wake uneasily and tiptoe to their doors, pausing with our hands outstretched, unable to advance or retreat. We think of the long years of childhood, the party frocks and lollipops, the shimmer of trembling bubbles in summer air. We dream of better times" (*The Knife Thrower* 52).

In the title story, an audience witnesses the disturbing act of the knife thrower Hensch. Hensch is skilled at provoking the voyeuristic appetite of his audience. He strips his assistant by pinning her clothes to a wooden partition as she still wears them: "She began to wriggle both shoulders, as if to free herself from the tickling knives, and only as the loose gown came rippling down did we realize that the knives had cut the shoulder straps. Hensch had us now, he had us" (9). Nevertheless, the use of the plural first-person voice explores how the audience itself is complicit in Hensch's increasingly dangerous stunts. Audience members eventually become part of the spectacle, coming up to be artfully cut by "the master" (13). The show concludes with a girl named Laura receiving "the final mark, the mark that can be received only once . . ." (15-16). Hensch's target falls, prompting the audience to fidget in but never relinquish its role as passive witness: "As we left the theater we agreed that it had been a skillful performance, though we couldn't help feeling that the knife thrower had gone too far" (17).

"Kasper Hauser Speaks" contrasts with the title story in the way it works against the audience's inertia. Here, the spectacle talks back to his audience. Kasper's gratitude at being rescued from savagery is not without an undertone of regret, even hostility. Like the narrator of "Penny Arcade," Kaspar struggles with the diminishment of his senses, which, in the latter case, have been sharpened during his mysterious captivity. Before he is "able to distinguish apple, pear, and plum trees from each other by the violent smell of their leaves. . . . The touch of a hand affected me like a blow" (*The Knife Thrower* 206-07). Now he finds "the unpleasant acuteness of my sensations weakened, until at present they are nearly normal . . ." (207). His progress is marked by ambivalence: "Sometimes I feel that I am slowly erasing myself, in order for someone else to appear, the one I long for, who will not resemble me" (210). This erasure implicates his audience, whose passivity here is turned against itself; witnessing Kaspar's progress, it is confronted with the malleable margin demarcating the supposedly civilized. This ambiguity is reflected in Kaspar's closing statement, which straddles the line between contrast and comparison: "Thank you for listening to me today, and if in the course of my remarks I have said anything to offend you, please forgive poor Kaspar Hauser, who would not harm the meanest insect that crawls in dung—far less you, ladies and gentlemen of Nuremberg" (210).

The adoption of *The Knife Thrower* as part of the French national secondary-school teachers' certification exam for literature in English gave critics in that country the occasion to delve further into the collection's style and structure. The study guide *Steven Millhauser, une écriture sur le fil* (A Writer on the Edge) appeared in 2004. Edited by Anne Ullmo, the volume features contributions by Cécile Roudeau, Françoise Sammarcelli, Bruno Monfort, Jean-Yves Pellegrin, and Marc Chénetier.

Roudeau compares Millhauser's fictions to the sculpture of Alexander Calder. Like a Calder mobile, whose free-floating parts are held together by the force of gravity, the constituent elements in Millhauser achieve a fragile equilibrium through the tension of opposing forces (13-14, 16). In "Balloon Flight, 1870," for example, the first-person narrator is suspended between earth and sky, between the integrity of his individual and national identity and complete dissolution as he journeys farther away from earth (17, 19). This quality of suspension is even evident on the sentence level; the opening of "The Knife Thrower" explains and obscures the strange appeal of Hensch's death-defying act (21-22), while language becomes increasingly meaningless in "Balloon Flight" (32-33). The latter story's disoriented narrator muses, "There in that blackness, all's without meaning; whether I strive or sleep; yawn or bleed; accomplish my mission or drift to the moon" (*The Knife Thrower* 149). Observes Roudeau: "The short stories of Millhauser, unsteady architectures of words, suspended between earth and sky, are thus, in their structure, in the manner of Calder's mobiles, compositions of unstable equilibrium and of movements that, in their very beginnings, are already vexed" (20). At the same time, instability is not the only hallmark of the author's short fiction: "If the stories of Millhauser are mobiles, the writer . . . has known, sentence after sentence, how to challenge language—as before him Calder had challenged wood, steel or iron wire, and daring outrageousness, bending the line, how to make his writing the place where meaning arabesques" (20).

Sammarcelli, in her essay "Les voix sans origins chez Steven Millhauser" ("Voices without Origin in the Work of Steven Millhauser"), argues that the stories in *The Knife Thrower* evoke the fantastic through the use of impersonal narration, passive voice, and a rhetoric of rumor. These result in speculative, prevaricating narratives of futile nostalgia (such as "Sisterhood"), undermined authority, and confused reality (40-41, 43). An effect of timeless and generalized uncertainty is created in "Beneath the Cellars of Our Town," in which a community's residents ruminate on the mysterious subterranean passages that exert such a powerful influence on life aboveground. This effect is accomplished through the use of the iterative voice (43-44), in which repeated events are represented as singular, ongoing circumstances, e.g., "As small children, we are brought down to the passageways by our parents, who hold us tightly by the hand and point at the dim-shining globed lamps, the soaring walls, the sharply turning paths" (*The Knife Thrower* 213). Even when Millhauser does not employ these strategies, he accomplishes similar effects. "Paradise Park" may consist of distinct episodes in the creation of the ultimate theme park, but the story is nevertheless disorienting in the way it makes the particular banal through repetition (Sammarcelli 44). And in the decidedly personal narrative "Kasper Hauser Speaks," the narrator taunts us with Borgesian play: if this human curiosity is created by his audience, the audience itself must partake of his strangeness (50). Rather than immersing the reader in the banal, Millhauser creates "an escape, in all senses of the term, and an effect of eeriness, the proliferation of unidentified voices favoring hesitation—and, as one knows, hesitation is connected with the fantastic . . ." (39).

The use of historical and antiquated motifs in *The Knife Thrower* is by no means incidental, contends Monfort in "Steven Milhauser [sic], une esthétique du périmé?" ("An Aesthetic of the Outdated?"). Millhauser's fairground attractions are analogous to the act of reading fiction, in which the audience can experience dramas free of risk. As in the title story, where audience members are ostensibly provoked and protected by the knife thrower's skill, "The contract of fiction consists, then, of two elements: one 'really' throws but 'falsely' risks since it is all well and good to simulate risk against which one is protected" (59). But this fictional contract carries a risk of its own—Graum's automatons take on an unsettling reality at the conclusion of "The New Automaton Theatre"; actors hired to merely simulate riffraff eventually threaten visitors to "Paradise Park" (61, 67-68). The inside and outside of fiction are also blurred by ambiguous narrators whose knowledge of reported events resemble the reader's, and by the use of eclectic lists that bring together attractions from disparate times and places (64-65, 70-71). Observes Monfort: "fiction is susceptible to pulling back from a fictional universe that no longer necessarily obeys the rules of 'as if,' where the game might eventually cease to be a game, in which case, that which begins as a game ends or threatens to end as reality" (59).

In "Entre désir et désastre: l'écart dans *The Knife Thrower* de Steven Millhauser" ("Between Desire and Disaster: The Gap in Steven Millhauser's *The Knife Thrower*"), Pellegrin discerns a fundamental dialectic in the fiction akin to that described by Pascal Quignard: the negation of the real which, paradoxically, returns us to the real. The story of Harter, a womanizer, in "The Way Out," for example, illustrates the former negation; the protagonist's romantic disappointment is told using a distanced narrative voice, the omission of information from both Harter and the reader, and flashback, a device that in effect begins the story after it has already ended (82-83). The second part of the dialectic is seen in "Beneath the Cellars of Our Town," in which descent to the town's mysterious tunnels serves as a prelude to eventual ascent (Pellegrin 87-88).

In a brief afterword to the collection, Marc Chénetier discusses the value of studying Millhauser's fiction, a body of work that resists theorizing: "hasn't it been explained to us at length and persistently that pleasure is heightened by knowing the magician's 'tricks,' that what is lost in naivety, one gains, paradoxically, in wonder?" (96).

—P. P.

Novellas

"Is it possible not to be drawn to the novella? Everything about it is immensely seductive," said Steven Millhauser in a 2003 interview with Jim Shepard (par. 1). Millhauser was, of course, speaking as a writer. His readers do not necessarily agree. As has been amply established elsewhere in this overview, the reception of Millhauser's work—novels, novellas, and short stories—has been mixed in this country, but popular critics seem especially confused by the novellas. The reasons for this are dispiritingly predictable; however, considering them may establish why the novellas are a form important both to Millhauser personally and to serious readers of his work.

A 1993 *Library Journal* review of *Little Kingdoms* characterized novellas in general as "often arous[ing] the suspicion that they're something that failed to be longer or shorter. . . . [O]ne more often expects something polite, whimsical, and pleasant in the novella format." Despite this reviewer's conviction that Millhauser's work in this novella triptych consists of "odds and ends," he deigned to acknowledge that the book contains "just enough fine writing . . .

for the money" (Geary 157-58). Another *Library Journal* review, published in 1999, did not stoop to such naked commodification; instead it confusedly called *Enchanted Night* a "novel," despite the fact that its subtitle is *A Novella*. The reviewer then complained that it is a "wisp of a story" (Leiding 134), though again acknowledging the presence of beautiful writing. We cannot know whether the reviewer complained because she felt the book was an inadequate example of a novel or because she disliked novellas as such. In any case, neither of these reviews tells us anything about the books except that they contain good writing, when, in fact, it is the novellas' structural dynamics—individually and as an oeuvre—that set them apart.

The novella remains virtually invisible in the United States in commercial terms, despite some notable exceptions. More attention has been paid in the academy, but conversations there still tend to turn on generic definition, on which there is no consensus (J. H. E. Paine, in his 1979 study *Theory and Criticism of the Novella*, titles one of his chapters "Forms of the Novella: The Hazards of Category"). In fact, Millhauser—wisely, for a writer making formal innovations—accepts length as the only legitimate definition of the novella. Its "shortness encourages . . . the close-up view, the revelatory detail, the single significant moment" while at the same time "invit[ing] the possibility of certain elaborations and complexities forbidden by a very short form . . ." (qtd in Interview, *Bomb*). In other words, the novella allows both the descriptive richness and the structural complexity for which Millhauser's work has become celebrated.

"The close-up view" is an apt term for Millhauser to use about his own work, for he has established a novella oeuvre that explores, in particular, the complex relation between sight and space, on the one hand, and memory and the temporal on the other. The triad, especially the romantic/sexual triad, is present in thematic and structural terms throughout Millhauser's work. However, as a somewhat indeterminate form—one that yearns for both length and compression, one that is neither novel nor short story—the novella is perhaps itself an instantiation of a "third way" (and thus the essential third point, or third angle, of the novel-novella-short story triangle). In any case, Millhauser's novellas constitute a rich field for exploring how the relationship between space and time is treated in his fiction.

Millhauser has published two novella triptychs (*Little Kingdoms* [1993] and *The King in the Tree* [2003]), and one freestanding novella, *Enchanted Night* (1999). According to his own criterion—length—the short stories "August Eschenburg" (*In the Penny Arcade*), and "A Game of Clue" (*The Barnum Museum*) also may be said to fit the definition, and they will be discussed here as well.

Little Kingdoms (1993)

Michael Dirda, in a favorable review of *Little Kingdoms* in the *Washington Post Book World*, says of Millhauser that "no one alive, except perhaps James Salter or John Crowley, can write more beautiful prose" (par. 1). Other reviews make similar observations: an anonymous *New Yorker* reviewer says Millhauser "records the imaginative life with the luminous strokes of a landscapist and the draftsmanship of a mapmaker" (99). Irving Malin called it "one of the truly amazing books written by an American writer in the last three decades" (212). According to Dirda, the "common reservation[s]" about Millhauser's work—"Aren't his tales . . . just a little precious and ethereal . . . ? And isn't Millhauser himself somewhat obsessed with childhood and its sense of wonder?"—are not particularly valid. He perceives that the "fanatical particularization" of Millhauser's tales is his "great strength" *because* of the narrative potency of Millhauser's descriptive approach:

> He can imbue his descriptive details with the evocative power and excitement of runaway narrative. "The Princess, the Dwarf, and the Dungeon," in this new collection, delivers repeated shivers of erotic menace and violation—yet almost nothing sexual really happens. But then it doesn't have to. . . .

Dirda's remark also points to the erotic charge present in most of Millhauser's work (and belies the assumption that Millhauser is "obsessed with childhood and its wonder," insofar as this obsession is assumed not to include the erotic).

Dirda perceives what some American reviewers and critics either seem to overlook or fail to acknowledge—that the novellas "subtly question *each other* about imagination and power" (par. 11, emphasis added). In fact, all of Millhauser's work does so. As Marc Chénetier points out in his 2003 study *Steven Millhauser: La précision de l'impossible* (The Precision of the Impossible), the consistency found across what at first may seem to be a heterogeneous oeuvre arises from its "obsessions, the throbbing recurrence of a handful of topics and questions beyond the apparent variety of subjects and situations" (10). Primary among these obsessions is the imagination, but not, as has been often assumed, as opposed to the "real." In fact, it is the zone in which, as Millhauser himself has said, "the familiar begins to turn strange. Where things cease to be themselves, where they begin to turn into something else, which has no name . . ." (Interview, *Bomb*).

Though sometimes relegated to footnotes, numerous mentions are made of "The Little Kingdom of J. Franklin Payne" in Arthur Saltzman's 2001 article "A Wilderness of Size," about Millhauser's

1996 novel *Martin Dressler*. Saltzman refers to the character Payne to elucidate his contention that, like both characters and the architectures they inhabit in Millhauser's fiction, the Vanderlyn Hotel is, as Saltzman puts it, "in the thick of things yet marvelously apart" (597). Payne, too, as he works in his study in a turret, is "separated from the life of the house but [felt] that he drew secret strength from the floors below" (*Little Kingdoms* qtd. in Saltzman 597n4). The theme of spatial configuration and its effect on temporal aspects of fiction—in other words, that of how boundaries in time intersect with boundaries in space—is one that will also be explored in Millhauser's second novella triptych, which may be read, in many ways, as an extension and companion to the first.

As the *New Yorker* reviewer put it, "[Millhauser's] 'little kingdoms' include the imaginative realms that his characters inhabit" (99). According to Saltzman, "for Millhauser, borders between fact and fiction, reality and dream are unreliable (even undesirable) retaining walls for personality" (603n10). He refers to the central conceit for J. Franklin Payne's newspaper comic "Figaro's Follies," in which the monkey Figaro, in each strip, devises a new way to violate the strip's panel frames: in one case, each frame contains a door that allows him to walk into a new panel "with a different shape: the first panel led into a circle, the circle led to a tall, thin tube, the tube opened onto a stairway, the stairway led to a small box, and a door in the box opened to a hot-air balloon with a basket, in which the monkey stood with a spyglass trained on the reader" (38). Whether these boundaries are always undesirable is arguable; the hot-air balloon appears in Millhauser's later short story "Balloon Flight, 1870," but in this case it is, rather than an escape vehicle, a "yellow monster" (151) that carries the protagonist into the overwhelming vacancy of the sky: "Here at the world's end, give me the sight and touch of things: shape of a hand, curve of a chin, weight of a stone, the heft of earthly things. Edges! Edges!" (156). Indeed, Payne himself sometimes distrusts his own boundary-breaking (in his guise as a little monkey):

> when he had entered the world of four black lines, which he broke apart and reassembled any way he liked, so that his impish monkey seemed the very expression of his longing to break free of some inner constraint, then he felt a craving for the lines and shadows of the actual world, as if the imaginary world threatened to carry him off in a hot-air balloon on a voyage from which he might never return. (39)

This oscillation between the oppressive world of the concrete and the vertigo of utter freedom—this mistrust of settling too easily into one world or another, of reifying the method by which one perceives—

creates both thematic tension and narrative momentum in much of Millhauser's fiction. Chénetier examines this phenomenon in mostly structural terms. He compares Millhauser's fictional technique to a Möbius strip: "the reader, who follows the sentence like a finger follows the back of the strip, finds herself without rupture or jolt on the back of the world described, having passed imperceptibly to the other side without realizing that torsion allowed the passage" (*La précision* 62). The key to this torsion, which is the dynamo powering the reader's adventuring between worlds, is the accumulation of meticulously exact description: "Quantitative accumulation 'naturally' produces the qualitative jump necessary for the passage from the world of the possible to that of the impossible" (*La précision* 62). Chénetier uses as an example one of the many remarkable descriptive scenes in "The Little Kingdom of J. Franklin Payne":

> Somewhere beyond the rain-haze he and Stella and Max and Cora were walking in checkered sunlight on a green, wooded path, but when he arrived home he had to drag his feet through piles of red and yellow leaves; the wind howled as he climbed the stairs to his study; from the high windows he could see the ice skaters on the river, turning round and round, faster and faster, until they were a whirling blur—and emerging from their spin they sat back lazily in sun-flooded rowboats, their straw hats casting blue shadows over their eyes. (73)

This momentum will eventually carry the narrative into the story's ultimate scene, in which past and present are, somewhat transcendentally, somewhat agonizingly, conflated into the screening of Payne's masterwork of animation; the *Virginia Quarterly Review* characterizes this withdrawal as "moving and pathetic" (Rev. of *Little Kingdoms* 24). The agony is that of dreadful loneliness and creative abundance occurring in exact simultaneity. The novella is erotic, as are the other two novellas, not in the explicitly sexual sense but in the sense that everything lures, "seduces" the reader to wander more deeply into the forest of the narrative and the worlds that bloom there in the undergrowth, and at the same time makes more explicit that this territory is dangerous and capable of betrayal.

Seduction and betrayals also figure strongly in "The Princess, the Dwarf, and the Dungeon," as does Millhauser's exploration of the gaze. The novella is divided into short sections; the longest is about five and a half pages long, and most are less than a page. Each section is titled, with a heading run into the text in capital letters; these titles are short and reflect sometimes one aspect of the section, sometimes another (the first three are "The Dungeon," "The Castle," and "Tales of the Princess"). All reinforce the slight remove the reader feels, as does the use of the first-person plural pronoun (to which Millhauser has said he is "increasingly drawn" ["An Interiew"]). They also reinforce the sense of the voyeuristic: everyone, in this novella, watches everyone else, or wishes to (with the exception of the Princess, who is endlessly watched). The townspeople cannot observe the interior of the castle directly, but they speculate at length about past and present courtly doings; the Prince enlists the dwarf Scarbo to spy on his wife, the Princess, whom he has ordered to offer nightly temptations to his former friend the margrave. Only the dungeon rats (being sightless) are indifferent.

Most contemporary reviews of *Little Kingdoms* singled out this novella as a beautifully written exploration of the themes of jealousy and revenge, one that plows up the soil of the fairy-tale format to reveal the charnel ground below it. *The Virginia Quarterly Review* compared it both to the "aloof play of Borges" and to the "elliptical rage of Browning's 'My Last Duchess'" (Rev. of *Little Kingdoms* 25); Daniel Green referred to it as an "outright fairy-tale," but one whose "inhabitants are as subject to uncertainty and disappointment as any character in the more abject fictional universe depicted by the minimalists" (par. 4). Green also compared the novella to Robert Coover's *Pricksongs and Descants*, noting, however, that Millhauser's work "does not so much deconstruct the fairy tale's explanatory power as explore it" (par. 9). Irving Malin said simply that it "contains elements of a fairy tale, [but] the narrative calls into question the meaning of continuity, process, movements of life" (212). Frederic Tuten noted in *The New York Times Book Review* that the novella explores the theme of authenticity and replication: "embedded in this story is the narrator's meditation on the art of his [indeterminately medieval] time, paintings so lifelike as to cause a dog to lick the portrait of his master" (9:1). The novella is also concerned with betrayal, not only in the sexual sense but because, being duplicitous, lies themselves function as a replica of the truth. This theme will also be explored in the later novella "The King in the Tree," which extends many of the themes in "The Princess, the Dwarf, and the Dungeon." Of course, an examination of duplicity must also include (as most of Millhauser's work does) an examination of transgression.

In his chapter "The Management of Desire," Chénetier identifies desire or lack as a general motive force in Millhauser's fiction:

> a Millhauser work is born from malaise, of a feeling of lack. It nourishes itself and expands, trying to fill this lack. It moves toward a paroxysm which might promise a new way of knowing, then, exhausted by [its own] excess, muted by the inexpressable, butting against the insoluble, it gives way to a new attempt to conquer the imaginary space, whereupon . . . it destroys itself by dissolving the forms it had so meticulously arranged to reach that point. (*La précision* 89)

This trajectory accurately describes "The Princess, the Dwarf, and the Dungeon," in terms of both the townspeople and, especially, the jealous Prince, whose restlessness consists of a fundamental and perverse desire to suffer by unjustly accusing his wife, the Princess, of trysts with his closest (and this in the chivalric sense) friend, the margrave. He proceeds to do so, and just at the point of crisis (when, if he would allow the "paroxysm" to take place, he might enter some new "way of knowing"), he destroys his own perceptual framework by dissolving the "forms"—the arrangements, that is, he has commanded regarding the Princess and the margrave—that he himself established. In other words, the Prince cannot allow any situation to come to fruition on its own. Closure is never achieved. The Princess is imprisoned in the tower for all time, but does not die (and achieve closure in that sense); the margrave chips away at his tunnel leading away from the dungeon, without ever gaining his freedom (though—who knows?—someday he may).

In any case, this has the effect of turning the dynamic of desire back upon the voyeuristic townspeople; never content with the state they have achieved, they oscillate ceaselessly between restless-ness and quiescence in "an aesthetic and epistimological variety of Penelopism (*La précision* 89): "We do not know what it is, this thing we lack. We only know that on certain summer afternoons, when the too-blue sky stretches on and on, or in warm twilights when the blackbird cries from the hill, restlessness comes over us, a dissatisfaction. . . . Then we turn to the castle . . ." (138). Thus the collective restlessness underscores the townspeople's isolation from the unreachable and unreadable castle, just as the Prince has allowed his restless imagination to isolate him from the margrave and the Princess, who are imprisoned in both space and time.

The tragic stasis of the novella's end is recycled into romantic myth, as the first-person plural narrator describes how the tales of the Princess, the dwarf, and the dungeon evolve: "secondary ver-sions" known as "cellar tales," "which have not been able to survive in the full light of day, continue to carry on a hidden life, and give rise to growths of a dubious and fantastic kind" (165-66). These muta-tions, these mushroom tales, offer alternate endings to the legend: the Princess and the dwarf bear a child; the margrave grows black wings and "one day . . . appears in the sky above the river as a black angel of death" (166). These variations are not given weight by the narrator, who has his own impulse toward closure. The penultimate section, titled "A Day Will Come," describes the eventual apocalyptic return of the margrave, who will wreak vengeance on the castle and the town. Yet it is no more clear that the narrator knows this will occur than that the Prince knew his wife had been unfaithful. This lack of certainty enables the community to deploy the story of the

Princess, the Prince, and the margrave (as well as the dwarf and the dungeon) in the ways they find useful as a group. As Millhauser said regarding the first-person plural point of view, "what interests me [about the 'we'] is the way moral indecisiveness or questioning may be given more weight or significance by attaching itself to a multiple being" (qtd. in "An Interview"). In many ways, the narrative "we" here functions as an exploration of this "indecisiveness or questioning." Appropriately, there is no decision or answer. The novella's last phrase itself allows the dynamic oscillation of meaning to continue: in the town, "sunlight and shadow fall equally" (173).

Irving Howe's afterword for an early publication (in *Salmagundi*) of "Catalogue of the Exhibition: The Art of Edmund Moorash (1810-1846)" observes the difficulties of using a "vertical" form such as a catalog (which is "a series of discrete items discussing particular paintings and only secondarily providing information and insights about the artist . . . and those near him" [112]) in a fictional narrative. Like the first-person plural narrator in "The Princess, the Dwarf, and the Dungeon," this form puts us at a remove from the melodramatic action. Howe says that, despite initial frustrations as he attempted to locate a connection between the catalog form and the dramatic narrative, he concludes that "[Millhauser] deliberately chose to keep his actions at a certain, an optimal, distance because what interested him, I now think, is a cultural situation in which talented but troubled people become so introverted, so deeply in the depth of obsessions, that the capacity for spontaneous life begins to dwindle radically" (114). In other words, the characters in Moorash's paintings and in his life have reached the same crisis, or stasis, point as the personages in the preceding two novellas. Again, betrayal and desire, and their relationship to the creative (and created) world, figure strongly, but this time the theme of romantic excess and the violent potential of art are explored more overtly.

Millhauser, in correspondence with Howe, confirmed that Edmund Moorash is "entirely an invention," as are the contemporaneous Phantasmacist (which the catalog's narrator dryly calls "a minor and short-lived school" [181]) and Diabolist movements. Moorash, whom Millhauser has said he wanted to be "an American equivalent of Turner" (qtd. in Howe 113), lives, like Wordsworth, with his sister (Elizabeth) in a remote lakeshore cottage (in this case, in upstate New York). Another brother-sister couple, William and Sophia Pinney, build a cottage on the opposite shore; much entanglement ensues, and eventually blood is spilled. With drama this vivid, narrative distance may be helpful. However, like Howe, critics have been uncertain of the form's efficacy and bothered by the narrative's tone. The *Virginia Quarterly Review*, which calls the novella a "less successful tale [than "The Little Kingdom of J. Franklin Payne"] of the psychic cost of artistic integrity" (24), also characterizes its prose as "all too convincingly academic" (it also dislikes its "rigidly symmetric" structure [24-25]). It seems clear that narrative distance, and the novella's structure, have much to do with critics' willingness to accept other aspects of the novella, including the thematic. The catalogue form manages to keep the reader at a triple remove from the action (through the assumption of the presence of an artificial setting—a museum exhibit; through awareness of the catalogue's author's own academic interest in Moorash and his circle; and through the funneling of much of the core narrative's emotional content through the paintings themselves, with the counterpoint of extracts from Moorash's sister Elizabeth's journal). This triple remove acts both to evoke the narrative suspension and oscillation typical of all three of these novellas and to make us aware (through the catalogue-author's slightly prurient academic gaze) of our own voyeurism, and the mercilessness and clumsiness of the public gaze upon the private lives of artists.

The narrator of "Catalogue" is far less self-aware than the "we" of "The Princess, the Dwarf, and the Dungeon," and this has the effect of making the narration more transparent—despite its structure as catalog notes—and the characters more vivid. Too, the novella's principle characters are not in the indeterminately distant, mythical past, as the middle novella's characters may be; they are only a century outside living memory, and dates scattered throughout the catalog effectively pin them down in time. (As Dirda points out, "A careful reader will have noted early on that all the main characters die in the same year" ["Worlds"].) This has the effect of allowing the reader to become absorbed in the action in a way that feels less mediated, despite the novella's unconventional form, while the formal structure still acts to frame the melodrama and allow the reader to experience it in a more nuanced way. In other words, the structure opens the action to interpretations more dynamic than the simple symbology at which the academic narrator hints.

A recurring theme in the novella is art's violent potential: early in the catalogue (in the description of painting no. 8), the narrator quotes the journal of Elizabeth Moorash, the artist's sister: "a painting strikes you *all at once*, with its full force, instead of dispersing its effects, [Edmund says]. A painting *strikes a blow*. William [Pinney], smiling: Is art then so dangerous? E: Painting is devil's work—let the beholder beware!" (191). Indeed, this is, ultimately, the effect of Moorash's last painting, a self-portrait, though it is in physical terms the victim of rage as well as its cause. In his chapter "Portrait of an Artist among Artists," Chénetier points out that the novella's core narrative, that of Moorash, is set in a century known both for its fascination with movement and its desire to push static visual techniques and technologies—painting and photography—toward movement (impressionism and experimental animation, respectively), as was explicated by Hausenstein, August Eschenburg's rival and underwriter (see *In the Penny Arcade* 39; Chénetier, *La précision* 53). Chénetier locates corresponding structural tensions in "Catalogue," in terms of the way this story's "montage of journal extracts, letters, historic citations, descriptions . . . has the double effect of superimposing 'the life and the book,' [of] inviting the made and the represented to melt under the reader's gaze" (54). This layered narrative technique is also thematically supported by descriptions of Moorash's painting, which utilizes impasto and other layering techniques to destabilize distance and contour. Narrative is also made ambiguous; despite the catalog-writer's attempts to limn for us the personalities of Moorash and the other principal characters, even Moorash's portraiture, according to Chénetier, explores representation *and* motion and stasis: "the personages represented figure *one moment* in their mutual relationship" (55, emphasis added).

Moorash's aesthetic, "dominated by the dissolution of contours, evanescent or mixed forms, fusions, distortions, and oneiric dispersions, [and] the confusions of levels of representations and tonalities" (Chénetier 55), both drives the narrative dynamic and suspends it. The fiction, like Moorash's self-portrait (as our catalog-writer points out in the last entry, no. 26), "seems to hover in a limbo between art and biography, between the realm of imperishable beauty and the realm of decay" (239). The spilling of blood and the breaching of boundaries in this novella bespeak a dynamic of transgression and yearning.

A survey of these novellas and their reception should not overlook the marked lack of response to Millhauser's very gentle but acute sense of parody (and of humor) within them. Though much has been made of the formal parody of *Edwin Mullhouse*, the cultural parody of *Portrait of a Romantic*, and the linguistic parody of *From the Realm of Morpheus*, which uses many Elizabethan locutions, these responses concern themselves more with superficial "marks" of parody than the ways in which it is part of the basic dynamic of Millhauser's work. Parody and humor are, after all, another sort of duplication, this time involving exaggeration: repetition and variation, miniaturization and gigantism all can, and sometimes do, function humorously in these works. But always, with Millhauser, the exaggeration is so subtle that as soon as it shows itself to be such it has begun to melt into something new (most of the time, a sympathetic appreciation of even his least sympathetic characters' impulse toward redemptive adventuring). As are all aspects of his work, it is beautifully modulated, and never announces itself so loudly that it outshouts the central "adventure" of the tale. Yet it is inescapable.

Enchanted Night (1999)

In his 2003 interview with Marc Chénetier, Steven Millhauser said, in the course of an exchange about the relative "darkness" or "light" of his books, that "art is connected in my mind—in my body—with a sense of enhancement, of radical pleasure, of affirmation, of revelry. Darkness is the element against which this deeper force asserts itself. It may even be that this force deliberately seeks out darkness, in order to assert itself more radically" (par. 12). *Enchanted Night,* a 130-page novella, the only one of Millhauser's to be published separately, seems either to be embraced or dismissed by popular critics for its relative "lightness." (L. S. Klepp, writing for *Entertainment Weekly,* called Millhauser "a poet not of punitive ironies but of gentle imaginative consolations" [61].) Published in 1999, six years after *Little Kingdoms* (and following *Martin Dressler* and its Pulitzer Prize, and correspondingly greater critical notice for Millhauser's work), it is a thematic departure from the first triptych. For those who had become accustomed to the quasi-Gothic hauntedness of Millhauser's fiction, *Enchanted Night* may have seemed far less complex.

Yet the novella seems to have resulted from a relatively challenging experiment: an effort to find a form that would allow the use of "many different voices" ("An Interview"); also, "the conception of the work was musical—a theme and variations on a summer night." In some ways, like music, the novella functions as a sort of stop-time: Millhauser says, referring to book's epigraph by Ben Jonson ("Lay thy bow of pearl apart / And thy crystal-shining quiver. / Give unto the flying hart / Space to breathe, how short soever," from "A Panegyre," written in 1603) that "in *Enchanted Night,* I gave the flying hart—the restless heart—a little space to breathe. Day will come soon enough."

The musical (or lyrical) aspects of the novella have been noted by a number of critics. Alan Cheuse, in a National Public Radio broadcast, said, "There are a hundred pages of lyrical prose in this novella, but their meaning escaped me until I . . . read them aloud. Millhauser's modernistic summer night sonata is as much a treat for the ear as it is for the eye." The *Virginia Quarterly Review* called it "part fairy tale, part tone poem" (64); Donna Seaman noted its "light and playful poetic prose" (233). Tobin Harshaw's review in the *New York Times* highlights one of two supernatural occurrences: the presence of mysterious flute music that, though "Perhaps it is only birdsong, there in the dark trees" (15), nonetheless will draw the children from their beds before the night has finished. Millhauser has said that the novella is, "in a sense, an elaboration of" his earlier short story "Clair de Lune" (qtd. in Chénetier, "An Interview"), with which it shares a similar setting; however, *Enchanted Night* has a far more self-consciously musical structure, with its choruses and recurring motifs. "Songs" are assigned to the different actors, from a teenage boy to the field insects.

The music of the language, too, is exquisitely modulated. In the scene in which the teenage boy Danny is ravished in his sleep by the moon-goddess, the text heightens the surprisingly explicit physicality of the moment with constructions—"Heart-stirred she rests, the goddess sharp-wounded" (98)—that adopt the syntax of Old English alliterative verse, with its oral form and its celebration of the embodied world. Later the lyricism shifts to a style more fluid and impressionistic: "Dark and sweet, dark and sweet, the night-notes draw the children deeper into the woods, past tree trunks fat as elephant legs, under branches that run like ink against the blue night sky . . ." (114). Indeed, Claude Debussy's aesthetic haunts this novella, more even than it does Millhauser's story "Clair de Lune." Impressionist languor is evoked through the lyricizing of Millhauser's precise descriptions, which also has the effect of slowing the reading. This languor and the poetics by which it is achieved appeal more to some critics than to others (Harshaw believed the languor "handcuff[s]" Millhauser [15]; Ben Marcus, in his *Village Voice* review, disliked the "overblown bursts of lyricism" that "coat . . . the characters in a thick, nostalgic sheen" [90]). Once again, traditionally realist expectations are unselfconsciously applied to Millhauser's work, with the predictable result that these expectations are disappointed.

Finally, though the novella may, as Brian Evenson said in his review, "lack the impact of Millhauser's best stories and novels," it seems "a perfect book with which to ease someone into the work of this most important American writer." As Evenson says, "it stands in relation to Millhauser's more ambitious work in the same fashion that . . . Saramago's *The Tale of the Unknown Island* stands in relation to his: the author's characteristic impulses, concerns, and gestures are there but gauzily transfigured as fairy tale" (181).

The King in the Tree (2003)

This, the most recent of Millhauser's books, has garnered the mixed reception of his other novellas. It consists of the title novella, a reworking and extension of the Tristan and Isolde myth; "An Adventure of Don Juan," in which Don Juan is subject to a reversal of his customary conquest-without-emotional-attachment; and "Revenge," a monologue written in a contemporary setting in the voice of a widow who subtly and powerfully lures her late husband's lover into the darkest of psychological traps.

The romantic triangle is, in these novellas, explored in terms of design—in terms of how the perpetually shifting dyads forming and re-forming in the three-way connection operate to create narrative dynamic and destabilize everyone's, including the reader's, notions of what can be known. "Revenge," at base, explores epistemology—and consequently replication and the "real." "Revenge" also seems to have garnered the strongest critical responses, and the most mixed. It has been called, variously, "a gothic masterpiece" (Miller 7); "the weakest of the three novellas" (Rev. of *The King in the Tree* 85); a "hand-wringing masterpiece" (Freeman EE.03); "a powerful tale of shattered identity" (Paddock); "a cluster bomb hidden in the folds of a monologue" (Annan 25); and the "best" of the collection (Troy Patterson, *Entertainment Weekly*). Many critics who have difficulty with the novella find the tone off-putting; Marvin J. LaHood, in a review for *World Literature Today*, called the voice of the widow, "at its worst," one of "shrill despair and vituperativeness" (95). LaHood frames his comment in terms of plausibility (he maintains that it is not clear that the dead husband's mistress would tolerate such vituperation). Even reviewers who were generally impressed by the novella noted, and even seemed a bit frightened by, its tone.

The novella was published too recently to have generated a great deal of study, but what serious attention has been paid (that is, beyond reviews) tends to examine how it may explore replication and epistemology. One useful starting point may be to examine how Millhauser's work explores realism (and the real) to begin with.

Marc Chénetier says that, in Millhauser's work, realism has a "very special status, which invites [us] to trust it as a form of support and at the same time defies its own limits. Art necessarily resorts to artifice, which is a condition of the enlargement of the conscience: giving its dimensions to another reality. Any art must ... declare its artifice; this does not alter its ontological status" (*La précision* 64). In fact, he says,

> Millhauser thinks so little of the distinction between art and artifice that one of his stories insists on "the mimetic *or* illusionist tendency of our art" ["The New Automaton Museum," *The Knife Thrower* 93]. Exploring the different possible stages and refinements of mimesis, he draws from (and through) the absolute precision of replicas until he has inventions that, going beyond resemblance, seek the truth and beauty of the represented, yet at the same time demonstrate via two distinct methods that if one takes seriously the powers of mimesis, realism is a failure of the artistic imagination. . . . One will see that, in the end, Millhauser exceeds realism. . . . (Chénetier, *La précision* 64-65, emphasis in Millhauser quotation his)

Chénetier proposes a "mimesis of the fantastic" (65) as one of
Millhauser's foundational themes and projects. If we take Chénetier's
conviction that artistry (and replication) is of the first importance
to Millhauser and apply it to "Revenge," it allows us to reframe our
evaluation of its qualities, and the widow may take her place among
other Millhauser "artists." Her creation is, of course, vengeance, and
she achieves it through a spatial and temporal reframing of her
house, which, through a "house tour" for her husband's mistress,
she renders a permeable, unsafe zone for the *unheimlich*. The house
admits both the past and the future in uncanny ways, through its
traces of the destroyed marriage and the presumed suicide of both
the mistress and the widow.

The novella is also a conceptual descendant of "A Game of Clue,"
with which it shares both thematic preoccupations (the secrets we
keep, transgression and betrayal, and the impossibility of complete
revelation) and setting and structure (both tales are set within a
house, whose various rooms have not only emotional but narrative
significance). The narrative techniques used in the two stories are
very different: "A Game of Clue" uses a close third-person point of
view that shifts among not only the human players but their Clue
counterparts—Professor Plum et al.—who are treated realistically.
This use of focalization reinforces the distance between the characters' epistemologies and the consequently mysterious nature of
existence. Millhauser's use of the third person allows the reader to
view all the characters' secrets, but these secrets themselves become
clues to larger secrets, which remain unsolved. This novella's pre-
dominant tone is one of incipience; aggression, though present, is
veiled. It is concerned with metaphysical purity, in the form of David
Ross, the fifteen-year-old whose birthday is the occasion for the game
of Clue; he is an adolescent, a state Millhauser finds fascinating:

> It feels a tug in two directions: back toward the completed world of
> childhood, from which it is permanently banished, and forward toward
> the unknown realm of adulthood, which it both craves and fears. . . .
> Fiction conventionally presents adolescence as a time of sexual awaken-
> ing, but for me it feels like the very image of spirit in all its restless
> striving. (qtd. in Chénetier, "An Interview")

"Revenge," too, presents characters in liminal states, but their
liminality's emotional tenor is far different. Fully committed to
adulthood and all its knowingness, the mysteries in "Revenge"
are solved, but the spirit, condemned to continuing in its "restless
striving," has no choice but to plunge toward oblivion. The close
focalization and blurring of point of view and bodily boundaries
make, in some ways, "Revenge" an inside-out "Game of Clue": the
latter is in part a meditation upon our inevitable separation, and

the fact that when we are joined, what we share is often that very separation and our complete subjection to unsolvable mystery; the former dissolves the separation violently and completely, but evokes the ultimate separation of death.

Millhauser has said that he is fascinated by fiction's role as a means of seeing, in its most straightforward sense:

> the world is there, presenting itself to us ceaselessly, and yet it remains largely invisible. I remember being struck by a passage in a philosophy book that pointed out how no object is completely present to sight. If you look at a cube, you can only see three sides. The passage went on to distinguish seeing from imagining—in imagination, I immediately apprehend all six sides—but for me the simple fact that objects don't reveal themselves completely to sight became a symbol for the general invisibility of the world. (qtd in Interview, *Bomb*)

In "Revenge," the axis of sight, or space, always threatens to dissolve into the axis of time, or narrative. The house becomes a space that admits not only secret rooms—attic, cellar—but spatializes, or layers, time itself: the events of the past haunt it. "Robert's ghost is sitting right there, where you're sitting now," the narrator tells the mistress, "and my ghost is sitting here, listening to his strangled confession" (13). Ghosts, in fact, are a special form of replication, in that they replicate the past in the present.

The monologue approach also destabilizes space, because it bifurcates the reader's point of view: it both locks the reader into the widow's point of view and, because address is made in the second person, we are also, horribly, in the shoes of the dead man's mistress. The reader's only clues about how she reacts must come from the widow's statements themselves ("You seem upset. Of course you ought to be" [13].); there are few such statements, and they are necessarily oblique or fragmentary. The character of the mistress, therefore, must be almost wholly inferred by the reader. In a sense, the reader is given no choice but to *become* the mistress—and another uncanny triangulation is established: the reader, the mistress, and the widow.

Replication is a theme explored with great nuance in this tale, as well as the other two novellas, and this is where the fantastic is evoked in the novella. Large parts of the widow's monologue are devoted to recounting her compulsive imaginings, after his confession, of her husband's affair and of the mistress's character. The real and the monstrous are taken apart and recombined using the material of the two women's bodies (at one point the widow imagines herself without legs, as a mermaid—"nothing below my waist" [33]—and shortly thereafter, after spying on the mistress through a window that blocks the mistress's top half, makes the mistress a "mermaid in reverse, legs below and fish scales above" [38]).

It is also productive to view "Revenge" in relation to the two other novellas in the collection, which extend the exploration of replication in the love-triangle and also explore the intrusion of the past upon the future. "An Adventure of Don Juan" launches Don Juan Tenorio on the only possible adventure left for him, which is, rather than conquest, being conquered. As in *Martin Dressler* and "Catalogue of the Exhibition," two sisters are involved; one, Mary, is married to Augustus Hood, a prosperous member of the Somerset gentry with a fondness for artificial environments. The second sister, named Georgiana, at first interests Don Juan less than Mary. Georgiana engages in frequent philosophical discussions with Hood, whose estate is permeated (at ground level and below) with what Hood calls "living representations" (73): a ruined priory, Arcadia, a Saxon forest, Elizabethan groves, a hellish underworld (located below ground) and an Elysium (also underground). Don Juan also, at one point in the novella, descends, via a hollow oak tree, into his own past: a perfectly formed underground Venice, constructed for his delectation by Augustus Hood (117-18).

In this tale, Don Juan's interest comes eventually to rest on the unmarried sister, Georgiana. She frustrates him, and (the humor is subtly played) he sulks, grows despondent, "flings himself" on various couches, and jumps out of windows rather than using the door (this last is a variation of one of Don Juan's Venice escapes, but without the cuckolded silk merchant with unsheathed sword and the plunge into the canal). The depth and uncontrollable nature of his affection for Georgiana is strikingly at odds with his experience of himself as a person. As Edward Hower said, "To Don Juan, Georgiana represents the turbulent world of emotion, the experience of romantic love that has been missing from his life of sexual conquest" (231). To be sure, she represents a sense of destabilization and vulnerability; the Don is unaccustomed to this kind of obsession. Meanwhile, Mary Hood has fallen deeply in love with Don Juan, although he has come to rely on her for guidance in his pursuit of Georgiana. All the while, Augustus Hood, another of Millhauser's artists of mimesis and illusion, not only constructs vanished or mythical worlds but also presides over a house whose boundaries are, increasingly, indistinguishable from these simulacra. In a scene close to the end of the novella, Hood recounts the story of a laborer who becomes trapped in an underground tunnel and, after much labor with his pick, emerges in what he believes to be China (it is actually an abandoned simulacrum of a Chinese temple). "For say," Hood says to Georgiana, Mary, and Juan, during a dusk stroll by the river (which serves as another fictional way of connecting not only space but also past and future), "a man reads of China, dreams of China, and does not go to China. And say another man hacks his way through a wall and enters a Chinese temple. Now riddle me this: which China is more real?'" (129). Hood extends the riddle with several more scenarios, to which Georgiana responds. Unusually, though, Juan too has his say on the matter: "A fifth man . . . travels to China. He likes the country, travels for many years, and never returns home. *Poco a poco*—mmm, little by little—his early life becomes vague, dreamlike. He too has never traveled to China. He has always been there" (129). Indeed. Immediately prior to this exchange, Juan has experienced a crisis in which both place and time seem to be dissolving (but not dissolving completely). He is caught in this peculiarly liminal state: "Who was he? Who? He was no longer Don Juan. He had wandered away from himself, he couldn't find his way back. Who are you? I am the one I no longer am. *Basta!* He would *have his life*" (128). He determines that night to go to Georgiana's room and have her one way or another.

But when he sets out for that chamber, he finds that he is in utter darkness and disoriented in the enormous house, with its "long and sometimes turning corridors, its various wings, each with so many rooms . . . its many stairways going up or down, its galleries, its hidden chambers reached only by passages known to servants long since deceased" (131). His confusion increases as he relies only on touch and not sight: "He tried to picture the drawing room carefully in his mind, but the imagined furniture kept shifting and sliding about. . . . He continued forward, through the room that ought to have been the drawing room, holding out his hand in empty space. It was an odd immensity of space, as if he had accidentally stepped through a door into a black meadow—and who was to say he had *not* stepped into a meadow . . . ?" (132).

After several more disorienting turnings, he happens upon Mary, who, carrying a candle, does not say where she is going. Juan does not detain her but holds to his determination to reach a destination, and he eventually arrives at Georgiana's room. However, it is not the "Georgiana's room" he or the reader has anticipated. As he draws aside the bed curtains (of what has become a "dream-bed"), he sees Georgiana in bed with her brother-in-law Augustus Hood.

Juan's trip through the darkness, in its effect on the reader, resembles the severely limited point of view in "Revenge," in which the reader never really "sees" the house as a whole, but only as a sequence of rooms and passages. Each journey not only dissolves ideas of spatial configuration, but undermines the idea of temporal destination as well. In the end, Juan flees England, "that legendary land composed entirely of fog" (63). But "destination" has become so undermined in this novella that the fiction leaves him (literally) in-between.

Between-ness, indeterminate futures, the nature of story itself—all continue to be explored in the final, title novella. Though this retelling of the Tristan and Isolde myth does not depart radically from previously developed variants (as "An Adventure of Don Juan" does), its concerns with time, and especially prediction, are notable. In this tale we are, through the observations of Thomas of Cornwall, our narrator, plunged into a situation in which suspense mounts not because we are awaiting one awful outcome (we already know the ending of the story). Rather, we are whirled from one set of expectations to another. As King Mark of Cornwall's suspicion of his new queen (her name is spelled Ysolt here) and his nephew Tristan grows, he deliberately thrusts them into situations in which their honor will be tested. We suspect (again, because we know the legend and because Thomas implies as much) that Ysolt and Tristan are betraying the king deeply and constantly. Yet the king, unable to contemplate what he will be forced to do if he confronts the truth, continues to allow himself to be deceived. It is an excruciating game of cat and mouse, in which the immediate, not the long-term, future is completely unstable. The long-term future, too, is indeterminate; we have only a schematic in our minds: we know the two lovers will be banished, we know things will not end well—but the particulars depend on the causal chain that veers and swerves. Tristan and Ysolt at first manage to convince the king that they are innocent; the king's chief steward Oswin raises suspicions; the court dwarf Modor (who "betrays everyone and is universally detested" [149]) does as well; Thomas himself sees the pair walking at night in a moonlit orchard. The king banishes Tristan; Tristan returns and is once more in favor. As we follow these dramatic twists and turns we are once again tied to a narrative point of view that does not allow us a long perspective; Thomas writes in journal entries, and does not know the outcome until we do ourselves. Eventually, the pair is caught, but evidence of real betrayal is not presented until twenty-six pages before the end of the 101-page novella. By that point Tristan has been banished and returned, and then the pair banished (and, once more, returned). In other words, proof comes far too late to make it surprising to anyone, least of all the reader.

Triangles, those most unstable of shapes, saturate the novella. When King Mark, demented with jealousy and grief, imprisons himself after banishing Tristan and Ysolt, he presides over a triumvirate of spiders, which forms one-third of a larger triumvirate: "Here is my court: three spiders, a raven, and a fly." Thomas himself gives us a clue as to the dynamic in play: "The love of Tristan and the Queen has always flowed around and against the King. Banished from the court, alone in the forest, did they find themselves sometimes thinking of him? . . . In order for their love to flourish—in order for them to love at all—do they perhaps need the King?" (208).

In this novella, labyrinths and secret enclosures figure strongly; the castle wall is honeycombed with chambers and tunnels, and the orchard is another labyrinth with a thousand secret "rooms." These chambers and tunnels are sites of reconfiguration of triangles. For example, Ysolt is lured by Oswin to his secret grotto; Thomas has alerted King Mark, and they follow Oswin and the queen to the underground lair; as they burst into the chamber they see that Tristan has protected the queen's honor and holds Oswin at sword-point (181-82). Thus Tristan is reinstated at the court for the first time. However, the Millhauserian trope that reinforces narrative instability here is the replica. On banishing Tristan and Ysolt, King Mark commands an "artificer," Odo of Chester, to make a replica of the absent queen: a polychrome statue, with an elementary automaton-feature: her extended arm may be raised and lowered via a lever in her back. The statue is kept in a chamber in an inner labyrinth, concealed behind a cloth painted with a likeness of the king. Even here, the dynamic returns to three: as Odo the artificer pulls a cord, "slowly the cloth divided, breaking the image of the King in half. The two cloths had been placed side by side so artfully that I had not been able to detect the jointure" (195). In addition to creating another threesome (the two halves of the king and the queen), this scene shifts the suspense from a horizontal axis—time's arrow—to a vertical axis: concealment and duplication. In fact, as the scene ends, the king is "unnaturally still. His arm was raised as if frozen in the act of reaching toward the Queen, his head erect, his eyes wide, his lips parted as if in speech" (195-96).

The replica here acts as a stop-time. Indeed, there is nothing the king wants more than to stop time's inevitable progression toward tragedy. One more replica will be involved before the end of the book: Tristan marries a replica "Ysolt," Ysolt of the White Hands. This marks the endgame, when all components of the set, all players who are members of a triangle, are in the "wrong place." As Thomas points out,

Across the sea, the Queen lies awake in the royal chamber. All night long she thinks of the new bride, of Tristan asleep in the arms of his wife. In Tristan's chamber the King lies awake; he is thinking of the Queen alone in her chamber, of Tristan laughing with his bride. Here, in Tristan's castle, Tristan lies restlessly beside the beautiful Ysolt, the Ysolt who is not Ysolt, who can never be Ysolt, who by daring to bear the name Ysolt has doomed herself to lie beside him untouched, unloved, and unforgiven. Ysolt of the White Hands lies white and motionless under the coverlet. Her hands are crossed over her breasts. Her eyes remain open in the dark. (231)

This replica Ysolt also acts as a stop-time. Her lie to the wounded and ailing Tristan—that the first Ysolt has not cared enough to see him before he dies—kills him. The only continuity subsists in Thomas's pen: the last words of the novella are fitting:

> I dipped my quill in the ink of the oxhorn, shook off a drop with a single sharp dip of the wrist. I pulled my candle closer and bent over the page, my head bowed as if in prayer. I, Thomas of Cornwall, prince of parchment, lord of black ink, king of all space, summoner of souls, guardian of ghosts, friend of the pear tree and the silence of waves, companion to all those who watch in the night. (241)

"August Eschenburg"

If we use Millhauser's length criterion, "August Eschenburg" is a novella, and has structural commonalities with other Millhauser novellas. In terms of thematic richness, it is foundational to Millhauser's oeuvre, and deserves far more critical attention than it has been given thus far.

Its titular protagonist is one of Millhauser's solitary male artists. The son of a watchmaker, Eschenburg, after seeing a performance by the itinerant magician Konrad, becomes fascinated with Konrad's exquisitely constructed automata. He turns from his instruction as a watchmaker's apprentice to constructing his own automata. His figures eventually attract the attention of Herr Preisendanz of the Preisendanz Emporium, a large department store in Berlin, who recruits Eschenburg to create figures for the store's display windows. Eschenburg's work is spectacularly successful until he is undermined by an unscrupulous imitator, who provides automata for the newly opened competing store, Die Brüder Grimm.

The competitor's automata, because they are imitations of Eschenburg's imitations, are replicas of replicas, and, in a sort of machinic devolution, are degraded both in terms of the quality of their imitation (they are much coarser than Eschenburg's) and their performative aspects (their purpose is to titillate, and, as in all pornography, they do so by fragmenting the body: the focus is not on how the body, as a whole, replicates a human form, but on how the exaggerated buttocks or breasts draw the eye). Eschenburg's automata cannot compete with such decadence. He is fired and returns to his small town, Mühlenburg, and his watchmaker father.

It is at this point that the novella's form begins to transcend the ordinary, and it does so in terms of both the text's comments upon teleology and closure and in the way the text's structure echoes these concerns. Eschenburg's return to Mühlenburg is not unpredictable. However, the appearance of his competitor Hausenstein at the village is, and from this point forward the story does not follow

a predictable trajectory. Hausenstein is an aesthete with a degraded
and cynical vision:

> Nietzsche, bless his romantic soul, had invented the Übermensch, but
> Hausenstein had countered with a far better word: the Untermensch.
> . . . [B]y it he meant the kind of soul that, in the presence of any-
> thing great, or noble, or beautiful, or original, instinctively longed to
> pull it down and reduce it to a common level. The Untermensch did
> this always in the name of some resounding principle: patriotism, for
> example, or the spirit of mankind, or social progress, or morality, or
> truth. (36-37)

Hausenstein is also, of course, a hybrid: he appreciates Eschenburg's
art—that is why he has come to find him—but produces what he
knows is "trash" (34). He is one of Martin Dressler's predecessors
as the romantic businessman who is drawn irresistibly toward
increase. That Eschenburg allows himself to be convinced to return
to Berlin and establish an automaton theater there (Das Zaubertheater, which will feature Eschenburg's automata but be underwritten
by Hausenstein) results in a fusion. It is no longer clear, between the
two men, who is the "original" and who the replica; Eschenburg's
superior productions are dependent upon Hausenstein for their ability to have being in the wider world. In other words, Hausenstein's
actions, cynical though they may be, allow Eschenburg's automata to
come to life; yet Hausenstein needs Eschenburg, perhaps, as Eschenburg himself speculates, as an ideal in which to found his cynicism
and as both a cure and preservative for his ennui (37).

The ramifications of Hausenstein's and Eschenburg's relation to
each other and to their respective automata for doubling and replication are wide. However, if we are to return to our theme of triangles
and a fictional "third way," we will also find much to appreciate in
"August Eschenburg." Two images early in the story may serve as
starting points. First, Eschenburg in his childhood was fascinated
with a "cruel and marvelous toy": a paper figure which, when a
live bird was trapped inside it, appeared to come alive. This crude
automaton is "far better" than tamer animated toys, and it is partly
because it is genuinely alive—animated by a living creature. These
paper figures are a reversal of Hausenstein's pornographic automata:
the outside is a "man" animated crudely and fearfully by the bird
trapped inside; the unpredictable, tortured, clumsy movements of
the man are unpredictable and tortured precisely because the creature inside's responses are so complex and because the stakes are
nothing less than life and death. Hausenstein's automata are, above
all, predictable in both their identity as automata (he is not trying
to pass them off as perfect imitations of real people; rather, they are
parodies) and in their performative aspects: the swaying buttocks,

the overt sexual encounters delight partly because there are no sur-
prises involved except the usual ones. Eventually, of course, it is this
crudity that undoes Eschenburg's own automata; he discovers that
Hausenstein has been operating an automaton theater competing
with his own creation, and that this second theater's revenue—based
on the attraction of Hausenstein's degraded figures—is what keeps
the first theater afloat.

Yet there is something even more striking about the Zaubertheater and this story. Marc Chénetier points out that, because of
rhetorical strategies such as the use of terms like " 'First of all . . .
and then . . . and soon' "

> [the fictional dreams are] condemned to open-endedness, unfinished-
> ness, to infinite extension, to the eternal, which they necessarily join,
> like [these dreams' products] and like the texts which bespeak them:
> "Yes, the art of the automaton was a magical art, for when all was said
> and done there was something mysterious and unaccountable about
> clockwork: you breathed into the nostrils of a creature of dust and lo!
> it was alive. And so the art of clockwork was a high and noble art: the
> universe itself had been constructed by the greatest clockwork master
> of all, and remained obedient to mysterious laws of motion. And on
> the moving earth, all was ceaseless motion: wind and tide and fire."
> (Chénetier, *La précision* 52-53; Millhauser, *Penny Arcade* 61)

Thus Eschenburg and Millhauser's other artists are condemned
to ceaseless motion: there is no closure, no biological death—only
weariness.

If the trapped bird enacts the beating of life within the machine,
Konrad the Magician, Eschenburg's earliest inspiration, signifies the
artist condemned to the "ceaseless motion" of natural law. Having
discovered that Hausenstein himself operates the Black Boot, a
theater of crude and sexualized automata that competes with (and
finances) the Zaubertheater, Eschenburg packs a few of his figures
and becomes a wanderer much like Konrad.

The point in the novella at which closure might logically occur is
when Eschenburg is on the way back to Mühlenburg, having discovered that the Zaubertheater is no longer operating. On the last leg of
the trip, when he is awaiting a coach, he rests at the base of a tree.
Impulsively he buries his suitcase (which contains his automata) in
the leaves; this act precipitates a melancholy meditation upon his
life and fate in terms of the machinic and the biological, in terms
of accident and design. Eschenburg finds that he cannot reconcile
anything about what has happened to him. "And so it had all come
to nothing. He had given his life away to a childish passion. And
now it was over" (63).

He sleeps, and this would seem an appropriate point at which

to end the story. Yet the novella cannot close so neatly. Eschenburg awakes and cannot find his suitcase, and in this moment of
disorientation, time itself seems suspended in the vacuum created
both by the arbitrary nature of a mechanistic universe and by his
sudden loss of memory and ability to orient himself in terms of a
logical chain of causality. Then, says the text, "He remembered"
(63), and the remembering restarts the clock. There is to be no rest
for Eschenburg the artist. "A short while later, he picked up his
suitcase and started back to the coach house" (64). Like the novella
form, like, as Chénetier remarked, the dreams of all Millhauser's
artists, he is condemned to "infinite extension, to the eternal" (*La
précision* 52).

"A Game of Clue"

This novella, in its tone, setting, and theme, tempts comparisons
to American realists such as John Updike. Yet it succeeds on the
basis of the extent to which the reader accepts not only the physical
and psychological realism of the primary story—a family drama,
subtly enacted through an evening of Clue played on the porch of
the family house in Connecticut—but also a secondary tale which
involves the characters on the board: Miss Scarlet, Professor Plum,
Colonel Mustard, Mrs. Peacock, Mr. Green, and Mrs. White.
    The novella is divided into short sections, an innovation Mill-
hauser will use in later novellas such as "The Princess, the Dwarf,
and the Dungeon" and "Catalogue of the Exhibition: The Art of
Edmund Moorash (1810-1846)." The section headings (run into the
text) may, if isolated and read sequentially, be read as hints or clues
themselves. For example, if we examine, somewhat arbitrarily, the
first thirteen headings—"The board"; "The table"; "Jacob"; "Pray
forgive me"; "The library"; "Marian"; "Tokens and weapons"; "The
porch"; "David"; "Doors and passages"; "The pleasures of secret passages"; "A woman of mystery"; "A warm night in August"—we can
see that they imply certain events and tensions in both the primary
(Connecticut) and secondary (Clue) narratives, and can themselves
be read as a sort of incipient "shadow narrative," one that never quite
comes to life but still haunts the fiction.
    The fifth section, typical of descriptive sections throughout the
novella, uses exact, meticulous, nearly clinical language:

> Viewed from above, the LIBRARY is a symmetrical figure that may be
> thought of as a modified rectangle: from each of the four corners a
> small square is missing. The resulting figure has twelve sides. As in
> all the rooms, the furniture is pictured from above and drawn in black
> outline. Thus the lamp on the central table reveals only the top of its
> hexagonal shade. . . . (*Barnum Museum* 12)

This meticulous description serves not only to instantiate the setting for readers, but also, through its verticality (both because it is a description that lacks the "horizontal" forward momentum of conventional narrative and because it enables the readers to share with the players the sense of looking downward—on a vertical axis— into a subterranean world), serves to establish an alternate path into the story. That is, like the "secret passageways" in the game itself, it forms a narrative secret passageway that allows us entrance to the second story, that of the Clue characters.

Our first glimpse into the secondary narrative occurs in a section titled "Pray forgive me": Colonel Mustard has disturbed Miss Scarlet, whom he will shortly attempt to seduce. The characterization in this passage is not noticeably different from that in the primary-story sections. The colonel is, certainly, a coarse, scheming philanderer, and his personality contrasts sharply with those of the players—Jacob, Marian, and David Ross, as well as Jacob's girlfriend Susan Newton—who surround the game board. Yet he is as dimensional as they are.

His entrance underscores the fact that the primary-narrative characters—Jacob, Marian, David, and Susan—have no control over the world of the Clue characters; they see that world only in its dimmest outlines, through the tools of the dice and the cards and the schematic drawing on the board. They must guess at the outcome, just as they must guess at the outcome of the game that is occurring among themselves, in which each person (through close third-person narrative that shifts among the characters) speculates about the motives and aims of the others. For example, the youngest character, David, who is celebrating his fifteenth birthday, is (poignantly) obsessed with whether his brother Jacob will participate in a ritual they have enacted on David's previous birthdays: staying up late together and talking. Marian speculates on Jacob's motives for bringing his girlfriend Susan Newton to a family celebration. Susan speculates on Jacob's state of mind and on David and Marian in general. Two games of Clue—one on the board, one in the Connecticut house—are played at once.

Psychological gulfs separate both the Rosses and Susan Newton and the group of Clue characters. Alienation is the order of the day for both primary and secondary narratives, an alienation growing from insoluble secrets. Neither the Clue characters nor the players nor we can discern exactly what will happen in the future, even after the game is "won" by the youngest Ross, David. In other words, we know who, where, and with what implement the murder was committed, but the secrets of the Clue characters' hearts remain obscure, and, indeed, they seem trapped in an endless physical space (the mansion) and an ongoing drama that has no discernible outcome. Like other Millhauser replicas, they are condemned to a sort of machinic eternity, which breeds new secrets even as others are solved. The human players' feelings are clearest to us, but the overwhelming impression is one of isolation and yearning. Susan Newton is alienated, having been treated coldly by Jacob and by his sister, who resents her presence at a family gathering; Marian, the sister, is alienated by Susan Newton's presence and by her own sense of her life's "waste and drift" (13). Marian regrets accusing her brother Jacob of selfishness for bringing Susan and for arriving at the family home several hours late; the weapon she used against her brother—her accusation—has turned upon and wounded her. David longs for time alone with his brother Jacob and is oppressed by his own sense of waste: the game of Clue is flawed; the cards cannot be divided evenly among four players. Susan Newton's presence has made it so the games "won't count" (17). Jacob himself vibrates with anger, tension, and a bitter and black frustration; only twenty-five, he finds himself already riven by the impossibility of choosing between what he feels called to do (he has taken a year off to write, but is drastically blocked) and his other alternative (completing his doctorate and forgoing writing for good). In the end, his frustration is with the impossibility of biological life: he will not live long enough to be both writer and scholar.

Professor Plum, who walks the secret passageways below the Clue mansion, provides a structural counterpoint to the Ross parents, Martha and Samuel, who sleep upstairs as the others play Clue on the porch. The professor allows himself to be seduced by the passageways, which are (with the doors) the "secret life of the game," because they allow the character's tokens to enter and leave the rooms, the sites of the action (17). Yet they have an importance superior to this, which is that they are pleasurable and seductive. That they seduce the professor is not surprising, because all the characters in this novella are seduced by secrets they are not allowed to know, secrets that, like the professor's passage, are never ended—made into knowledge rather than secret—by disclosure. The point of the game of Clue is the clues themselves, which are all located on an axis other than the conventional narrative. The passageways lead nowhere and thus do not, as secret passageways should, reveal secrets—including where they will eventually lead. Up in the attic other secrets are stored: childhood toys, which evoke not only the childhoods of the players but family history. Marian's grandmother's toy German schoolroom, though (perhaps appropriately) disarranged, evokes not only the connection between grandmother and granddaughter but between a historic before and after, demarked by immigration and identity shifts. In addition to memory, the school evokes history, including history's tendency to submerge the past's secrets in its relentless forward momentum. The attic toys also include the token for Professor Plum. Thus the professor, who wanders the passageways below the mansion in the secondary narrative, and his symbol—the lost token that rests in an old shoebox above the heads of the Rosses and Susan Newton in the primary story—form not only a vertical axis but a narrative suspension or lack of closure: in the final scene the secondary story slows, gels, and fades, but achieves no real "end." Instead, in the last line, Professor Plum is simply "fading among his fading passageways" (60).

No secrets will be resolved, for the Rosses or Susan Newton, for the Clue characters, or for the reader. Instead, the Clue board established a passageway between the imaginary and the real, but like the passageways Professor Plum wanders, it is not clear where these passageways lead. The Clue characters are condemned to endlessness; the Rosses and Susan Newton are all too aware of their own biological being and the ending that implies, and the impossibility not only of discovering but also of telling secrets. What both sets of characters have in common is the proliferation of clues that, if eventually they reveal their secrets, at the same time establish the structure that ensures more clues will arise, accumulate, and lead their own mysterious, whispering lives.

—D. A.

Interpretive Approaches

Criticism in English of Steven Millhauser's work, though not abundant, varies widely in terms of approach. This may be because Millhauser's novels, short stories, and novellas pose interpretive questions, both as a body of work and individually, with which American critics are unaccustomed to dealing—at least in an American writer. The sheer range of Millhauser's work—from the overtly fantastic to realistic (if strange and uncanny)—is itself daunting. Classifying his work is not easy or, perhaps, possible, and this fact can flummox critics whose project relies on traditional classification or taxonomy. For example, the introduction of the supernatural does not reduce the sense that Millhauser's realism is authentic. His 2003 novella "Revenge," in which there is no particle of identifiable magical realism, still manages powerfully to evoke the uncanny. Its method has something in common with Poe and Kafka, but its literary inheritance also includes John Updike. Dreiser and Hawthorne have been named as Millhauser's precursors; so (often) has Borges. The romantic sublime also has a place in his fiction, but this sublime operates very differently from what is usually called to mind by that term.

In terms of narrative, too, easy interpretive strategies are rare. Though much of Millhauser's work concerns itself more with trope than with formal experimentation, questions concerning the nature of time and of causation are frequently raised via these tropes. In the instances in which Millhauser does make use of formal experiment—"Klassik Komix #1," for example, as well as "Catalogue of the Exhibition: The Art of Edmund Moorash (1810-1846)"—the experiment's basis is in genre hybridity rather than overt narrative disruption, metafiction, alternative history, and so on (though narrative is, of course, affected by the genre experimentation).

In short, negotiating some of these dynamic binaries—the realistic versus the fantastical; biographical fiction versus the purely invented—can lead to interpretive cul-de-sacs. Scholarly critics tend to adopt one of two broad approaches. The first group attempts to trace authorial intention (and usually includes some measure of biographical criticism in this attempt), and/or tries to discern Millhauser's place in the literary/historical pantheon (should he have a place on the shelf next to Borges or to Hawthorne?) In other words, this group primarily tries to elicit the significance of Millhauser's works as literary/cultural productions or artifacts. The second group tends to focus more on textual criticism and less on literary history, authorial intention, or biography. That is, they examine the method or poetics by which the fictions themselves operate. (Not surprisingly, the second group has a somewhat easier time.)

In 1991 (just after the 1990 publication of *The Barnum Museum*), the journal *Salmagundi* devoted a significant portion of its fall issue to Millhauser, and Mary Kinzie's lengthy essay is one of the first extensive treatments of Millhauser's work as a whole. In terms of this discussion, Kinzie's essay is in some ways paradigmatic: she is attempting to reconcile Millhauser's early novels (especially *Edwin Mullhouse* and *Portrait of a Romantic*) with *In the Penny Arcade* and (especially) *The Barnum Museum*. Because the novels encourage the reader to find parodic elements in them (*Edwin Mullhouse* for obvious reasons, and *Portrait of a Romantic* for the reason that Arthur Grumm and his companions at various points skirt the edge of self-parody), they also encourage searches for influence and for authorial intentions. The story collections, however, do not, and Kinzie's aim of proving her "conviction that [Millhauser] was wrestling with and trying to extend the literary example of Borges" (132) is frustrated by Millhauser's own contention that Kafka, particularly *Letters to Felice*, has been a far greater influence.

However, Kinzie is also an early identifier of Millhauserian stylistic and narrative traits that other critics have since commented upon, and in her investigation of the Borges connection she uncovers some of the paradoxes that must be addressed in any Millhauser criticism. She notes that Millhauser applies the "smaller-scale techniques of fictional realism to a largely notional as opposed to a realistic landscape" and thus creates "his own subtle, clever, funny, breathtaking, and delightful mode of magical realism" (116). However, she cannot reconcile Millhauser's use of minimalist characterization with the fact that "Millhauser's work is perfectly riveting," and spends much of the essay approaching the problem through the Borgesian criteria for fantastic literature. In the end, she leaves her question about characterization mostly unanswered. However, the fact that she has raised it tells us much about the discomfort American critics and readers feel when they try to respond to this highly original work whose fictional operations can appear mysterious and, indeed, magical.

It is perhaps in keeping with Millhauser's own fictional poetics and perhaps ultimately most useful to allow that the imaginative engine that drives Millhauser's work is in fact structural and thematic tensions—between "real" and fantastic, casuistry and existentialism, replication and originality, miniaturization and gigantism, minimalism and maximalism, the horizontal and the vertical, the catalogue and the dramatic narrative, suspension and closure, childhood and adulthood, and so on, ad (almost) infinitum. In fact, Millhauser himself, in a recent interview, points out that dual and competing preoccupations with the fictional and the real (and perhaps by implication realism and the fantastic) have always obsessed us:

Americans have always been notoriously practical, while at the same time they're consumed by visions—a contradiction that strikes me as characteristic of hope-crazed conquerors in a new land. Cut down your trees, build your cabin, dream your dream. The great American novel is *Moby-Dick*, a visionary masterpiece filled with minuscule realistic details about whaling. As for realistic fiction: it comes late to America and is actually quite foreign, a delayed importation of French naturalism. In this sense, a writer like Hemingway is radically un-American, a betrayer of the tradition represented by Hawthorne and Melville. Any art form that blurs the distinction between reality and fiction is as American as apple pie. ("Questions")

In terms of explorations of the text, the realistic/fantastic (marvelous, uncanny) binary, in all its instantiations, may be plotted along two axes: space (under which we may include all stylistic characteristics) and time (enacted through narrative).* Insofar as the American hunger for forward momentum is sometimes expressed through

---

* This essay will not undertake a thorough narratological analysis, but will instead establish a few broad principles that will, it is hoped, be helpful both in understanding the negative popular responses to Millhauser's work and in suggesting further avenues of critical exploration.

the desire for a good story, many popular critics are bothered by what they have termed a certain sense of stasis in Millhauser's fiction. This discomfort seems to be related to Millhauser's extreme descriptive precision, which also frequently draws charges of art-for-art's-sake preciousness. These charges frequently seem to derive from a fear of coming to a stop and looking, with care and attention, around ourselves—which is one of the things Millhauser's fiction does. Ultimately, this careful looking in Millhauser's fiction itself constitutes a kind of narrative. Cécile Roudeau (among other critics) has established that Millhauser's descriptive precision is not simply "beautiful writing," but also, via displacement, frequently functions *as* the narrative dynamic in Millhauser's work. Again, Roudeau compares Millhauser's work to Calder's mobiles; the fictions are not, she says, "simply . . . marvelous stories told by an illusionist of genius, but also . . . playful and fragile architectures [that] defy the rigidity and weight of the (verbal) material [of which they are constructed] . . ." (13). She draws specific and detailed comparisons of Millhauser's fictional technique with the functional aesthetics of the mobiles. "The Knife Thrower" is compared with Calder's "Vertical Out of Horizontal": "The horizontalness, the linearity of a classic narration emerges from a verticality of incessant reprise. . . . With Millhauser, it seems that the 'next' is always first an 'again.'" Variations in linguistic motifs—"the same words return: [he] 'raised his arm and threw' [or] 'tossed' or again 'flung' . . ."—underlie the narrative dynamics: the text "oscillates thus around a point of equilibrium that is also one of *displacement* (and it is this that permits the story to 'advance')" (15, emphasis added).

Roudeau's insight is valid across most of Millhauser's oeuvre. Displacement is constitutively related to two of Millhauser's fictional techniques, listing and repetition. In fact, neither listing nor displacement nor repetition occurs alone, because none is possible without displacement (listing because of its cumulative effects—each item is successively displaced by the next, as Arthur Saltzman points out in "In the Millhauser Archive"; repetition because it must occur across time—otherwise it would be simultaneity—and each successive repeat displaces the one that occurred before it). Thus I would submit that descriptive precision—along with lists, replications, and other techniques that require or are driven by such precision—not only creates a different and more complex *view* of time but in fact creates a new kind of fictional time in Millhauser's narratives. It is this unfamiliar fictional time that drives critics' displays of anxiety, which are frequently cloaked in dismissal and, occasionally, outright vituperation. It is not a lack of narrative dynamic that bothers people. It is that Millhauser's is a new narrative dynamic—a genuine formal innovation.

Clues to understanding this formal innovation may perhaps be found in the author's own critical preoccupations, which focus upon three related topics (all crucially related to displacement): replication, miniaturization, and repetition (across narrative or across time, as opposed to the repetition involved in replication). In "The Fascination of the Miniature" (1984) Millhauser points out that this fascination has not only to do with the miniature's tininess but also with the fact that it is, unlike the gigantic, "without dread" (34). Further, the miniature, in order to fascinate (and not simply to tire) must include "thoroughness of execution, richness of detail"; in other words, "the miniature *seizes* the attention by the fact of discrepancy, and *holds* it by the quality of precision" (34, original emphasis). This last phrase almost exactly replicates the way Millhauser's fiction itself works: the dynamic relation of the "real" to the "imaginary" seizes our attention, and our attention is held by the precisely described imaginary and real world.* The precise descriptions constitute their own kind of narrative dynamic.

Replication, too, has been defined closely by Millhauser ("Replicas," 1995). Though replication is "an act of radical unoriginality" (and therefore "subverts the Romantic idea of originality by insisting on total imitation" ["Replicas" 51]), it nevertheless seeks to duplicate its original exactly. If it succeeds completely, though, without revealing itself to be a replica, it is no longer really a replica but a "false original" (53). Therefore,

The replica may thus deceive us for a time, but it must also undeceive us. Ideally, a certain moment will be reached when the spectator, confronting the ambiguous object, experiences a wavering or hesitation: caught between belief in the object and a secret doubt, the spectator will experience an almost metaphysical uncertainty. The true art of replication lies in imitating an object so perfectly that it may be mistaken for an original, while at the same time it reveals its falseness. (54)

Millhauser names a number of methods by which this may be accomplished: falseness of material; geographical incongruity; the scale model (as Millhauser points out, an instance of the miniature); trompe l'oeil, the wax apple, the photograph, the Platonic object, the movie set, and more, on through the idols of Epicurus, and, last, memory (which, of course, has implications for the ways in which Millhauser plays with the vertical and horizontal aspects of narrative) (54-59). There are degrees of exactness in these replications.

---

* Douglas Fowler, in his 1996 essay "Steven Millhauser, Miniaturist," has examined Millhauser's fiction as instances of the miniature and as "a world that demands our most serious attention" (140).

In terms of Millhauser's fiction, though, his next set of observations has interesting implications:

> by pointing beyond themselves to another world that by contrast is felt to be genuine, replicas create in those who look at them a feeling of restlessness and desire. In the very act of revealing their nature, they leave us dissatisfied. And yet by presenting themselves frankly as imitations, by offering themselves as playful or made-up versions of serious objects, replicas present themselves also as seductions or temptations. Because we needn't take them seriously, they offer us release from the oppression or solemnity of actual things. (59-60)

Along with this release comes danger: at heart, replicas, in their "hidden arrogance," want to "secretly undermine the world of primary objects," to "claim superiority by virtue of their playfulness" (60). In fact, the power of replication, as "a branch of the dark and many-branched art of illusion . . . lies precisely in the conflict between two forces: the thrust away from imitation and toward a superior, authentic world, and the equal and opposite thrust away from that ceaselessly summoned world toward a world of alluring artifice" (60). In this dynamic, we allow the real to be ceaselessly displaced by the artificial, but the "feeling of restlessness and desire" the replicas evoke invites us to replace the replication with the real. The dynamic is a narrative one; the nature of replication is descriptive. Where these axes cross is where Millhauser's fiction occurs.

Although Millhauser himself has not written about listing per se, it is perhaps his most radically innovative technique. It is also one frequently responsible for critics' imputing a "static" quality to Millhauser's fiction. Saltzman's 1996 essay "In the Millhauser Archives" (reprinted in 2000 as chapter 3 of his book *This Mad "Instead": Governing Metaphors in Contemporary American Fiction*) is the most extensive exploration in English of how Millhauser's lists function. As Saltzman says, "For Millhauser, lists are conspicuous interfaces where art and life, systems and surge, the magical and the mundane coalesce"; significantly, also, lists, as always "arbitrar[y] and incomplet[e]," are a location for "imminent spawn" (50). Saltzman productively examines several Millhauser works—"The Barnum Museum," "A Game of Clue," and *Edwin Mullhouse*—in terms of lists' "sustained crossbreeding of inventory and invention" (55). He maintains that the list is another form of "scrupulous distortion," to use pseudobiographer Jeffrey Cartwright's words, and operates with a complexity comparable to that of metaphor (61). In other words, lists suspend narrative in some ways but open it up in others. Like Roudeau, Saltzman points out that the descriptive precision of lists enables the interpenetration of time and space: a list's "arbitrariness

[and] incompleteness" implies movement, alteration, accumulation: all narrative qualities (50).

The public appetite for abundance—expressed in Millhauser's fiction through lists—is not new, and one would think that, especially in an acquisitive twenty-first century American culture, lists would be particularly satisfying. (Lists are also, of course, a quintessentially American fictional technique—*Moby-Dick*'s cetological catalogs are only the most striking example.) However, Millhauser's fictions expose a dangerous side of listing, for the lists not only temporarily suspend time but also overcome it: time's relevance (or irrelevance) is determined along this cumulative, spatial, vertical axis, and not the other way around. They force the reader not only to attend to this vertical axis but also to allow this vertical axis temporarily to undermine the primacy of the horizontal, forward-driving narrative. In other words, rather than being appended to a forward-moving narrative, the lists take over the narrative and force the reader to shift not simply her definition of causation and event but her notion of how these principles may be bodied forth in a "fiction."

This phenomenon is present not only in Millhauser's fictions viewed as narrative constructions but thematically as well. In some ways, the destabilizing of time by the oscillations created through listing is a kind of sublime—it is uncontainable because neither the spatial nor the temporal has primacy. The maximalization of detail that intensifies the spatial is similar to the maximalism pursued with such energy by Martin Dressler. Saltzman's 2001 essay "A Wilderness of Size" usefully explores how maximalism can become a sort of American sublime: "Americans have enjoyed a national heritage of presumption, whereby we may choose to regard every promontory as an exclamation point. As a result, our confrontation with the Uncontainable does not so much dwarf as endow us" (590). *Martin Dressler,* though, as Marc Chénetier has pointed out, concerns an artist of the technological, and the technological always becomes exhausted, yet at one and the same time does not die a biological death. Its trajectory is indeterminate, as most of nature's is not.

Millhauser's own 1994 essay on Thomas Mann's *Tonio Kröger* demonstrates even more deeply the importance of repetition and variation in relation to time. This close reading of Mann's novella explores the ways in which repetition and variation, in the form of the leitmotif, serves as a way of "binding together the various parts of [the author's] tale—a method that cuts across chronology, that serves to *halt or defeat the relentless advance of fictional time*" (199, emphasis added). Millhauser does not here refer to any of the effects I have named above vis-à-vis creation of a new sort of fictional time; rather, he is talking about a writerly problem: "A fifty-page story that covers nearly twenty years and is arranged chronologically risks a dissipation of its effects, risks, that is, becoming scattered or diffuse; and a writer committed to such a scheme must continually strive to overcome the dispersive tendency of his narrative" (199). In Millhauser's statement, it is in this sense and this sense alone that the leitmotif serves to "halt or defeat the relentless advance of fictional time." Yet the halting and defeating of fictional time is crucial to stories that occupy a much smaller chronological space than does *Tonio Kröger*.

This is so in part because the leitmotif, in cognitive terms, functions in somewhat the same way as memory. "At the moment of repetition, past and present become one, or rather are held in the mind separately but concurrently. For an instant, confluence abolishes chronology. Time is deceived, outwitted, overcome" (Millhauser, "Some Thoughts" 200). Yet the leitmotif is more effective than flashback because there is no "creaking of machinery in its entrances and exits" (although flashback has the one practical advantage of being able to reach into a past outside the temporal range of the text itself) (202). Moreover, leitmotif, because it functions as temporal synecdoche, "will also summon forth past settings or situations or even entire scenes—a whole cluster of pasts. In this way the past of the text is continually carried forward into the present" (202).

Millhauser's sensitive discussion of repetition in Mann has several implications for his own work. Insofar as leitmotif is present in Millhauser—and it is, in abundance, especially in works that take place over a long span of time (such as *Martin Dressler*)—it functions in just these ways. (Millhauser is so fond of leitmotif that he often repeats phrases or sentences word for word at different points in a novel, novella, or short story.) However, leitmotif is integrated into the text in the way a list is not. Lists, once again, seem to the reader vertical rather than horizontal: they imply a stoppage of time, yet an instantiation of narrative through (as Saltzman puts it) their "arbitrariness and incompleteness" (50). They are, in important ways, a *real* stoppage: while the listing is taking place, no conventional narrative motion except what is implied by their arbitrariness and incompleteness takes place. Yet the reader is aware that the lists may be sleight of hand: the narrative may be occurring behind or alongside the listing (while the reader is absorbed in the catalogue, the action may be occurring offstage, or just beyond the reader's peripheral vision). In either case, the list induces an experience of time that is outside most readers' experiences. As Saltzman puts it, "Lists reinforce this paradox: all transcendence is tied to the roll call of integers; conversely, the surface tension of components may enable the imagination to exceed the rim of the real, the way water overfills the glass without spilling" (53). This function extends to time itself, and makes time into a form of the sublime: we are in the world of story, yet we can no longer use the world of story, or narrative, to contain time.

However these binaries operate in Millhauser's fiction, it is clear that they are far more than and far different from simple aesthetic self-indulgence. They demand much more from the author (in terms of technical prowess and writerly courage) and the reader (in terms of willingness to enter this fictional world) than the kind of psychological realism to which we are most accustomed. In the end, it is Saltzman's lovely metaphor of the water swelling momentarily above the rim of the glass that best embodies the breathlessness the reader feels at certain moments in Millhauser's fiction: when the impossible has actually occurred somehow, occurred palpably in one's own sensorium.

—D. A.

Works Cited

Adams, Timothy Dow. "The Mock-Biography of Edwin Mullhouse." *Biography* 5.3 (1982): 205-14.

Allen, Bruce. Rev. of *Around the Day in Eighty Worlds*, by Julio Cortázar, *In the Penny Arcade*, by Steven Millhauser, *The Handmaid's Tale*, by Margaret Atwood, and *The Good Apprentice*, by Iris Murdoch. *Saturday Review* June 1986: 74.

Annan, Gabriele. "Cold Comfort." Rev. of *The King in the Tree: Three Novellas*, by Steven Millhauser. *New York Review of Books* 50:13 (14 Aug. 2003): 25.

Balz, Douglas. "A Collection of Cunning Escape Routes for Fleeing the Mundane." Rev. of *The Barnum Museum*, by Steven Millhauser. *Chicago Tribune* 5 Aug. 1990: 7. 1 June 2005 <http://galenet.galegroup.com>.

Barrineau, Nancy Warner. "Theodore Dreiser and *Martin Dressler*: Tales of American Dreamers." *Dreiser Studies* 30.1 (1999): 35-45.

Bautz, Mark. "Short Stories to Savor from a Master Technician." *Washington Times* 24 Sept. 1990. 16 July 2005 <http://lexisnexis.com>.

Bennett, Tony. *The Birth of the Museum: History, Theory, Politics.* London: Routledge, 1995.

Birkerts, Sven. Rev. of *Martin Dressler*, by Steven Millhauser. *Yale Review* 85.1 (1997): 144-55.

Borges, Jorge Luis. "Parable of the Palace." *Dreamtigers*. Trans. Mildred Boyer and Harold Morland. New York: Dutton, 1964. 44-45.

Boyd, John D. "The Double Vision of *Edwin Mullhouse*." *Biography* 11.1 (1988): 35-46.

Bradfield, Scott. "The Grand Cosmo." *Times Literary Supplement* 3 Apr. 1998: 23.

Burroway, Janet. "Heartbreak Hotel." *New York Times* 12 May 1996, late ed., sec. 7: 8. *LexisNexis* 23 June 2005 <http://lexisnexis. com>.

Charles, Ron. "Desperation and Discomfort in the Lap of Luxury." *Christian Science Monitor* 15 Oct. 1997: 8. *EBSCO* 21 June 2005 <http://ebsco.com>.

Chénetier, Marc. *Beyond Suspicion: New American Fiction Since 1960.* Philadelphia: U of Pennsylvania P, 1996.

—. *La précision de l'impossible.* Paris: Belin, 2003.

—. "Synthèse." Ed. Anne Ullmo. *Steven Millhauser, une écriture sur le fil.* Villeneueve d'Ascq: Presses Universitaires du Septentrion, 2004. 93-97.

Cheuse, Alan. Rev. of *Enchanted Night*, by Steven Millhauser. "All Things Considered," Natl. Public Radio (23 Dec. 1999). 20 Apr. 2005 <http://proquest.umi.com>.

Cochoy, Nathalie. "*The Knife Thrower and Other Stories*, de Steven Millhauser: l'écriture au couteau." *Études anglaises* 56 (2003): 467-481.

Cortázar, Julio. "The Instruction Manual." *Cronopios and Famas.* Trans. Paul Blackburn. New York: New Directions, 1962. 3-5.

Crowley, John. "Underground with Mirrors and Mermaids." *New York Times* 12 Oct. 1986, late city final ed., sec. 7: 9. *LexisNexis* 20 July 2005 <http://lexisnexis.com>.

Cusac, Anne-Marie. "The Best Books of 1997." *Progressive* Jan. 1998: 38. *EBSCO* 21 June 2005 <http://ebsco.com>.

Dirda, Michael. "In Which Wonders Never Cease." *Washington Post* 18 June 1990, Style: B1. *LexisNexis* 16 July 2005 <http://lexisnexis. com>.

—. "Journey to the Center of the Earth." *Washington Post Book World* 21 Sep. 1986, final ed. *LexisNexis* 20 July 2005 <http://lexisnexis. com>.

—. "Worlds within Worlds." Rev. of *Little Kingdoms: Three Novellas*, by Steven Millhauser. *Washington Post Book World* 3 Sept. 1993: 5+. 27 June 2005 <http://galenet.galegroup.com>.

Dooley, Patricia. Rev. of *From the Realm of Morpheus*, by Steven Millhauser. *Library Journal* 1 Sept. 1986: 216.

Dunn, Robert. "First Love and the Last Automatons." Rev. of *In the Penny Arcade*, by Steven Millhauser. *New York Times Book Review* 19 Jan. 1986: 9.

Eliot, T. S. "The Love Song of J. Alfred Prufrock." *The Complete Poems and Plays 1909-1950.* New York: Harcourt, 1971. 3-7.

Evenson, Brian. Rev. of *Enchanted Night*, by Steven Millhauser. *Review of Contemporary Fiction* 20.2 (2000): 180.

Fowler, Douglas. "Millhauser, Süskind, and the Postmodern Promise." *Journal of the Fantastic in the Arts* 1.4 (1988): 77-86.

—. "Steven Millhauser, Miniaturist." *Critique* 37.2 (1996): 139-148. *EBSCO* 22 Nov. 2004 <http://ebsco.com>.

Freeman, John. "A Couple of Lovely Romance Works: Art of Betrayal, Deceit Permeate These Collections." Rev. of *The King in the Tree: Three Novellas*, by Steven Millhauser, and *Darts of Cupid*, by Edith Templeton. *Denver Post* 9 Feb. 2003: EE 03.

Geary, Brian. Rev. of *Enchanted Night*, by Steven Millhauser. *Library Journal* August 1993: 156-57.

Green, Daniel. "Two Fabulists." *Georgia Review* 49.3 (Winter 1995): 960-67. 27 June 2005 <http://galenet.galegroup.com>.

Harshaw, Tobin. "Pay the Piper." Rev. of *Enchanted Night*, by Steven Millhauser. *New York Times Book Review* 14 Nov. 1999: 15.

Hebel, Udo J. "Performing the Spectacle of Technology at the Beginning of the American Century: Steven Millhauser's *Martin Dressler.*" *The Holodeck in the Garden: Science and Technology in Contemporary American Fiction*. Ed. Peter Freese and Charles B. Harris. Normal, IL: Dalkey Archive, 2004. 192-211.

Herrero-Olaizola, Alejandro. "Writing Lives, Writing Lies: The Pursuit of Apocryphal Biographies." *Mosaic* 35.3 (2002): 73-88.

Howard, Maureen. "Semi-Samizdat and Other Matters." Rev. of *Fools and Other Stories*, by Njabulo S. Ndebele, *Awaiting Trespass: A Passion*, by Linda Ty-Casper, *Antonia Saw the Oryx First*, by Maria Thomas, *A Sport of Nature*, by Nadine Gordimer, *Three Farmers on Their Way to a Dance*, by Richard Powers, *Visitants*, by Randolph Stow, *More Die of Heartbreak*, by Saul Bellow, *The Enchanter*, by Vladimir Nabokov, *Foe*, by J. M. Coetzee, and *In the Penny Arcade*, by Steven Millhauser. *Yale Review* 77 (1988): 243-58.

Howe, Irving. Afterword. "Catalogue of the Exhibition: The Art of Edmund Moorash (1810-1846)" by Steven Millhauser. *Salmagundi* 92 (1991): 110-14.

Hower, Edward. "Hidden Worlds." Rev. of *The King in the Tree: Three Novellas*, by Steven Millhauser. *World & I* 18.6 (2003): 230.

Irvine, Anne. Rev. of *Martin Dressler*, by Steven Millhauser. *Library Journal* 15 Apr. 1996: 123.

Kakutani, Michiko. Rev. of *From the Realms of Morpheus*, by Steven Millhauser. New York Times 17 Sept. 1986, late city final ed.: C24. *LexisNexis* 20 July 2005 <http://lexisnexis>.

—. "The Love that Is Misery and Madness." Rev. of *The King in the Tree: Three Novellas*, by Steven Millhauser. *New York Times* 28 Feb. 2003: E2:52.

—. "Perceptions of Marvels." Rev. of *In the Penny Arcade*, by Steven Millhauser. *New York Times* 11 Jan. 1986, late city final ed., sec. 1: 12.

Kasper, Catherine. "Steven Millhauser's American Gothic." *Denver Quarterly* 36.3-4 (2002): 88-93.

Kinzie, Mary. "Succeeding Borges, Escaping Kafka: On the Fiction of Steven Millhauser." *Salmagundi* 92 (1991): 115-44.

Klepp, L. S. "Enchanted Night." *Entertainment Weekly* 7 Jan. 2000: 61.

LaHood, Marvin J. Rev. of *The King in the Tree: Three Novellas*, by Steven Millhauser. *World Literature Today* 78:3.4 (2004): 95.

Lavoie, Thomas. Rev. of *In the Penny Arcade*, by Steven Millhauser. *Library Journal* Jan. 1986: 103-04.

Leavitt, Caroline. "Looking beyond the Bestseller List for the Perfect Present . . ." *Boston Globe*, 8 Dec. 2002: D6.

Leavitt, David. "The Unsung Voices." Rev. of *In the Penny Arcade*, by Steven Millhauser, and *Days, An Amateur's Guide to the Night*, and *Oh!*, by Mary Robison. *Esquire* Feb. 1986: 117-18.

Leiding, Reba. Rev. of *Enchanted Night*, by Steven Millhauser. *Library Journal* July 1999: 134.

Malin, Irving. Rev. of *Little Kingdoms: Three Novellas*, by Steven Millhauser. *Review of Contemporary Fiction* 14.1 (1994): 212.

Mangaliman, Jessie. "A Character in Search of Criticism Turns to *Architectural Record*." *Architectural Record* 185.10 (1997): 37. *EBSCO* 30 Nov. 2004 <http://ebsco.com>.

Marcus, Ben. Rev. of *Enchanted Night*, by Steven Millhauser. *Village Voice* 26 Oct. 1999: 90.

McLaughlin, Robert L. Rev. of *Martin Dressler*, by Steven Millhauser. *Review of Contemporary Fiction* 16.3 (1996): 185-86.

McGrath, Patrick. "Artists and Automatons." Rev. of *The Knife Thrower and Other Stories*, by Steven Millhauser. *New York Times* 10 May 1998, sec. 7. *LexisNexis* 10 July 2005 <http://lexinexis.com>.

McQuade, Molly. Rev. of *Martin Dressler*, by Steven Millhauser. *Booklist* 1 Apr. 1996: 1343-44.

Miller, Laura. "Theme Parks of the Mind." Rev. of *The King in the Tree: Three Novellas*, by Steven Millhauser. *New York Times Book Review* 9 Mar. 2003: 7.

Millhauser, Steven. *The Barnum Museum*. Normal, IL: Dalkey Archive, 1997.

—. *Edwin Mullhouse: The Life and Death of an American Writer, 1943-1954, by Jeffrey Cartwright*. New York: Knopf, 1972.

—. *Enchanted Night*. New York: Crown, 1999.

—. "The Fascination of the Miniature." *Harper's* May 1984: 33-34.

—. *From the Realm of Morpheus*. New York: Morrow, 1986.

—. *In the Penny Arcade*. Normal, IL: Dalkey Archive, 1998.

—. Interview with Jim Shepard. *Bomb Magazine* Spring 2003: 1-5. 18 Feb. 2005 <http://bombsite.com>.

—. "An Interview with Steven Millhauser." By Marc Chénetier. *Transatlantica: Revue d'études Américaines* [American Studies Journal] March 2003. 7 June 2005 <http://etudes.americaines.free.fr/transatlantica>.

—. *The King in the Tree.* New York: Knopf, 2003.

—. *The Knife Thrower and Other Stories.* New York: Vintage, 1998.

—. *Little Kingdoms: Three Novellas.* New York: Vintage Contemporaries, 1993.

—. *Martin Dressler: The Tale of an American Dreamer.* London: Phoenix, 1996.

—. *Portrait of a Romantic.* New York: Washington Square Press, 1977.

—. "Questions." E-mail to Alicita Rodríguez. 21 Sept. 2005.

—. "Re: Hello." E-mail to Alicita Rodríguez. 2 Mar. 2005.

—. "Replicas." *Yale Review* 83.3 (1995): 50-61.

—. "Some Thoughts on *Tonio Kröger.*" *Antaeus* 73-74 (1994): 199-223.

Monfort, Bruno. "Steven Milhauser, un esthétique du périmé?" Ed. Anne Ullmo. *Steven Millhauser, une écriture sur le fil.* Villeneuve d'Ascq: Presses Universitaires du Septentrion, 2004. 55-78.

O'Hara, J. D. "Two Mandarin Stylists." *Nation* 17 Sep. 1977: 250-52.

—. "*Portrait of a Romantic.*" *Library Journal* 1 Aug. 1977: 1679.

Paddock, Christopher. Rev. of *The King in the Tree: Three Novellas,* by Steven Millhauser. *Review of Contemporary Fiction* 23.1 (2003): 136.

Patterson, Troy. Rev. of *The King in the Tree: Three Novellas,* by Steven Millhauser. *Entertainment Weekly* 700 (14 Mar. 2003): 71.

Pearson, Michael. "*Edwin Mullhouse*: Re-flexing American Themes." *Critique* 27.3 (1986): 145-51.

Pellegrin, Jean-Yves. "Entre désir et désastre: l'écart dans *The Knife Thrower* de Steven Millhauser." Ed. Anne Ullmo. *Steven Millhauser, une écriture sur le fil.* Villeneuve d'Ascq:Presses Universitaires du Septentrion, 2004. 79-91.

Porée, Marc. "Le Royaume de Morphée." *La Quinzaine Littéraire* 581 (1991): 10.

Postlethwaite, Dianne. "Cities of the Mind." *Nation* 262.18 (1996): 68-72. *EBSCO* 21 June 2005 <http://ebsco.com>.

Rev. of *Edwin Mullhouse: The Life and Death of an American Writer, 1943-1954, by Jeffrey Cartwright,* by Steven Millhauser. *New Republic* 16 Sep. 1972: 30-31.

Rev. of *Enchanted Night,* by Steven Millhauser. *Virginia Quarterly Review* 76.2 (2000): 64.

Rev. of *In the Penny Arcade,* by Steven Millhauser. *Booklist* 1 Jan. 1986: 658.

Rev. of *The King in the Tree: Three Novellas,* by Steven Millhauser. *New Yorker* 24 Mar. 2003: 85.

Rev. of *Little Kingdoms: Three Novellas*, by Steven Millhauser. *New Yorker* 7 Feb. 1994: 99.

Rev. of *Little Kingdoms: Three Novellas*, by Steven Millhauser. *Virginia Quarterly Review* 70.1 (Winter 1994): 24.

Richwine, K. N. Rev. of *In the Penny Arcade*, by Steven Millhauser. *Choice* July-Aug. 1986: 1677.

Rieckmann, Jens. "Four: Mocking a Mock-Biography: Steven Millhauser's *Edwin Mullhouse* and Thomas Mann's *Doctor Faustus.*" *Neverending Stories: Toward a Critical Narratology.* Ed. Ann Fehn et al. Princeton: Princeton UP, 1992. 62-69.

Rifkind, Donna. "Stories for a Stormy Night." *Wall Street Journal* 24 Apr. 1996, Eastern ed.: A12.

Roudeau, Cécile. "Steven Millhauser, une écriture sur le fil." Ed. Anne Ullmo. *Steven Millhauser, une écriture sur le fil.* Villeneuve d'Ascq: Presses Universitaires du Septentrion, 2004. 11-37.

Saltzman, Arthur. "In the Millhauser Archives." *Critique* 37.2 (1996): 149-60. *EBSCO* 22 Nov 2004 <http://ebsco.com>.

—. *This Mad "Instead": Governing Metaphors in Contemporary American Fiction.* Columbia: U of South Carolina P, 2000.

—. "A Wilderness of Size: Steven Millhauser's *Martin Dressler.*" *Contemporary Literature* 42.3 (2001): 589-616.

Sammarcelli, Françoise. "Les voix sans origins chez Steven Millhauser." Ed. Anne Ullmo. *Steven Millhauser, une écriture sur le fil.* Villeneuve d'Ascq: Presses Universitaires du Sepentrion, 2004. 39-54.

Schuessler, Jennifer. "Steven Millhauser: The Business of Dreaming." *Publishers Weekly* 6 May 1996: 56-7.

Seaman, Donna. Rev. of *Enchanted Night*, by Steven Millhauser. *Booklist* 96.2 (1999): 233. 20 Apr. 2005 <http://proquest.umi. com>.

Sheppard, R. Z. "Trump, the Early Days." *Time* 10 June 1996: 82. *EBSCO* 21 June 2005 <http://ebsco.com>.

Sheridan, David. "The End of the World: Closure in the Fantasies of Borges, Calvino, and Millhauser." *Postmodern Approaches to the Short Story.* Ed. Farhat Iftekharrudin et al. New York: Praeger, 2003. 9-24.

Shklovsky, Victor. "From 'Art as Technique'." *Modernism: An Anthology of Sources.* Ed. Vassiliki Kolocotroni, et al. U of Chicago P, 1999. 217-21.

Simson, Maria. "Forecasts: Fiction Reprints." *Publishers Weekly* 12 Feb. 1996: 74.

Smith, Dinitia. "Shy Author Likes to Live and Work in Obscurity." *New York Times ProQuest.* 9 Apr. 1997: 13. 7 June 2005 <http://proquest.umi.com>.

Stade, George. "Reality Gripped by Fiction." *New York Times Book Review* 2 Oct. 1977: 13+.

"Steven Millhauser." *Contemporary Authors Online*. 2004 ed. 27 June 2005 <http: galenet.galegroup.com>.

"Steven Millhauser." *Dictionary of Literary Biography*. 1978 ed.: 337-39. 27 June 2005 <http: galenet.galegroup.com>.

"Steven Millhauser: Introduction." *Contemporary Literary Criticism*. 27 June 2005 <http:galenet.galegroup.com>.

Todorov, Tzvetan. *The Fantastic: A Structural Approach to a Literary Genre*. Ithaca: Cornell UP, 1975.

Tuten, Frederic. "The Last Romantic." Rev. of *Little Kingdoms*, by Steven Millhauser. *New York Times Book Review* 3 Oct. 1993: 79.

Ullmo, Anne. *The Knife-Thrower and Other Stories*. Paris: Armand Colin, 2003.

—, ed. *Steven Millhauser, une écriture sur le fil*. Villeneuve d'Ascq: Presses Universitaires du Septentrion, 2004.

Ward, Andrew. "Kaspar Hauser." *FeralChildren.com*. 8 Aug. 2005 <http://www.feralchildren.com/en/showchild.php?ch=kaspar>.

Zaleski, Jeff. Rev. of *The King in the Tree: Three Novellas*, by Steven Millhauser. *Publishers Weekly* 20 Jan. 2003: 55.

Cohabitation:
On "Revenge," by Steven Millhauser

Danielle Alexander

> *Now my aim is clear: I must show that the house is one of the greatest powers of integration for the thoughts, memories, and dreams of mankind. The binding principle in this integration is the daydream. Past, present, and future give the house different dynamisms, which often interfere, at times opposing, at others, stimulating one another. In the life of a man, the house thrusts aside contingencies, its councils of continuity are unceasing. Without it, man would be a dispersed being. It maintains him through the storms of the heavens and through those of life. It is body and soul. It is the human being's first world. . . . And always, in our daydreams, the house is a large cradle. . . . Life begins well, it begins enclosed, protected, all warm in the bosom of the house.*
> —Gaston Bachelard, *The Poetics of Space* (6-7)

Steven Millhauser's unsettling novella "Revenge," first published in *Harper's Magazine* in 2001, is a psychological drama with narrative implications that extend far beyond its careful realism. Its fabula—a woman whose husband has died in an auto wreck puts her house on the market in order to lure the late husband's mistress into a confrontation—is inherently dramatic. Yet what distinguishes the novella is how it deploys domestic space to metonymize—for both the reader and for the victim of the narrator's revenge—the indeterminacy of the past, whether that past is defined as memory, a causal chain of events, or time itself. This essay will explore how Millhauser's "Revenge" evokes both the spatial and temporal uncanny to accomplish these ends.

The post-Freudian and postromantic uncanny has always been concerned with time as well as with space. In his collection of critical essays *The Architectural Uncanny*, art historian and architecture critic Anthony Vidler points out that psychologist Ernst Jensch, whose views on the uncanny influenced Freud's own, posited "intellectual uncertainty" as the root of the *unheimlich*. This uncertainty arose from a lack of spatial orientation or, in contemporary idiom, the feeling of being lost or "turned around" in one's environment. Schelling, however, joined space and time in his discussion of the uncanny when he proposed that the Homeric sublime was formed by the repression of the uncanny *over the course of time*:

> Greece had a Homer precisely because it had mysteries, that is because
> it succeeded in completely subduing that principle of the past, which was
> still dominant and outwardly manifest in the Oriental systems, and in
> pushing it back into the interior, that is, into secrecy, into the Mystery
> (out of which it had, after all, originally emerged). (Vidler 26)

Repetition, which conflates time and space, frequently in itself
constitutes the uncanny. Vidler credits De Quincy with the first
articulation of the romantic "spatial uncanny," which is "displayed
in the abyssal repetitions of the imaginary void" (37). These abyssal repetitions are instantiated in De Quincy's reading of Charles
Nodier's short story "Piranèse." The story's abyssal palace interior,
through which Piranesi climbs endlessly, only to find that at the
summit he is once again at the foot of what appears to be (but may
not in fact be) the same palace, evokes both dread of the void and
the ecstasy of the Romantic sublime. Interestingly, as Vidler points
out, the "site" of De Quincy's own laudanum-induced reveries was a
"simple white cottage, formerly owned by Wordsworth, in the valley
of Grasmere" (37).

Gaston Bachelard, in his 1958 work *The Poetics of Space*, posits
another kind of site that collapses architecture and temporality:
the oneiric house, the house of "dream-memory" (15). In Bachelard's
philosophy this is the "crypt of the house that we were born in," and
is the site of the reciprocal relationship between thought and dream.
This house is not, strictly speaking, uncanny—as the psychological
residue of the house of our birth, which allows us access to "the *real
being* of our childhood" (16), its dream has more in common with
reverie than nightmare. As Bachelard says in the quotation that
begins this essay, the house, in daydream, is a cradle: "Life begins
well, it begins enclosed, protected. . . ." This "beginning well" may
also imply a certain order, a certain continuity—a trust that the
past will remain past, that events once experienced will not recur
unexpectedly, and that the future, whatever else it holds, holds the
daydream of the cradle-house to protect us. The uncanny obtrudes
when a real house becomes, instead of protection from the past, a
site at which the locus of self—the self determined by memory—is
uprooted; when that uncanny house is the oneiric house transformed,
it displaces the very basis of identity.

In "Revenge," an ordinary house in which a marriage once flourished is gradually subsumed by an uncanny version of itself—by
its own double, a place in which, as Vidler says, "[what] at any
moment seemed on the surface homely and comforting, secure and
clear of superstition, might be reappropriated by something that
should have remained secret but that nevertheless, through some
chink in the shutters of progress, [has] returned" (27). The revisions

of the past that must be undertaken by the narrator, and by the reader, destabilize time and allows the "something that should have remained secret" to seep, and then flood, the house and the psyche of all concerned. Ultimately, though, the "houses" that are breached are bodies—that of the narrator, the other woman, and, of course, the late husband.

The setting for Millhauser's novella is not a cottage in the Lake Country of England but an unidentified university town that seems to be located in upstate New York or New England. The unnamed first-person narrator—the woman whose unfaithful husband Robert has died in an auto accident—is selling her house; the potential buyer, and the person addressed throughout the novella, is the late husband's mistress (also unnamed). The first-person address establishes from the outset a claustrophobic delimiting of narrative distance. The environment, too, is claustrophobic. The exterior of the house is not described; instead we (who, because we are addressed as "you" by the narrator, stand in for the woman with whom the late husband had the affair) are guided through the house one room at a time in sections corresponding to the house's rooms and passageways. The paragraph that ushers us into the novella, and the other woman into the house, is worth quoting in its entirety:

> This is the hall. It isn't much of one, but it does the job. Boots here, umbrellas there. I hate those awful houses, don't you, where the door opens right into the living room. Don't you? It's like being introduced to some man at a party who right away throws his arm around your shoulders. No, give me a little distance, thank you, a little formality. I'm all for the slow buildup, the gradual introduction. Of course you have to imagine it without the bookcase. There isn't a room in the house without a bookcase. (3)

First-time readers will be unaware that the bookcase, the umbrellas, and the boots are, as synecdoche for the quotidian materiality of marriage, already uncanny instantiations of the past. So, too, is the subtle announcement (couched in chatty, almost familiar language) that the reader, and the other woman, will not be allowed access to the "living" room, but will be introduced to the interior gradually, with "a little distance, a little formality." In fact, the other woman does not yet know that her host, the narrator, is aware of the affair her late husband was having, much less that she herself was his partner.

The narrator very quickly establishes the first instance of repetition in the form of doubling. As she takes the other woman's coat, she says, "Oh, I like it. It's perfect. And light as a feather. Where*ever* did you find it? . . . I'll just hang it right here, next to mine. It must look very empty to you, all those hangers side by side. Those are my late

husband's hats. . . . One day I cleared out all the coats. . . . But I left
the hats. I couldn't touch the hats" (3). The narrator conflates herself
with the other woman by hanging their coats side by side; the twin
coats are topped uncannily by the dead man's hats. This is the first
of many instances of doubling and mutilation and dismemberment:
here the coats, like flayed skins, are empty.

Having neatly summarized the progress of her grief (and thus
limned the first outline of the uncanny house that will subsume both
people by the end of the novella), the narrator conducts the other
woman through the living room, the architectural space in which
most couples greet guests and thus display their public identity to
the world. Here the narrator establishes that her marriage was a
home, that she was happy, that the living room was a site of the
heimlich: "Imagine a fire going . . . the wind rattling the windows
behind the curtains—and one of those Chopin melodies that feel like
sorrow and ecstasy all mixed together pouring from the keys—and
you have my idea of happiness" (5). This is also a fairly neat description of De Quincy's romantic sublime, in which the storm pounds
outside while the interior of his Grasmere cottage serves as a "secure
vantage point from which to start his interior journeys" (Vidler 37).
It is in the living room, too, that the husband's duplicity (and the
uncanny house this duplicity constitutes) begins to invade, to contaminate the real house. A mere four paragraphs after the narrator
establishes "[her] idea of happiness," she tells the other woman how
the *unheimlich* began to seep inside, in the form of the narrator's
doubt of her husband: "I found myself thinking, on the couch—or
not really thinking: it was more like the shadow of a thought: Could
it be that Robert . . . ? I immediately felt embarrassed, almost . . .
ashamed, as if I'd been caught in some unpleasant act. But there it
was. The little thought-shadow" (7).

The seepage of the uncanny becomes far more noticeable in the
next paragraph, in which the narrator offers to the other woman
another doubling. This time, it takes the form of a split chronology: a
"story" the narrator tells the other woman of an "imaginary" woman
to whom, the narrator says, "nothing happen[s]." In other words,
this is a woman who has conquered the temporal and its depreda-
tions, and a woman who, the narrator says, is "not like me—not like
me at all" (7). This is, of course, a distressing occurrence; neither we
nor the other woman understand the point of telling the story. This
distress is intensified as the narrator, in a separate, two-sentence
paragraph, says, "That's my story. Do you like it?" (7). This odd,
disingenuous, childlike (or childish) remark points forward into the
future of the novella we are now reading—we assume that we will be
able to make sense of both the story and the question when more is
revealed to us. We are not sure, either, at this point, if the question is

meant to be rhetorical. In any case, the implied answer is that nothing ends well, yet we do not have a cause-effect chain with which to make sense of this answer. In this sense, the question has already implied its answer, yet remains mysterious (in the ancient, uncanny sense), both to the reader and the other woman—into whose point of view we have once more been thrust.

We are at this point barely seven pages into the novella, yet the uncanny house has not only been established but we have also begun to see the extent to which it contaminates the real house. We begin to sense, too, that the narrator is still struggling against this contamination, even though it has already taken place, by conflating herself with the husband's mistress, whom she also wishes to destroy, as we will shortly see. The narrator's revenge will not be simply to reveal to the other woman the emotional devastation the late husband's affair has caused. She will also attempt to appropriate the architecture of the other woman's body: to physically merge with and subsume her.

The mistress and the narrator make their way to the kitchen, in which the narrator offers the other woman a homely and domestic cup of tea. But this gesture toward the *heimlich* only prepares us for another invasion by the *unheimlich*. Selling the house, the narrator tells the other woman, rattles her: "it's like stirring a pile of leaves with a stick—you never know what's going to come slithering out" (10).

Not only the narrative space of the house has here been breached; by now it is also clear that the narrative is constructing in the reader uncanny duplications. The reader must revise her or his conception of the causal chain at work in the story repeatedly. Every new revelation from the narrator forces both new readings and an increasing mistrust of these new readings (as the depth of the narrator's rage, and the awareness she is edging us, as well as the other woman, toward a psychological abyss). The increasing destabilization of temporality is first discernable in the kitchen. The narrator here reveals to the other woman not only that she knew of her late husband's infidelity, but also that she knows the other woman was his partner. Thus historicity is destabilized: the past the other woman thought she knew was false, just as the past the narrator thought she knew (until her husband's affair was revealed) was false. In addition, the "true" historical narrative—that the husband had an affair, and that the narrator was aware of it as it occurred—is, for both women, situated in lies and duplicity. The conflation of truth and lies in this matrix fully implicates the reader as well. In the kitchen section, subtle shifts in focalization reveal that the reader is being slowly contaminated by the uncanny. Again, the narrator addresses the other woman in the second person—as "you"—thus achieving a narrative conflation of the reader and the other woman, and in the kitchen scene, the narrator addresses the other woman (and the reader) in increasingly manipulative (and directive) ways: "That's when I learned it was you. You seem upset. Of course you ought to be. . . . Do you know what else he said? He told me you were nothing to him. *Don't say anything.* He told me you were a body, just a body" (13, emphasis added). The narrator thus informs the other woman that she is "just a body"—not only sexual but fragile, easy to dispose of. The narrator also, through her responses to the other woman—"You seem upset" and "Don't say anything"—splits the focalization. We momentarily occupy the narrator's point of view as we imagine the other woman demonstrating her distress (that is, her "upsetness") in some physical sense. Yet, because of the second-person address, we must also remain situated in the other woman's point of view, especially in the sense that (if this is our first reading of the story) we are at as great a disadvantage as the other woman: we have suddenly understood that the narrator herself has knowledge that we do not. We may also suspect that the narrator will, before the end of the tour, subject us to her view of the affair, of her husband's motivation—and who knows what other unwelcome knowledge.

This epistemological layering becomes more complicated through the order in which the narrator releases information. She informs the other woman that the house is haunted, in the midst of her revealing that she is aware of the other woman's role in the affair. The focalization here slips quickly between past and present, between the narrator and the other woman. First, tea is offered. As the two women sit, the narrator (over the course of two pages, with appropriate side trips into the state of the garden; of course, the narrator "lost half my forsythias" the previous year [10]) describes her increasing sense that the husband was "withholding something" (10). She attempts to attribute this withholding to difficulties her husband is having with a book he is writing. Eventually, the husband confesses to the affair. The narrator's description of her inability to take in this terrible news—her initial impulse to comfort the husband—is not only deft, but constitutes another sort of doubling. The other woman, no doubt, is experiencing her own disorientation, as she realizes that the narrator has known of the affair for some time, and that she will be expected to behave sympathetically toward the narrator, who has been both betrayed and widowed in the recent past. The reader sympathetically experiences both women's grief and discomfort in flashes that alternate so rapidly they constitute a sort of dreadful shimmering.

The paragraph about the haunting is positioned exactly at the place (and in the narrative moment) in which the other woman (and the reader) will be most disoriented, in which she must be revising her idea of the past and the present. Thus the meaning of the haunting may also slip between the traditional—the house has a ghost, just the same as the house has bookcases—and what the narrator actually means, which is that the affair has not simply stopped time but evacuated it of its meaning:

> All houses are haunted. It's just that some are more haunted than others. Robert's ghost is sitting right there, where you're sitting now, and my ghost is sitting here, listening to his strangled confession. The air is full of ghosts. At night you can hear them: sifting through the house, like sand. (13)

Not only does this assertion increase the level of claustrophobia, it too, has metanarrative implications. The fabula itself is disrupted in that it can be read vertically as well as horizontally: the layers of plot occur simultaneously (the husband, in spectral form, is always "sitting right there," and the narrator's ghost listens to him; by implication all events in the house are always already occurring).

Category confusion intensifies as they move to the next part of the house—the porch, of which the narrator says, "The whole idea is to be outside and inside at the same time. That's what a porch *is*" (14). Increasingly, the insides and outsides of bodies will also be mixed: a series of atemporal yet increasingly real bodily mutilations and dismemberings is about to ensue. After her husband's confession, the narrator tells the other woman, the narrator went to the porch and sat down: "I felt dead. At the same time my mind was very sharp and alert. . . . Robert had killed me, a quick stab to the heart, and I'd come out on the porch to watch myself die. Why wasn't I dead? . . . Or maybe the dead have their thoughts, as well as the living. Do you think so?" (15). The conflation of the two bodies and the erasure of boundaries continues as the narrator recounts the ways in which she tries both to escape and to control the confusion of identity and epistemological disorientation she experiences. She describes her attempt to make sense of the affair by, at one point, considering (perhaps seriously) an invitation to the other woman to join them in their marriage bed: "Sure, why not? We have a big bed—there's room for one more. I'll make punch and sandwiches" (17). The narrator's strategies, it quickly becomes clear, are aimed at possession of the other woman. First the narrator "becomes" her late husband, and "trie[s] to imagine you as Robert would: a desirable body. I . . . undressed you, in my mind. I looked at you. I . . . did things to you" (18). Soon the narrator has metamorphosed herself into a man: "My hips shrank. My arms grew hard. I was a lovely man: tense, dangerous" (19). Then, via a move that is perfectly believable (in realist terms) and that functions as a second haunting (this time by a living person, the narrator), the novella is drawn into the uncanny. The

narrator informs the other woman that, one night after she learned
of the affair, she actually invaded the other woman's house and stood
over her with a knife in her hand.

> Then I was there, in front of [. . .] your house [. . .]. The back door at
> the top of the steps: locked. But the cellar door—really, people ought
> to be more careful, why only the other day . . . It opened so easily, as
> if you'd been expecting me. Were you? Up the little stairs. Moonlight
> in the kitchen. [. . .] Everything was strange. The edges of the plates
> in the dish rack caught in the moonlight. I realized that I was in an
> enchanted cave. [. . .] I went in [to your bedroom]—just like that—and
> stood over the bed, looking at you. I was surprised to see a knife in
> my hand. (21-22)

This scene (which in this quotation has been radically compressed)
suspends time through a meticulous inventory of what the narrator
sees, hears, thinks, and feels as she makes her way toward and into
the other woman's house. ("Go awaaay, my voices sang in me. Oh
staaay, my voices echoed. I took in the front porch—wicker sofa, the
two plants hanging like . . . oh, like anchors . . . and shutters . . . with
those little grooves in them" [21].) This fine-grained description,
along with the occasional use of ellipses, decreases the narrative's
momentum but increases the sense of dread: if we are, indeed, in
the point of view of the other woman, this account will be horrifying.
Yet more horrifying, though, is the doubling that occurs at the end
of the scene. The narrator has referred to the other woman's house
as "the house of the wicked witch." However, by the end of the scene,
as she stands over the other woman's bed with a knife in her hand,
a swap has occurred:

> suddenly I was the wicked witch and you were . . . only you. A woman
> sleeping. I looked at you. I tried to make you dream me. I saw some-
> thing in my hand. I left the room and never looked back.
>   That was our first meeting. (22-23)

The other woman discovers that she has *all along* been haunted by
the narrator, who will return to her house more than once before the
husband dies and the affair ends. The revenge has invaded the past:
it has contaminated, and poisoned, the other woman's memories of
that most intimate of states, sleep. And the revenge will engulf the
future. The other woman never stood—it seems—a chance.
    The house, too, has been doubled. Because the narrator has
invaded the other woman's house and brought with her the future,
she has made a liar out of the other woman's house: it did not tell her
the truth about its ability to keep her safe, as it were. It thus betrays
the other woman; it is duplicitous; it says one thing and means

another, and lets bad dreams in through the cellar door. Thus the narrator and the other woman's house, as well as their bodies, have become conflated: they let in the dangerous past and the dangerous future, and destroy the present by evacuating it of meaning. The houses are an architecture of dread, and what is most dreadful are the ways the houses participate in the continued mutilation of the two women's bodies.

The narrator shows the other woman the dining-room table on which the narrator and Robert once made love and that the narrator, after she learned of the affair, stabbed with a screwdriver, forever rupturing its horizontal plane and allowing an intermixture of the past (the table was inherited from Robert's mother) and the future (the marriage will be ruptured, and all parties—the narrator, the other woman, and Robert—will be "murdered"). Of course, the stabbing is another occasion to disfigure (or kill) the other woman: "As I gouged the mahogany with that screwdriver, I thought of many things—the time, long ago, when Robert and I made love on the table, the time when we were happy and lighthearted—but most of all I thought of you. I imagined the table was your face" (30).

After they leave the dining room and its ruptured table and ascend the staircase toward the most private part of the house, the narrator describes another reversal: she points out the stair upon which she stumbled and fell, tumbling all the way back to the ground floor.

> Have you ever fallen down a flight of stairs, out of sheer—I suppose it was sorrow. A sorrowful fall. I remember everything: a feeling of just letting everything go, that sense of release, it was almost exhilarating, like floating up in the air, except that my head was banging against the banister and my body was a big awkward lump with arms and legs sticking out all over the place. (31)

In addition to directional confusion ("like floating up in the air") and the house's complicity in injuring her body, the stairs, a transitional area, prompts a memory for the narrator of a young man in her past as she lies, vulnerable and exposed: "there I was, lying with my skirt up, looking like some woman trying to seduce some man. Then I tried to remember the last time I'd made love to Robert. It seemed a long time ago. But was it really that long? And then out of nowhere I thought of Tom Conway" (31). This memory, of the narrator and Tom Conway enfolded in a peaceful stasis that seems in certain ways close to Bachelard's description of the oneiric house, will return later in the novella and provide a counterpoint to the increasingly chaotic universe of the present house. For the moment, though, the two women's tour of the upstairs rooms increases the mutilations and ruptures of both body and identity—and, again, the house is complicit.

After she learned of the affair, the narrator tells the other woman, she noticed that the mirror in the upstairs bath allowed her to view only her top half. "That was one of your cruelest thefts," she tells the other woman, "stealing my bottom half" (33). After the two have moved into Robert's study, appropriately, the narrator slips into Robert's point of view: "That fall he began teaching again, three days a week, but he'd always rush right home. Make sure nothing happened to the crazy wife. A girl can fall down the stairs, you know. She can get dizzy in the bathroom. She can fall out a window and break her pretty neck. Razor blades have been known to cause trouble in the most well-regulated families. A house is a dangerous place . . ." (36). We begin to read this passage as a threat to the other woman somewhere in the fourth sentence; by the fifth sentence, and the words "break her pretty neck," the menace is unmistakable.

The narrator will find where her bottom half has gone in one of her nocturnal visits to the other woman's house. Through the other woman's bedroom window, with the blind drawn halfway down ("as if to keep me from spying," says the narrator [38]), the narrator sees

only part of you, from a little above the waist to about mid-thigh. You were wearing an Indian-print skirt with a wide red belt. I thought of my bathroom mirror: I was the woman without a bottom half, and you were nothing but a bottom half. Then I imagined you were a mermaid in reverse, legs below and fish scales above, and the idea struck me as so absolutely incredibly hysterical that really I nearly died laughing. (38)

The fact that the other woman's top half has become fishlike dehumanizes her; bodies are now also in the zone of dream. The use of synecdoche in the description—"fish scales above"—erases the woman's top half completely (if read literally, we have nothing *but* scales, which are impossible to envision in bodily form). If the description prompts the image of a fish's morphology (gills, abdomen?) atop a human lower abdomen and torso, it means that nothing human is left of the other woman but her genitalia. The narrator has endowed her with a fishlike brain and sensibility.

At this point in the novella, at least three killings have been committed. The first is on page 15, when Robert "kills" the narrator and she goes out to the porch to die. The next occurs on page 22, in which the narrator stands over the other woman's bed (and murders the integrity of her memory of peaceful sleep). Then, on page 38, as we have just seen, the other woman is cut off at the waist and made monstrous. These deaths are actually numbers two, three, and four, though; the first occurred on page 12. What we did not know at the time we read the passage (it is the paragraph about the haunting, in which the narrator says "Robert's ghost is sitting right there, where you're sitting now . . .") is that Robert was dead long before he died in the auto accident. "What do you do when you're dead-alive and your husband is a ghost?" the narrator asked on page 16. She refers not to the day of the house-tour but to the moment after her husband's confession. This killing has the effect of, once again, pulling time inside-out for the other woman. If the husband has been dead since the confession, she has had an affair with a ghost.

The bedroom—the heart of the house, and of the marriage—is last on the tour of the second floor. The reader is not greatly surprised when the narrator invites the other woman to lie on the bed beside her: "We can have a nice pillow talk, like girlfriends in junior high" (42). The tension, throughout the novella, has reached its pitch partly through the careful modulation of the focalization, and here again we are torn from the narrator's point of view and hurled into the other woman's. "Take my hand," the narrator says. "All right then. I'll take yours" (42). And there we lie, a split reader, both in the narrator's point of view and the other woman's, as the narrator talks about how she received the news of her late husband's death ("Killed by black ice. The black ice of his black-hearted icy wife" (42)); about her late husband's problems with impotence at an early stage of their marriage ("Here's a secret. Don't tell anybody" (42)); and about another secret: "I know you've slept in this bed. With my husband, of course. Don't you pull away from me" (43). The argument that preceded the husband's death on the icy road seems, indeed, to have been touched off by the narrator's immediate perception that the marriage bed has been violated.

The narrator then escorts the other woman to the attic. Here we will return to Bachelard for a moment, because his readings of the significance of cellar and garret may assist in our interpretation of the novella's remaining scenes.

Bachlard maintains that, at least in the European psyche, the house is "imagined as a vertical being" and, further, as "a concentrated being. It appeals to our consciousness of centrality" (17). The two poles of this verticality are, of course, the cellar and the attic. For Bachelard, too, the attic is the site of rational thought; it supports the roof, which gives shape to the house and, in more basic terms, shelter. The roof is visible to the public; it has an identity it shares with the world. "In the attic it is a pleasure to see the bare rafters of the strong framework. Here we participate in the carpenter's solid geometry" (18). Bachelard also opposes the attic to the cellar, which is, he says, "first and foremost the *dark entity* of the house, the one that partakes of subterranean forces. When we dream there, we are in harmony with the irrationality of the depths" (18).

The attic in the narrator's house fails to meet both these criteria. It is not "rational," not related to the outside world; in fact, it is

profoundly private. It also does not participate in the orderly vertical polarization Bachelard outlines. Instead, it conflates birth and
death: it is where the narrator shows the other woman the rafter
from which she attempted to hang herself, as well as her own and
Robert's childhood artifacts. "Look: my old cradle," says the narrator; the oldest artifact points to the beginning of everything, and
is an inside-out, upside-down replica of Bachelard's cradle-house.
It is haunted by all manner of things: "Wings. Weensy little feet.
Children are right. Stay out of the attic. It's like walking around in
the head of a madwoman" (45). Indeed.

In the cellar, Bachelard says, "the impassioned inhabitant digs
and re-digs, making its very depth active" (18). In other words, the
psyche, in this description of Bachelard's, desires of the cellar, rather
than rationalization and closure, endlessness, boundarilessness.
This insight is already held in tension with the cellar's nature as
a suffocating place of entrapment. In "Revenge," it is, of course,
both.

It is, first, the site of the other woman's death, and contains her
dismembered body. "See that cabinet?" says the narrator, "Your
head again, hanging on a hook. Lovely she was, even in death. I
buried you here, under the floor. Under that ratty rug. And don't
look in the woodpile" (47). Indeed, the leaves have been stirred, and
much has slithered out. Here in the cellar, too, the narrator ensures
that the contamination of the narrative—both the other woman's
narrative and the reader's—is complete, by subsuming both the
other woman's body and her future. First, she reframes Robert's
car accident as a desperate flight (unsuccessful, as such flights usually are) against the intractable affair, which had, for him, frozen
both time and space. The narrator blames the other woman for her
husband's death, which may have been suicide, in effect if not in
intent (the text does not tell us): "An accident? Come on. . . . It was
Robert's way of solving the problem. . . . Yes! You! Murderer! You!
. . . I'm afraid you made a real mess of it . . ." (51). The narrator then
completes the conflation: she asks the other woman to kill herself.
"So you might as well get it over with. I think so. Do it. Do it. Do it.
Why don't you?" (51-52). They are now almost one person:

But sooner or later. One day or another. Somewhere down the line.
That sudden uneasiness as you look out a window. That moment of
panic when you climb the stairs. What will you do? How can you live?
Where will you go? There's nowhere to go. There's nothing to do. No
one to see. Don't you know? Why go on? And always the little voice
whispering in my ear, always the sad ghost rustling in the dark. That
is why I wanted to show you my house. To tell you who we are. So that
we would know. What to do. (52)

Perhaps the other woman will comply; we are left with the sense that it does not matter whether she does or not. And in fact, it does not "matter," and this is the ultimate effect of the uncanny: the uncanny house freezes both temporality and meaning. The other woman may return as a ghost—certainly this story already haunts us—but a ghost with no power, locked in an endless repetition of time. Near the end of this tale, which has created and occupied its own collapsed time/space site, the narrator says to the other woman:

> Here's a question for you. If you were a ghost, if you were a ghost in this house, if you were dead and came to live in this house, where would you hide? In the attic? Or in the cellar?
> Watch it. Watch your head (52).

Works Cited

Bachelard, Gaston. *The Poetics of Space.* Trans. Maria Jolas. Boston: Beacon, 1994.

Millhauser, Steven. "Revenge." In *The King in the Tree: Three Novellas.* New York: Knopf, 2003. 3-53.

Vidler, Anthony. *The Architectural Uncanny: Essays in the Modern Unhomely.* Cambridge, MA: MIT Press, 1994.

"a game we no longer understood": Theatrical Audiences in the Fiction of Steven Millhauser

Pedro Ponce

The Collective as Audience

Critics have previously noted the recurrence of first-person, plural narration in Steven Millhauser's *The Knife Thrower and Other Stories*. In the title story, a town's residents await the knife thrower's performance with a strange ambivalence: "Hensch, the knife thrower! Did we feel like clapping our hands for joy, like leaping to our feet and bursting into smiles of anticipation? Or did we, after all, want to tighten our lips and look away in stern disapproval?" (3). In "The New Automaton Theater," the narration combines plural and singular first-person narration in detailing a city's fascination with automaton art: "Our city is justly proud of its automaton theater. . . . Rather I mean that by its very nature our automaton theater is deserving of pride, for it is the source of our richest and most spiritual pleasure" (89). Anne Ullmo observes how the pronoun *we* "functions like a screen behind which the subject conceals itself" (34). Millhauser has spoken of the implications of such a screen in a 2003 interview with Marc Chéntier:

> What interests me is the way moral indecisiveness or questioning may be given more weight or significance by attaching itself to a multiple being. A single narrator might have multiple interpretations of an event, or might try to evade moral choice in numerous ways, but the same kind of uncertainty in an entire community becomes public, societal, even political, and carries a different weight. I would argue that the moral wavering of the "we" in "The Knife Thrower" is more disturbing than the moral wavering of an "I" would have been, or disturbing in a different way.

Ullmo also notes how the plural first-person reflects a communal voice, "incorporating a sort of *vox populi*" (34). But Ullmo qualifies this comparison by adding that this "narrative insistence put in place by Millhauser does not connote socially. It pertains more to an anonymous and collective consciousness which all western readers are able to identify with" (34). Françoise Sammarcelli sees the reader similarly implicated through the collective voice in "The Knife Thrower," "The New Automaton Theater," and "The Dream of the Consortium," which create "a situation of reception deteriorated over various [vocal] registers and including the reader in a vast public or an ensemble of witnesses or critics . . ." (49).

This essay intends to focus and extend such analyses by considering collective groups as audiences in Millhauser's fiction. Critics have frequently praised Millhauser in spite of his perceived neglect of the audience. In coming to such a conclusion about *The Knife Thrower*, Michiko Kakutani cites "Kaspar Hauser Speaks." In Millhauser's fictional monologue, the legendary feral child rescued in nineteenth-century Germany expresses his desire to be ordinary, just like his rescuers. Writes Kakutani, "The reader, sated with this volume's repetitious descriptions of the odd, the mysterious and the disturbing, might well echo Kaspar's sentiments. The reader, too, might understand how even the marvelous can become banal."

Such observations are striking, given how often audiences are invoked throughout Millhauser's work. As cited above, the narrative voices in "The Knife Thrower" and "The New Automaton Theater" represent or strongly identify with the audiences of different entertainments. Audiences also figure importantly in earlier collections; "August Eschenburg" (from *In the Penny Arcade*) and "Eisenheim the Illusionist" (from *The Barnum Museum*) each dramatize the complex relationship between an uncompromising artist and his audience. In the title novella from Millhauser's 2003 collection *The King in the Tree,* a satirical mime immerses its audience of courtiers in the scandal over a queen's suspected infidelity. These examples only cover theatrical audiences in Millhauser. Anonymous members of movie audiences are the protagonists of "Behind the Blue Curtain" and "Rain" (both from *The Barnum Museum*). The latter story depicts a theatrical audience figuratively; Mr. Porter, the protagonist, attempts to drive in a rainstorm but his wipers struggle futilely:

> A passing truck sprayed water against the windshield and for a moment Mr. Porter could see nothing but the lazy wipers, bowing left and right, left and right, like twin actors on a stage. The applause has died down, the audience is making its way to the exits, but still they bow, left and right, left and right, though the audience has left long ago and the lights are out in the deserted theater. (159)

As Tom Deignan has written of *The Knife Thrower*, Millhauser pays "important attention" to audiences in his work because "without audiences, consumers, or whatever you call them, there would be no art or artist, no store or entrepreneur" (283).

In the Millhauser Audience

Theorists of audience reception may vary in the content and scope of their investigations, but they are consistent in denying the existence of a monolithic audience—each is different. According to Henry Jenkins, "Other theorists speak of an 'ideal reader' or a 'subject position' created by the text, often assuming that textually ascribed meanings get reproduced fairly directly in spectator's heads"; the study of audience, on the other hand, is one in which "Text, context, and reader all play vital roles in shaping interpretation" (166). Susan Bennett echoes Jenkins in her analysis of theater audiences:

> theatre is not monolithic. . . . As we have seen, non-traditional forms of theatre practice have involved audiences in all stages of production, and have sought (rather than allowed) a central role for the spectator. More than this, such definitions of the audience's limited role skate past the ideological and social mediation of the cultural institution. The audience, by its physical presence as a group, is bound to the institution which produces theatre. . . . (93)

These caveats, while important to keep in mind, should not be seen as obstacles to audience research; instead, they invite researchers to adjust the scale of their projects accordingly: "Audience research has increasingly rejected large-scale generalizations about spectatorship, demanding a more contingent 'case-study' approach" (Jenkins 177). The case-study approach will inform the current consideration of Millhauser's fictional audiences.

This choice of approach, however, must be further refined. As discussed previously, Millhauser alludes to audience frequently in his work. The difference between live performance and film is significant, with implications for the study of their respective audiences: "The literary, as well as the filmic, text is a fixed and finished product which cannot be directly affected by its audiences. . . . In the theatre every reader is involved in the making of the play" (Bennett 22). It is this sense of involvement that arguably raises the stakes of a theatrical performance, not simply in terms of how it is received but how it works with or against the cultural context represented by the audience. As Bennett elaborates, "it would seem then that both an audience's reaction to a text (or performance) and the text (performance) itself are bound within cultural limits" (101). At the same time, "those limits are continually tested and invariably broken. Culture cannot be held as a fixed 'entity, a set of constant rules, but instead it must be seen in a position of inevitable flux" (101). In this way, the theatrical performance is unique in its potential for representing cultural flux as mediated by art.

Bennett's complex approach considers the numerous factors that may affect audience response before, during, and after a theatrical performance. Even before tickets are purchased, for example, audiences are already being implicitly influenced by what kind of show is being produced and who selects it: "Thus, questions arise as to how easy it is to produce a script, where to stage that script, and for whom. Those in a position of economic (and thus cultural) power control what is available through mainstream channels" (115). An audience's reception also depends on what kind of knowledge it carries into the theater, "the codes audiences are accustomed to utilizing, the conventions they are used to recognizing, at a theatrical event. Intelligibility and/or success of a particular performance will undoubtedly be determined on this basis" (112).

Once an audience member buys his or her ticket, other factors come into play before the houselights dim. "Cloakrooms, restaurants, and bars" in theater foyers offer more opportunities to socialize (and profit) as part of the theater experience (139). Even taking your seat has ideological implications; the familiar auditorium allows the spectator to maintain the private space of his or her seat in the midst of a larger group. Observes Bennett, "Such an effect is hardly surprising in light of the value accorded to the individual and his/her privacy in bourgeois culture. Neither is it surprising that oppositional theatre has determinedly sought to break up notions of space and to reinforce the social perception and response" (142).

During the performance proper, the audience's attention is drawn to the actors and the external aspects of a production—such as lighting and set design—in making meaning (149). As Bennett observes, "It is the combination of these signs which permits the audience to posit the existence of a particular fictional world on stage with its own dynamic and governing rules" (149). Bennett extends this observation to include the audience member as a kind of reader, whose interpretation of events onstage has implications for his or her understanding offstage:

> Like the individual reader, the audience inevitably proceeds though the construction of hypotheses about the fictional world which are subsequently substantiated, revised, or negated. The horizon of expectations constructed in the period leading up to the opening frame of the performance is also subject to similar substantiation, revision, or negation. (150)

After a performance, obviously, the audience signals the extent of its approval through applause (or lack thereof). Beyond this, there are two aspects of audience response that deserve mention here. According to Bennett, exiting the theater "may provide a welcome release and the end of interpretive activity. On the other hand, the buzz of an excited audience, slow to leave the theatre, continues the interpretive process and is likely to enhance the experience of that production in the individual's memory" (176). Subsequently, "audiences may follow up by reading the text (if available), by reading reviews, or (at a later time) seeing another production or even a subsequent movie adaptation. All these acts have the potential to reshape initial decoding of the production" (176).

These last two points are particularly relevant in considering the fictional audiences of Steven Millhauser. If there is one thing linking the spectators present at Millhauser's magic shows, automaton dramas, and other entertainments, it is the experience of leaving the theater—or, more accurately, trying and failing to leave the theater. If, as Bennett asserts, the stage is a forum for articulating and/or problematizing different kinds of cultural conventions, the theatrical audiences in Millhauser often feel the dramas they observe extending into their daily lives, an experience that shatters the safe boundaries taken for granted by spectators. Thus, Eisenheim's audience regards itself suspiciously after the illusionist causes a child to materialize from among the theater seats (*The Barnum Museum* 234). The narrator of "The Knife Thrower" perceives a disorienting slippage as he watches Hensch and his female assistant: "Black against black they stood there, she and he, bound now it seemed in a dark pact, as if she were his twin sister, or as if both were on the same side in a game we were all playing, a game we no longer understood . . ." (11). The theatrical audience, far from being peripheral, is central to questions of art and life, reality and fiction, provoked in readers by Millhauser's work as a whole.

"roast beef and French underwear": "August Eschenburg"

In terms of audience research, "August Eschenburg" is an anomaly. While later fictions dwell more on the audience's immediate and postperformance response, this story—which opens Millhauser's collection *In the Penny Arcade*—is also concerned with the social and cultural circumstances that help shape audience taste. These circumstances are articulated most scathingly by Hausenstein, August's jaded mentor. Hausenstein coins the term *Untermensch* (a play on Nietzsche's *Übermensch*) to describe "the precise level of vulgarity to which one must sink in order to gain the hearts of the modern masses—the German masses in particular" (35). According to the narrator, "the Untermensch was a strictly spiritual term, and by it [Hausenstein] meant the kind of soul that, in the presence of anything great, or noble, or beautiful, or original, instinctively longed to pull it down and reduce it to a common level" (35). By no means the most subtle cultural critic, Hausenstein later warns his idealistic pupil about the hypocrisy of the masses: "capitalism and history are both against you, if you persist in serving up visions of high beauty to an upright citizen of Kaiser Wilhelm's Reich. He won't stand for it for very long; give him his roast beef and French underwear" (53).

This grotesque representation of the audience—which in Hausen-stein's view desires both sustenance and titillation—is complicated by the character of August himself. His fascination with clockwork mechanisms and automatons is sparked by his attendance at a magic show as a youth. After a series of uninspiring tricks, Konrad the Magician announces that he will "shrink himself" onto a miniature stage (10). Konrad vanishes; in his place, an automaton magician performs a series of tricks. However crude, the figure fascinates August: "Indeed [the automaton's] face seemed so able to express the several emotions required of him that it was as if he were controlled not by an inner mechanism of wheels and levers but by a thinking mind; and it was above all this illusion of an inner spirit that was so remarkable in the performance of the clockwork magician" (13). On entering the magician's tent, "August saw at once that he had made a mistake: the magician was perspiring, the air was unbreath-able, the crowd was composed mostly of children and mothers" (10). Despite the distraction of an audience, August is able to enjoy the performance and discover his artistic passion: "To those few min-utes in a drab green tent, August ever after traced his devotion to clockwork art" (13).

The trajectory of August's career is marked by alternating periods of creation and public scrutiny, which, in the world of this story, are often mutually exclusive. August works late into the night at the Preisendanz Emporium, eventually moving into his workshop (22); his work on a female automaton consumes "untold hours . . . and she promised to be his finest creation" (29), despite Herr Preisendanz's concerns about productivity. Unlike the nontraditional performances described by Bennett, August's is an art that can only thrive in isola-tion. He risks his livelihood and reputation in order to perfect the art of "giving . . . the glorious gift of life" to the inanimate (30).

August's ideals are tested numerous times by an audience vulner-able to the profitable and sensational. His first automatons are made for the shop window of his father, a watchmaker: "Already people spoke admiringly of the sixteen-year-old boy's shrewd business sense, a form of praise that pleased old Joseph but made August secretly uneasy" (16). August's unease makes him afraid "that someday he would be exposed as a dreamer, a ne'er-do-well, a seedy magician in a drab green tent" (17). The image of the seedy magician recalls Konrad, who performs in a "dark green tent" (10). For August, being mistaken for a businessman debases his experience and production of art.

Over the course of the story, however, profit is never not a con-cern for the artist: "Preisendanz knew that the world of modern commerce obeyed one all-embracing principle: novelty. This prin-ciple was divisible into two laws: novelty is necessary, and novelty never lasts. The second law might also be phrased: today's novelty is tomorrow's ennui" (28). For the emporium's potential customers, novelty consists of knowingly treading the line between advertising and pornography. The merchandise displayed in the windows of Die Brüder Grimm, a rival store, is complemented by "a remarkable set of automatons" (26). Despite their obvious faults, they begin to draw attention away from August's work; their attraction "lay precisely in the degree to which they were able to appear decorous while conveying an unmistakable flavor of lasciviousness" (26). Two female figures, for instance are "dressed impeccably in the latest French fashion" while displaying "rumps [that] had been exaggerated in a manner approaching that of certain picture postcards" and "breasts [that] were of a kind rarely or perhaps never seen in natural females" (26, 27). Even though he completes his masterful female automaton, August is fired. Preisendanz hires "his crude rival" in automaton design, whose figures are displayed with the help of a bellows, "so that their dresses were pressed against their bodies and sometimes fluttered up" (31-32). August returns home to his father and his mechanical Fräulein never performs for Preisendanz. As Bennett notes in her analysis of audience response, "Economic factors often determine why particular products are available and constitute culture, and, more significantly, highlight once again the inextricable link between production and reception" (117).

August has a chance to foil the market when he is approached by his formal rival, Hausenstein, who "could not look forward with excessive ardor to spending the rest of his life in the production of rubbish for the likes of Preisendanz and the beloved German *populus*" (35). Hausenstein offers to subsidize a theater in Berlin for August's work, admitting "to a weakness for brilliance, on the rare occasions when he came across the real thing; and his wealth now permitted him to indulge a whim" (37). While the theater is ostensibly under the control of the artist, Hausenstein "had reason to believe that he would rake in a nice profit" (37). And his old cynicism is still evident in his choice of performance space: "It was not so much a theater as a small hall that, before Hausenstein had rented it for August's use, had seen a wide variety of arts and talents . . . Hausenstein, reciting this history gleefully to August, compared the stage with its red curtain to a redheaded whore welcoming all comers" (43). While Hausenstein "wished to admit standees," August refuses; instead "he continually rearranged the 121 seats, sitting in each one and worrying whether the view was good" (44).

August's first automaton show is a financial success: tickets sell out and August receives a standing ovation. August "[looks] with alarm at all the standing people" (46), but his show is more aesthetically successful than he seems to realize. During his Preisendanz days, he aims for "the precise imitation of all human motions" (25). Bennett notes how "Certainly theatrical performance encourages audiences to appreciate the actors' skill" (162). Measured by this standard, the Zaubertheater debut is entirely convincing, especially given the cast. August's automaton Pierrot, the scorned lover of Columbine, seems animated by something greater than the sum of his mechanical parts as he performs "a wild and silent dance, in which Pierrot with his dark eyes and broken lute seemed to soar above his despair and to dissolve in the beauty of the moonlit night. . . . Hausenstein, watching from the wings, saw that the audience was held" (45). Pierrot is followed by an interlude with an automaton pianist: "At the end the little pianist stood up and bowed gracefully. Someone called 'Encore!' and the cry was taken up, but the stern little pianist strode off the stage" (45).

August's success is only temporary, however. The audience soon moves on to other distractions, such as "spirit-rapping and demonstrations of the wonders of chemical science" (49). While August is steadfast in his use of "automaton art to express spiritual states . . . such lofty experiments were bound to seem rather confusing to all but the most stubborn adherents of the Zaubertheater" (50). A new venue—Zum Schwarzen Stiefel (At the Sign of the Black Boot)—finds a greater audience: "The theater itself was somewhat larger than the Zaubertheater—Hausenstein estimated a seating capacity of 180—and not only were all the seats filled but people stood along the walls . . ." (50). In August's theater, automatons—essentially props—seemed capable of transcending their inanimate state to express and provoke palpable emotions. At the Black Boot, the props *are* the performance, animated by shoddy workmanship and the baser impulses of the audience. The Black Boot's cabaret dancers may be mechanically rudimentary, but "care and attention had been lavished on their black silk stockings, their petticoats, their drawers, above all on their wriggling buttocks and bouncy breasts" (50-51). In another piece, an "automaton lady" is penetrated from behind by a male figure who "touched a lever in his side to release his belt" (51, 52).

August, who attends the latter performance, "rose and left" before it concludes (52). The artist's disgust is undercut by Millhauser's interesting use of analepsis within the scene. The narration states that "August left in the middle of the third piece" (51) but then goes back to detail the events cited above before August departs. Since, ostensibly, August is the focalizing character throughout this scene, the narration implies not only his disgust, but the sustained attention that precedes it. In a telling conversation, Hausenstein later reveals that he started the Black Boot in order to buttress the faltering Zaubertheater: "And let me tell you something, Eschenburg: you aren't that pure. You think you're the purest soul on earth, but you knew the theater was started with money I made from Preisendanz. Who cares if it continues courtesy of the Black Boot?" (59).

August again leaves Berlin, feeling "no desire for revenge, only a compelling need to be alone. He never saw Hausenstein again" (60). For a time, August tries his luck in other towns, "but the audiences were generally scanty and a little confused. People seemed to come out of curiosity, as they might come to see a ventriloquist, a Fireproof Female, or a magician, and the Automaton Theater left them with a feeling of puzzlement, as if they had expected something else, something a little different" (61). On his way back home to Mühlenberg, he passes through Berlin, where both the Zaubertheater and the Black Boot have closed down (61-62): "Hausenstein was right: automatons were dead" (61). The story concludes with August in Ulmbach, waiting for the coach to Mühlenberg. As he sits in a nearby wood, he buries "his rope-tied suitcase of automatons" under a thick pile of leaves (62). He reflects on what now seems like his wasted life: "His art was outmoded: the world had no need for him. And so it had all come to nothing" (63). Despite this, after a refreshing nap, "he picked up his suitcase and started back to the coach house" (64).

In tracking the vicissitudes of an artist's career, "August Eschenburg" finds hope—however limited—in the artist's persistence. There is also hope in the individual whose discernment can escape the common demands of the crowd. August may respond to the Black Boot's invitation to leer, but impelled by Hausenstein's pragmatism, he continues to pursue art on his own terms. He is not the only one; scattered among the indifferent crowds are those patrons who continue to attend the Zaubertheater. Later in the story, Marie, an automaton that August "had created . . . with tenderness, with something akin to love-anguish" (54), draws a mere fifteen spectators. After the performance, "August, who had silently come out to take a seat and watch the last few minutes, heard a young woman say to another woman: 'It's remarkable, but I think I could watch her night after night and never have enough'" (55). Such reception is hard-won in a world where art is hopelessly mired in commerce.

The artist in "August Eschenburg" must protect his work from his audience. In later fictions, Millhauser blurs the boundary that August struggles to maintain in order to test the limits of art's power to transcend and transform the world.

Beyond History: "Eisenheim the Illusionist"

The opening of Millhauser's "Eisenheim the Illusionist" appropriates the sober voice of a history text: "In the last years of the nineteenth century, when the Empire of the Hapsburgs was nearing the end of its long dissolution, the art of magic flourished as never before" (*Barnum Museum* 215). The authority suggested by the narrative voice is quickly undermined, however, as the facts are enumerated, such as they are:

> Eisenheim, né Eduard Abramowitz, was born in Bratislava in 1859 or 1860. Little is known of his early years, or indeed of his entire life outside the realm of illusion. For the scant facts we are obliged to rely on the dubious memoirs of magicians, on comments in contemporary newspaper stories and trade periodicals, on promotional material and brochures for magic acts; here and there the diary entry of a countess or ambassador records attendance at a performance in Paris, Cracow, Vienna. (216)

Eisenheim as historical figure eludes cohesive narrative. Eisenheim as entertainer also eludes, even as he enchants. From his beginnings as a cabinetmaker, "it is clear that Abramowitz gradually shifted his attention more and more fully to magic, by way of the trick chests and cabinets that he had begun to supply to local magicians" (218). His early shows demonstrate great skill with familiar illusions, such as Robert-Houdin's Mysterious Orange Tree, in which an audience member's handkerchief is magically removed and recovered from a small orange tree. While these tricks are entertaining, they are ultimately decodable, to adapt a term from Bennett; the illusion of the tree "depended on two separate deceptions: the mechanical tree itself, which produced real flowers, real fruit, and mechanical butterflies by means of concealed mechanisms; and the removal of the handkerchief from the trick box as it was handed to the spectator" (218). Eisenheim's "uncanny" Phantom Portrait, which emerges as if by magic from a blank canvas, is similarly explainable through subtly employed chemistry: "a canvas of unbleached muslin may be painted with chemical solutions that appear invisible when dry . . . the picture will appear if sprayed with a weak solution of prussiate of potash. An atomizer, concealed in the conjurer's sleeve, gradually brings out the invisible portrait" (219).

As Eisenheim becomes more original, however, his illusions defy understanding. The illusionist graduates from familiar tricks to materializations, objects and people apparently conjured by the power of his mind. After sitting onstage for fifteen minutes, he manages to conjure "a small box" out of thin air: "The applause was uncertain; people did not know what they had seen" (227, 228). The audience's impatience turns to distress after the illusionist offers the box for inspection: "One woman, reaching for the box and feeling nothing, nothing at all, stepped back and raised a hand to her throat. A girl of sixteen, sweeping her hand through the black box, cried out as if in pain" (228). One reviewer "considered and rejected the possibility of hidden magic lanterns and mirrors" in creating the effect (229). Several "placed Eisenheim beyond the world of conjuring and saw in him an expression of spiritual striving, as if his art could no longer be talked about in the old way" (229). Eisenheim's props emphasize this provocative new kind of illusion. He performs his first materialization behind a glass table, rendering transparent the magician's table that typically conceals the machinery of illusion. Bennett writes that "*mise en scène* is inevitably structured so as to give emphasis to a sign or sign-cluster intended to locate audience focalization on that aspect of the drama" (160). In the case of Eisenheim's otherwise bare stage, the *mise en scène* "meant the refusal of certain kinds of mechanical aid, the elimination of certain effects" (227).

Eisenheim's illusions unsettle the way audiences understand magic, but they also unsettle how they understand the known world. Starting with handkerchiefs and mechanical butterflies, illusion encroaches further and further beyond the stage. The boundary between stage and audience is an important one according to Bennett: "The stage-auditorium barrier can provide the secure position which permits reception" (163). Not surprisingly, this barrier is increasingly vulnerable as Eisenheim's power grows. One of his unique tricks calls for an audience member to stand in front of a mirror dressed in a red robe. The reflection initially complies with the spectator's gestures, but the illusion ends with the recalcitrant reflection stabbing itself to death: "all at once the ghost emerged from the glass, floated toward the startled and sometimes terrified spectator, and at the bidding of Eisenheim rose into the dark and vanished" (220). The Pied Piper of Hamelin calls for children to come onstage and disappear into "a cavelike opening"; when they return through a magic chest, they "told their parents they had been in a wondrous mountain, with golden tables and chairs and white angels flying in the air; they had no idea how they had gotten into the box, or what had happened to them" (221). Walter Uhl, the chief of police, gets involved after one audience volunteer "told his mother that he had been in hell and seen the devil" (221-22).

The illusions also extend to the acts of other magicians. Beneditti, who performs knockoffs of Eisenheim tricks, suspects his rival of tampering when one of his own shows suffers several embarrassing flubs. During a later performance, Benedetti disappears, prompting Uhl to investigate, to no avail: "Some said the unfortunate Benedetti had simply chosen the most convenient way of escaping to another city, under a new name, far from the scene of his notorious debacle; others were convinced that Eisenheim had somehow spirited him off, perhaps to hell" (223). Ernst Passauer proves himself a more serious competitor: "Unlike the impetuous and foolhardy Benedetti, Passauer made no allusion to the Viennese wizard; some saw in this less a sign of professional decorum than an assertion of arrogant indifference, as if the German [Passauer] refused to acknowledge the possibility of a rival" (223). Eisenheim responds to Passauer's taunting by "[remarking] casually that Passauer's hour had passed" (224). The excitement generated by the rivalry foreshadows Eisenheim's greatest trick: "The fate of the unfortunate Benedetti had not been forgotten, and it was said that if the demand for Passauer's next performance had been met, the entire city of Vienna would have become a magic theater" (224). Something akin to such a transformation occurs when, after his last show, "he tore off a rubber mask and revealed himself to be Eisenheim" (225).

Eisenheim finally goes too far as his materializations become increasingly elaborate. He manages to conjure apparently living beings out of nothing, including Elis: "Elis-fever grew to such a pitch that often sobs and screams would erupt from tense, constricted throats as the air before Eisenheim slowly began to darken and the beautiful boy took shape" (232). Elis's departure is similarly unsettling during "a particularly troubling episode, in which a young woman leaped onto the stage and began clawing the vanishing form" (232). Rosa, another apparition, offers to predict the fate of another audience member: "she said that he would cough up blood in November and would die of tuberculosis before the end of the following summer. Pale, visibly shaken, the young man began to protest angrily, then sat down suddenly and covered his face with his hands" (233). Bearing in mind Bennett's earlier description of the barrier around a stage, the materialization of a child from the audience takes on an interesting resonance:

> The child, a boy of about six, walked down the aisle and climbed the stairs to the stage, where he stood smiling at the audience, who immediately recognized that he was of the race of Elis and Rosa. Although the mysterious child never appeared again, spectators now began to look nervously at their neighbors. . . ." (234)

Uhl's rationale for arresting Eisenheim is also significant in light of Bennett's discussion of stage boundaries:

> The phrase "crossing the boundaries" occurs pejoratively more than once in his notebooks; by it he appears to mean that certain distinctions must be strictly maintained. Art and life constituted one such distinction; illusion and reality, another. Eisenheim deliberately crossed boundaries and therefore disturbed the essence of things. In effect, Herr Uhl was accusing Eisenheim of shaking the foundations of the universe, of undermining reality, and in consequence of doing something far worse:

subverting the Empire. For where would the Empire be, once the idea of boundaries became blurred and uncertain? (234-35)

Uhl's paranoia seems justified when he goes to capture Eisenheim. Sharing a stage with the illusionist, the police chief's authority quickly unravels as he becomes part of the show: "his hand fell through Eisenheim's shoulder, he appeared to stumble, and in a fury he began striking at the magician, who remained seated calmly through the paroxysm of meaningless blows" (236). Eisenheim's greatest trick is not necessarily his evasion of the authorities by dematerializing. Rather, it is the persistence of his illusions in the minds of his audience, who can no longer take reality for granted: "Some said that Eisenheim had created an illusory Eisenheim from the first day of the new century; others said that the Master had gradually grown illusory from trafficking with illusions. Someone suggested that Herr Uhl was himself an illusion . . ." (237).

Bennett describes how "The audience, through homogeneity of reaction, receives confirmation of their decoding on an individual and private basis and is encouraged to suppress counter-readings in favour of the reception generally shared" (164). She also details how, in experimental theater, "the lack of aesthetic as well as real distance prevented the establishment of a homogeneous response" (164). In the eerie conclusion of "Eisenheim the Illusionist," such a fragmented response is described by the narrator: "as precise memories faded, and the everyday world of coffee cups, doctors' visits, and war rumors returned, a secret relief penetrated the souls of the faithful, who knew that the Master had passed safely out of the crumbling order of history into the indestructible realm of mystery and dream" (237). The audience in this story is potentially destructive, but not in the same way as in "August Eschenburg." Instead of the sluggish masses of the latter story, "Eisenheim" reenvisions the audience as a forgetful but persistent guardian of resistance and possibility beyond the prevailing narratives of the state and its history.

The Audience Talks Back: *The Knife Thrower*

It is not until Millhauser's latest collection of short fiction that the theatrical audience acquires a voice of its own. In both the "The Knife Thrower" and "The New Automaton Theater," the narrative voice strongly identifies with the collective in expressing the longing, ambivalence, and discontent of its point of view. These stories represent two kinds of art in relation to their respective audiences. Hensch's gives the people what they want, however much they refuse to admit it. Heinrich Graum's automatons, by contrast, fulfill desires of which the spectator is not even aware.

In Bennett's analysis, the audience is a contradictory entity: "It is surely the case that while the theatre audience is a collective consciousness composed of the small groups in which spectators attend theatrical events, it is also a specific number of individuals" (164). By trying to capture this contradiction within a single narrative voice, Millhauser pushes fictional convention to the point of breaking. The collective voice is arguably realistic in reporting elements of a common external experience: "Hensch, the knife thrower! Of course we knew his name"; "No one ever outgrows the automaton theater" (*Knife Thrower* 3, 90). But inevitably, when reporting internal thoughts, the voice becomes much more problematic: "When we learned that Hensch, the knife thrower, was stopping at our town for a single performance at eight o'clock on Saturday night, we hesitated, wondering what we felt"; "And the new automatons begin to obsess us. They penetrate our minds, they multiply within us, they inhabit our dreams" (3, 110). The voice prompts Sammarcelli to ask, "What is this 'we' that introduces a plural homodiegetic narration and accompanies it with an effect of illusion, as if to deny the potential of sharing information tied to internal focalization? (the syntagm 'wondering what we felt' is in this framework one of the more unsettling)" (45). Sammarcelli's observation recalls Bennett's analysis of the delicate collective that makes up the audience: "Certainly the collective contract is a fragile structure . . ." (Bennett 165). Millhauser exposes this fragility by voicing the audience simultaneously as collective and individual; the integrity of this "already-constituted interpretive community" (Bennett 149) is threatened by the stage entertainments detailed in *The Knife Thrower*.

The threat to Hensch's audience is subtly different from the one faced by Eisenheim's. Both are confronted with spectacles that challenge the way they perceive reality, but in "The Knife Thrower," the audience's fascination is made eerily palpable through the story's point of view. Eisenheim's magic is, to an extent, undercut by sober attempted explanations of his magic. Hensch's tricks are swallowed whole; the reader experiences the resulting skewed perceptions on the page. His assistant, at one point, "held up something between her thumb and forefinger that even those of us in the front rows could not immediately make out" (7). The mysterious object turns out to be a butterfly, which the knife thrower "drove . . . against the wood, where those in the front rows could see the wings helplessly beating" (7). Hensch subsequently targets his assistant's gloved hands: "In the sudden silence she stood there with her arms outspread and her fingers full of knives. . . . Then slowly, gently, she pulled each hand from its glove, leaving the gloves hanging on the wall" (10). Next, he proceeds to mark his assistant, based on "the idea of the artful wound, the mark of blood that was the mark of the master" (4). "The knife stuck beside her neck. He had missed—had he missed?—and we felt a sharp tug of disappointment, which changed at once to shame, deep shame, for we hadn't come out for blood, only for—well, something else . . ." (11). But the master has in fact hit his target: "Then we saw, on her neck, the thin red trickle, which ran down to her shoulder; and we understood that her whiteness had been arranged for this moment. Long and loud we applauded . . ." (11).

In response to this last trick, the narration claims that Hensch "had carried us, safely, it appeared, into the realm of forbidden things" (11). But as suggested by the interview cited previously, Millhauser implies that the audience is at least in part allowing itself this passage. Hensch's increasingly transgressive performance—which eventually targets audience members—provokes little worry about physical danger. The assistant's wound, for instance, is interpreted as just part of her costume: "We imagined the white bandage under the black collar [of her dress]; we imagined other bandages, other wounds, on her hips, her waist, the edges of her breast" (11). And even after Hensch administers to an audience member "the final mark, the mark that can be received only once" (15-16), the audience is strangely distanced from the target's ominous fall "to the floor" (17): "As we left the theater we agreed that it had been a skillful performance, though we couldn't help feeling that the knife thrower had gone too far" (17). The exit from the theater represents an "end of interpretive activity" (Bennett 176), but it also represents an abdication of responsibility. The audience exploits the "stage-auditorium barrier" (163) and interprets Hensch's act as theater, studiously avoiding any specific consideration of actual consequences: "Of course the final act had probably been a setup, the girl had probably leaped smiling to her feet as soon as the curtain closed, though some of us recalled unpleasant rumors of one kind or another, run-ins with police, charges and countercharges, a murky business" (*The Knife Thrower* 18). But the collective's fragility has the last word in the story: "The more we thought about it, the more uneasy we became, and in the nights that followed, when we woke from troubling dreams, we remembered the traveling knife thrower with agitation and dismay" (18).

"The New Automaton Theater," by contrast, returns the Millhauser audience to a world where the boundary between stage and street is not so rigorously maintained. Bennett writes, "As the artist works within the technical means available and within the scope of aesthetic convention, so audiences read according to the scope and means of culturally and aesthetically constituted interpretive processes" (99). The audience depicted in "The New Automaton Theater," unlike that in "August Eschenburg," consists of serious consumers of the art form. Automatons are not just entertainment; they are part of a community's identity and knowledge:

> In childhood we are said to be attracted by the color and movement of these little creatures, in adolescence by the intricate clockwork mechanisms that give them the illusion of life, in adulthood by the truth and beauty of the dramas they enact, and in old age by the timeless perfection of an art that lifts us above the cares of mortality and gives meaning to our lives. (89-90)

Into this world comes Heinrich Graum, "this troubled spirit who has risen up in our midst with his perilous and disturbing gift . . . the very nature of his art throws all into question . . ." (97). After mastering the making of automatons, Graum stops for ten years. He returns with a Neues Zaubertheater, which eschews "mimetic brilliance" (107) for what at first appears to be shoddy craftsmanship: "The new automatons can only be described as clumsy. By this I mean that the smoothness of motion so characteristic of our classic figures has been replaced by the jerky abrupt motions of amateur automatons. . . . They do not strike us as human" (107-08). But there are those who see this clumsiness as a radical innovation; Graum's genius, according to this interpretation, is to bring machines to life: "they have the souls of clockwork creatures, grown conscious of themselves. The classic automatists present us with miniature people; Heinrich Graum has invented a new race" (109).

The implications of this creation are demonstrated through fragmented audience response, reflected in part by the narration, which modulates between analytical first-person singular and awe-struck plural:

> My laborious remarks obscure the delicate art they seek to elucidate. Nothing short of attendance at the Neues Zaubertheater can convey the startling, disturbing quality of the new automatons. We seem drawn into the souls of these creatures, who assert their unreal nature at every jerk of a limb; we suffer their clumsiness, we are pierced by inhuman longings. (109)

Besides presenting the audience with a new experience, the new theater alters perceptions of the old: "Gratefully we seek out the old theaters, but once we have felt the troubling touch of the new automatons we find ourselves growing impatient with the smooth and perfect motions of the old masters, whose brilliant imitations seem to us nothing but clockwork confections" (110-11). And, as with previous audiences studied here, the change in perception does not stop at the theater door: "our dreams have changed" (111). If the Neues Zaubertheater does not allow an easy exit for its audience, it is because it targets the underpinnings of a culture rather than those desires that are (however reluctantly) allowed to surface.

Disorder in the Court: "The King in the Tree"

The theatrical motif continues in Millhauser's latest work. In the title novella of his collection *The King in the Tree,* a king's court decides to entertain a visiting count with a mime. The mime occurs against the backdrop of a retelling of the Tristan and Iseult story. Millhauser's doomed lovers are Tristan and Queen Ysolt, who has just married the king, Tristan's uncle. The mime at first appears to be peripheral to the main story, but if one scrutinizes the mime and its effects on the characters, stagecraft becomes a central metaphor informing the narrative.

From the beginning, rumors connect Tristan and Ysolt: Thomas of Cornwall, the novella's narrator and "faithful counselor" to the king reports that "The Queen is a whore—cut off her nose. The Queen is lecherous—burn her. Such are the interesting remarks one hears at court" (141). These remarks connect the Queen to Tristan: "They are too much together. I do not like these rumors" (145). The King is steadfast in trusting his nephew, however: "the King has set [Tristan] over her as a protector" (147). His love for Ysolt is equally unshakable. Foreshadowing the role-playing that will soon affect the main players at court, Ysolt's hold on the King is reportedly so intense that he can no longer act as he should. The narrator observes, "Before his marriage to Queen Ysolt, the King was master of his countenance . . . Now, in that well-loved face, one can see adoration, suspicion, jealousy, yearning, sudden doubt" (142).

The King's suspicions are provoked by the mime, which features Modor, one of the King's dwarfs, and the Count's dwarfs, Roland and Bathsheba. Before relating the significance of the performance itself, Bennett would draw attention to the seating arrangement of Millhauser's characters: "A stage was erected on the dais, surrounded by seats for the King, the Queen, the Count, and the highest nobles of both courts; all others sat on benches in the lower part of the hall" (156). The seating reflects the court's hierarchy; Bennett observes how "proximity to, and visibility of, the stage is usually proportionate to the price paid for the seat. The cheapest seats are farthest away, often with a restricted view, and distance their occupants not only from the stage action but from the rest of the paying audience" (141).

If the seating arrangement in the novella reflects social hierarchy, the performance shatters this hierarchy. The drama that the dwarfs act out is all too familiar: "When Modor appeared, gasps and murmurs sounded. His brash impudence astonished me. He wore a brilliant crimson mantle edged with ermine—the unmistakable robe of the King. On his head sat a gilt paper crown" (157). Modor is joined by the two other dwarfs: "Enter Roland and Bathsheba. He wore the jeweled mantle of Tristan; from Bathsheba's shoulders hung the crescent-covered mantle of the Queen" (157). The audience's reaction is significant here; if such central characters of the court are recognized according to wardrobe, this in effect reduces their authority to mere stage signs. Modor makes the most of his onstage coup: "Now Dwarf King and Dwarf Queen leave the stage and Dwarf Tristan is seen groping his way among invisible trees. He stops, cups his ear. Ysolt appears. They embrace passionately. Beside me, the King drew in a sharp breath" (157). In a striking parallel to "The Knife Thrower" and "Eisenheim," stage intersects grotesquely with reality. Modor and Roland vie for the Queen's affection in what is supposed to be a mock swordfight: "Suddenly the edge of Modor's sword strikes Tristan's upper arm, cutting through the mail. Blood runs through the iron rings" (158). The play ends with Roland's decapitation.

The supplanting of stagecraft with actual violence is unsettling enough, but the mime also bleeds (figuratively) into the rest of the novella. Afterward, the King decides to do something about Tristan and Ysolt, despite the fact that there was "no evidence of wrongdoing" (159). He decides to set a trap for the lovers by spying on them. His resolution is undercut by Thomas's distinct sense that the King is merely filling a role: "As the King spoke, he became animated, as if the act of utterance were filling him with decisive energy, but his eyes remained melancholy, withdrawn, and—an impression that struck me—as if indifferent to the strategy he was urging" (160).

The King and the narrator spy on the alleged lovers as they meet at night in an orchard. Tristan protests to Ysolt that he has been unfairly maligned. The narrator suspects, however, that this scene is being staged: "I had the odd sensation that I was watching a court play" (162). Concludes the narrator, "So they declaimed, two actors under the moon. For I understood—suddenly and absolutely—that they knew they were being watched, up there in the branches" (163). As suspicion continues and the lovers become more blatant in their transgression, the King relinquishes further authority until he assumes the new role of cuckold: "It is not good to pity one's king" (168). Even when the suspected pair are on their best behavior, it could all be a ruse; the narrator believes at one point that "They had agreed, in the strength of their rapturous love, to abstain for a while from amorous dallying, out of pity for the King. It was as if they were so sure of themselves . . . that they could bear to be obedient" (205).

What sets Millhauser's novella apart from previous explorations of the porous border between stage and audience—art and life—is the ultimately positive influence that playacting has. The court is scandalized, but also energized, by the ensuing drama. After Tristan is caught lying with the Queen beneath a pear tree, he escapes, leaving both the Queen and her court bereft. The frustration of and desire for the disguises of the stage are demonstrated in a brief subsequent scene:

> Today, after the tables were removed from the hall, a blind harper from Brittany played for us. I watched the King and Queen staring fiercely at him, trying to penetrate the disguise. Even I, who saw at once it was not Tristan, studied him closely, wondering whether I had perhaps been mistaken, whether he had deceived us by changing the shape of his body.
>
> We are all waiting for him, the shining one. (221-22)

This sense of the dramatic continues when Thomas visits Tristan, who has remarried during his exile. Tristan sustains a spear wound during a skirmish with four brothers who have attacked a knight. The wound fails to heal; after a time, Tristan "believes that only [the Queen] can save him" (235). He waits for her arrival under circumstances that Thomas reads as stagy: "he has so arranged it that if the Queen is on the return ship, the sail will be white, but if she remains in Cornwall, the sail will be black" (235).

If Tristan seems to inhabit a drama of his own devising, Thomas does not see this as naive falsehood. Remarking on another occasion of histrionics, the narrator explains that "I do not mean that Tristan's gesture was insincere. On the contrary, it sprang from the deepest part of his nature. . . . If he loves, he has to love more than anyone on earth has ever loved, he must love as if there were nothing else. Ceaselessly he must overcome obstacles, including the obstacle of his own rectitude" (232). If Thomas is understanding of Tristan and the rest of the court's need for drama, such understanding stems from appreciating the disturbing alternative. After Tristan and Ysolt die—"She was throwing herself at death, rolling around in lovely death" (238)—the narrator listens to the sound of waves outside his window: "now and then, if one listens very carefully, one can hear something else, hidden between or within the waves, and revealed suddenly, as behind a swiftly drawn curtain: the nothing—the nothing—the nothing at all" (238). It is not surprising, then, that Thomas concludes his narration with his quill poised, a "king of all space, summoner of souls," ready to distill drama from the morass of his experiences: "No, I wasn't ready for sleep—I was ready for words" (242).

Bennett understands theatrical events in terms of two frames, an outer frame that "contains all those cultural elements which create and inform the theatrical event" and an inner frame that "contains the dramatic production in a particular playing space" (149). Where the frames intersect, the audience comes in: "It is the interactive relations between audience and stage, spectator and spectator which constitute production and reception, and which cause the inner and outer frames to converge for the creation of a particular experience" (149). Read in terms of its fictional audiences, the work of Steven Millhauser is anything but exclusionary. Rather, the audience itself becomes a stage on which art works to console and provoke, challenge and enchant, the world beyond the theater door.

Works Cited

Bennett, Susan. *Theatre Audiences: A Theory of Production and Reception.* London: Routledge, 1990.

Deignan, Tom. "Crossing the Line." Rev. of *The Knife Thrower and Other Stories* by Steven Millhauser. *World & I* Oct. 1998: 280-84.

Jenkins, Henry. "Reception Theory and Audience Research: the Mystery of the Vampire's Kiss." *Reinventing Film Studies.* Ed. Christine Gledhill and Linda Williams. London: Arnold, 2000. 165-82.

Kakutani, Michiko. "The Great Escape From Reality to Fantasy." Rev. of *The Knife Thrower and Other Stories,* by Steven Millhauser. *New York Times* 5 May 1998, late ed.: E9. *LexisNexis* 10 July 2005 <http://lexisnexis.com>.

Millhauser, Steven. *The Barnum Museum.* Normal, IL: Dalkey Archive, 1997.

—. Interview. *Transatlantica* 3 (2003). 10 Aug. 2005 <http://etudes. americaines.free.fr/transatlantica/3/Millhauser3.html>.

—. *In the Penny Arcade.* Normal, IL: Dalkey Archive, 1998.

—. *The King in the Tree.* New York: Knopf, 2003.

—. *The Knife Thrower and Other Stories.* New York: Vintage, 1999.

Sammarcelli, Françoise. "Les voix sans origins chez Steven Millhauser." *Steven Millhauser, une écriture sur le fil.* Ed. Anne Ullmo. Villeneuve d'Ascq: Presses Universitaires du Septentrion, 2004. 39-54.

Ullmo, Anne. *The Knife-Thrower and Other Stories.* Paris: Armand Colin, 2003.

Architecture and Structure in Steven *Millhauser's* Martin Dressler: The Tale of an American Dreamer

Alicita Rodríguez

Architecture is a vital component in *Martin Dressler: The Tale of An American Dreamer*, serving an almost metonymic purpose: a close analysis of architecture reveals not only its own function within the novel, but also the greater generic impulse of the novel itself. Though it seems that Martin finds his ultimate calling as a hotelier, what he truly discovers is his spatial drive, an obsession with both the mathematical and enigmatic aspects of construction. In some sense, Martin's increasingly complex forms recall the American building frenzy at the turn of the century, with its emphasis on skyscrapers, bridges, and world's fairs. But Martin's buildings are not so easily comprehensible, for every seemingly realistic detail is coupled with a fantastic element. There are two distinct levels to the architecture presented in the novel, the descriptive passages detailing the hotels' construction and the analytical reviews critiquing the hotels' style. This built-in architectural deconstruction creates a hermeneutical circle that emphasizes the importance of architecture's role within Martin's world, and, consequently, our own—that is, its significance in our critical discourse. This essay seeks to show how *Martin Dressler* uses architecture to achieve the fantastic, in its course acknowledging the novel's debt to the American sublime.

In "Performing the Spectacle of Technology at the Beginning of the American Century: Steven Millhauser's *Martin Dressler*," Udo Hebel argues that Millhauser's novel fictionalizes the American moment when technology and spectacle merged (192). According to Hebel, there were two distinct movements in turn-of-the-century America: an interest in technology, especially with large-scale construction and transportation projects, and in theatricality, notably with the fair industry. Martin gets caught up in the performance of modernity: "He is fascinated by contemporaneous technology and revels in fantasies of his own participation in wonderful acts of technological designing and engineering" (192). It is certainly true that Martin desires the up-to-date; at the Vanderlyn, he wants to install steam radiators and room telephones, electric elevators and private toilets (67-68). And later, when he envisions the New Vanderlyn, he is fascinated by the image of "an immense dynamo" (169). But Hebel neglects that Martin's technophilia is always tempered by a childlike playfulness, so what begins as admiration for the technologically advanced ends up as desire for the magical. For example, Martin's description of the Brooklyn Bridge slowly shifts from reality to imagination: "in the river between the two cities the bridge piers went down through the water to the river bottom and down through the river bottom halfway to China" (16). The first part of that image is accurate, for the piers do plunge to the bottom of the river, but the second part is childlike exaggeration. The problem lies with Millhauser's "mutual contamination," wherein the awe of the technological achievement is so great as to seem unbelievable, so that when readers receive the truly unbelievable information, they automatically integrate it with reality (Chénetier 61). Readers are so dumbstruck by the massive scale of the Brooklyn Bridge that it seems its piers may in fact reach China.

While Hebel does not ignore *Martin Dressler*'s shift into the fantastic, he instead ascribes it to another historical and cultural phenomenon: "In both its larger scheme and details, the design of the Grand Cosmo evokes the exhibits and attractions of the climax of late nineteenth-century American fair industry, the Chicago World's Columbian Exposition of 1892/93" (200). There are, of course, some interesting analogies to be drawn within Hebel's comparison, but the problem with this argument is that it conveniently ignores Millhauser's subtle implications of the fantastic prior to the appearance of the Grand Cosmo. Already, the very first hotel Martin constructs hovers between two realms: "Above the ground a great lobby stretched away: elevator doors opened and closed, people strode in and out, bells rang, the squeak of valises mingled with the rattle of many keys and the ringing of many telephones, alcove opened into alcove as far as the eye could see" (169). Here is another perfect example of Millhauser's ambiguous enchantment. First, notice the use of infinitude, for the lobby stretches away and the alcoves multiply as far as the eye can see—that is, indefinitely. Second, mark the self-animation of the objects, almost as in a fairy tale: the valises squeak and mingle as if of their own volition, and the elevator doors open and close without cause. Third, the musical quality of the image, with its emphasis on dinging, ringing, and clinking, grants the objects further life; they serve as a sort of orchestra, a soundtrack perpetually accompanying their own lives. Last, all of the images of opening and closing, rising and falling, and swinging (people striding, keys rattling) makes the scene machinelike—and isn't the threat of the machine that it will take on a power of its own?

Though Hebel never labels it such, his reading of *Martin Dressler* owes much to David E. Nye's concept of the "American technological sublime," as delineated in his book of the same name. In particular, Millhauser's novel seems to work within the "Geometrical Sublime," which has its basis in bridges and skyscrapers. Unlike the European sublime, with its emphasis on an individual's awe in the presence of great beauty—an astonishment "with some degree of horror" (Nye 9)—the American sublime implies a shared experience of nature or technology that signifies cultural greatness (32). In *Martin Dressler*, the geometrical sublime is most evident in Martin's hotels, which grow bigger and bigger, taller and taller—a movement toward gigantism that reaches its apex in the skyscraper. Just as the American sublime is a European concept transformed and manipulated by Americans into a demonstration of power, American architecture is a variation of Old World style enlarged and elaborated in its crowning achievement, the skyscraper. The designers of the first American skyscrapers "were deadly convinced that to be attractive and noble, an American design simply had to be European, only much bigger" (Messler 65). It's no coincidence that the architect Martin hires is Austrian. In fact, Martin's relationship to Rudolf Arling underscores America's "incurable inferiority complex" (Messler 64); Martin hires the architect despite being "irked by the imperious tone but attracted by an air of supreme confidence" (188). Their first collaboration, the Hotel Dressler, fulfills Nye's first condition of the geometrical sublime, as "Crowds came to stare at the block-long building" (205).

The criticisms that the Hotel Dressler inspire reveal both Martin's and Millhauser's aesthetic philosophy: "The Dressler itself, as the doubting journalist had pointed out and as Martin readily acknowledged, was a massive contradiction: a modern steel-frame building sheathed in heavily ornamented masonry-walls meant to summon up a dream of châteaux and palaces" (207). This "inner eclecticism," as Martin calls it, is found in both creations, Martin's hotels and Millhauser's prose. One of the reasons that the architecture is so troubling is that it cannot easily be classified; this too is the problem with *Martin Dressler*. In his book *Steven Millhauser: la précision de l'impossible*, Marc Chénetier concludes that Millhauser is an "ultra-realist" (111), because he is not satisfied with realism, but rather exceeds it (116). Millhauser uses realism to establish his "Other-worlds" (Chénetier 111): "he cleverly applies the smaller-scale techniques of fictional realism to a largely notional as opposed to a realistic landscape" (Kinzie 116). If we listen to Martin's explanations, they sound quite similar to Millhauser's. Martin claims that "the note to strike was pleasurable diversity, a sense of spaces opening out endlessly, of turnings and twistings, of new discoveries beyond the next door" (191-92). Millhauser says that what interests him "is the place where the familiar begins to turn strange" (Shepard). In each case, we have a thrust for change and a movement toward something else, though that something else is neither defined nor reached. There is an attempt at metamorphosis, but the drive remains more important than the end—both insist upon a state of flux where "fulfillment is always impending and always receding" (Saltzman 598).

Martin's hotels eventually merit their own reviews in *Architectural Record*. In a lengthy attack of the New Dressler, Martin finally feels "that his deeper intentions had been understood" (234): "The writer criticized the New Dressler as a hybrid form, a transitional form, in which the hotel had begun to lose its defining characteristics without having successfully evolved into something else . . ." (235). A later review of the Grand Cosmo finds fault with the hotel's inclusiveness. Since it is "everything but a hotel" (Rollo 261), it produces "an impression of confusion, of uncertainty" (Millhauser 268). The extended critiques of Martin's hotels in newspapers and architectural journals serve readers of *Martin Dressler* as a sort of interpretive guide for both the structure of the hotels and of the novel as well: in this way, they work as metatext. A close analysis of the architectural reviews illustrates Millhauser's own narrative style—an evocation of uncertainty—which, more importantly, reveals *Martin Dressler*'s genre. While the similarities between Martin's transformational New York and America's turn-of-the-century technological sublime prove numerous, we cannot draw a one-to-one correlation between a historical, cultural movement and Martin's spatial drive. This interpretation denies the novel's "incursion of the supernatural, the fantastic," without which we would be left with historical fiction (Saltzman 593).

Using the novel's architecture, many readers conclude that *Martin Dressler* is an allegory of the American Dream. The most obvious form of allegory is the fable, which usually concludes with a summary of its allegorical meaning (Todorov 64-66). This is clearly not the case with *Martin Dressler*. Allegory can appear in a subtler form, wherein the allegorical meaning is not directly divulged, although the story itself operates on a figurative rather than literal level (Todorov 66-69). In such an instance, Martin might obviously stand for something else, such as an American dreamer. His buildings might then be metaphors for gaining wealth or power. Beginning a story with an abstract formula gives it the effect of indirect allegory, especially if the narrative then seems like the explication of an idea (Todorov 69). Here *Martin Dressler* is guilty, for we learn at the very start that satisfaction "is a perilous privilege" (1). But the indirect allegory must still work from an extended metaphor or double meaning. When we read *Martin Dressler*, do we consistently believe that the literal story is effaced by a figurative meaning? And putting this into architectural terms, do the Dressler, the New Dressler, and the Grand Cosmo exist as buildings? Or are they simply stand-ins for a metaphorical meaning? Millhauser's initial abstraction, which might lead readers to label *Martin Dressler* an allegory, dissolves rather quickly—another instance of his tendency to approach a form or an idea, but not satisfy it.

The architecture of a building and the structure of a narrative share an underlying organization, a blueprint or pattern with discernible edges or boundaries. But what importance can the discovery of such an underlying form have? Gérard Genette answers this question eloquently: "Literary discourse is produced and developed according to structures it can transgress only because it finds them" (Todorov 8). It seems appropriate, then, that we should use Millhauser's architecture to uncover Millhauser's architecture; in other words, an analysis of Martin Dressler's buildings yields an understanding of *Martin Dressler*'s genre. Paradoxically, Martin's constructions are fuzzy, seeping, unfixed. Yet a study of their very transience solidifies the novel's form. It's as if the ghostly hotels emerge from the very real skeleton of their corporeal counterpart. And this is like so much of Millhauser's work: its hovering, its in-betweenness makes it difficult to classify, but that very uncertainty provides precious clues as to its essential form.

In *The Fantastic: A Structural Approach to a Literary Genre*, Tzvetan Todorov explains the fantastic genre, using its neighboring genres—known in translation as the marvelous and the uncanny—to define the term. Todorov maintains that uncertainty drives the fantastic: "it is hesitation which sustains its life" (31). Once a protagonist or reader decides on an explanation for the fantastic, the genre is replaced by the marvelous or the uncanny:

> In a world which is indeed our world, the one we know, a world without devils, sylphides, or vampires, there occurs an event which cannot be explained by the laws of this same familiar world. The person who experiences the event must opt for one of two possible solutions: either he is the victim of an illusion of the senses, or a product of the imagination—and laws of the world then remain what they are [the uncanny]; or else the event has indeed taken place, it is an integral part of reality—but then this reality is controlled by laws unknown to us [the marvelous]. (25)

The fantastic genre, then, exists as a springboard into other genres; rarely does the fantastic remain so, because there is little literature in which the underlying reason for the inexplicable event remains ambiguous. Todorov offers Henry James's *The Turn of the Screw* and Prosper Mérimée's "La Venus d'Ille" as examples of the pure fantastic (43). Because of Millhauser's architectural focus, Todorov's demarcation of the fantastic genre by a single vertical line proves most interesting (44):

| uncanny | fantastic-uncanny | fantastic-marvelous | marvelous |

In the above diagram, the fantastic "in its pure state is represented here by the median line separating the fantastic-uncanny from the fantastic-marvelous. This line corresponds perfectly to the nature of the fantastic, a frontier between two adjacent realms" (44).

But the fantastic is often an unused concept; we hear the term uncanny more frequently (Masschelein 54). The uncanny is usually ascribed to Sigmund Freud's 1919 essay, "Das Unheimliche." Many critics view Todorov's fantastic and Freud's uncanny as quite similar, which may partly explain the popularity of one term over the other (Masschelein 55). Both critics/terms share certain generic characteristics—hesitation/uncertainty, doubling/repetition, effacing/collapse of dream and reality—that dominate *Martin Dressler*. Todorov, however, delves into the generic distinctions in a way that Freud does not. There are two distinct movements in *Martin Dressler* in terms of its narrative and architectural structures: the novel toes the generic line, thus existing as the fantastic, by creating an architecture that effaces the distinction between the exterior and interior worlds. This struggle between two oppositional movements is echoed in the very characteristics of the fantastic that *Martin Dressler* displays: a dizzying doubling and multiplication; the morphing of foreground and background, particularly with the physical/architectural body; and the effacement of dream and reality. It is Millhauser's use of architecture that highlights the fantastic in Martin Dressler's series of hotels, which progressively double and multiply.

The first hotel that Martin purchases, the New Vanderlyn, has six stories (6x1); Martin's second hotel, the Dressler, has eighteen stories and a six-story tower (6x3; 6x4); the New Dressler, Martin's third hotel, has twenty-four stories (6x4); and the final hotel, the Grand Cosmo, has thirty stories (6x5). Furthermore, the hotels' underground levels and basements increase dramatically, so that the six stories of the New Vanderlyn double to become the twelve underground levels of the Grand Cosmo. Freud believes that "this inner *repetition-compulsion* is perceived as uncanny" (145), because it represents an involuntary force: "something repressed which *recurs*" (148). The number six appears again and again: in the "gilt hexagons" of the Vanderlyn (9, 24, 168), the six Metropolitan cafés (166), the six floors of architect Rudolf Arling's pleasure dome (186), the "half a dozen" shops in the New Vanderlyn (189), the "six vacation spots" in the New Dressler (231), and the "six top floors" of the Grand Cosmo (275).

The hotels grow in a seemingly impossible fashion until they appear infinite, but engineers and architects remind the reader that the structures imagined by Martin may possibly be constructed. Millhauser stresses the magnitude of these buildings by emphasizing the vertical and horizontal. The dichotomy of the two directional axes is introduced early in the novel: the first hotel is "a well-planned machine that drew all these people to itself and carried them up and down in iron cages and arranged them in private rooms" (24). Martin later imagines a city composed of moving trains and rising towers (111) and a hotel "rising and falling" (169). Because the buildings seem endless, we doubt the reality of the novel's world. Martin "urges the carpenters to find room for another shop, and another" (178) during the remodel of the Vanderlyn. And though the hotel already exists—a fact that underscores its finitude—more shops are later leased (190). Similarly, when Emmeline cries, "I want to keep going forever. Come on!" (197), we believe that her perpetual descent is possible.

But Millhauser tempers the potential magic of the buildings' expansion: "the consulting engineers had said it could be done" (250). Using modalizing expressions such as "could be" is typical of the fantastic genre, because such figurative language stresses possibility and ambiguity (Todorov 80). Additionally, the use of the past perfect tense calls into question the engineers' assessment of what is/was possible. Millhauser's use of multiplication and infinity creates a feeling of uneasiness and inexplicability. We remain unsure of the reality of *Martin Dressler*'s architectural world until the end of the novel and afterward; this uncertainty exemplifies Todorov's main condition for the fantastic.

The conflation of foreground and background—where the body ends and the environment begins—in the body/building metaphor also emphasizes the hesitation typical of the fantastic genre. For Martin, this effacement occurs in two ways: through the amalgamation of his own body and his hotels', and of women's bodies with one another and himself. Martin's hotels act as metaphors for his body:

> The warren of underground shops, where the dynamos churn and the servants toil, is like the hotel's subconscious; the ornate elevator is its spinal column; unseen turbines serve as its respiratory system; a gigantic furnace fires secretly in the sub-basement, digesting perpetually . . . Martin experiences an ecstasy of embodiment. (Saltzman 602)

The comparison is not meant to be subtle; Millhauser writes, "it was as if the structure were his own body" (170); and later, "as the first columns rose over the top of the excavation, Martin had the sudden sharp sense of the bones of his shoulders pressing upwards against his skin" (229). While the physical produces beautiful analogies, the spiritual comparison yields the most uncanny feelings.

✣ In *The Poetics of Space*, Gaston Bachelard establishes the connection between body and house, likening the underground to the subconscious. Thus verticality can be divided into "the rationality of the roof to the irrationality of the cellar" (18). Martin takes full advantage of people's subconscious desires in his multiplying underground. These multilevel basements allow Martin "to develop certain ideas that gave him a deep, almost guilty pleasure" (209). People begin to spread rumors about the underground levels, which "house darker and more disturbing entertainments" as people descend further. The catalog of "entertainments" recalls psychoanalytic repression in its penchant for the violent, sexual, and grotesque: dog fights, asylum inmates, brothels, wild children, living statues, intoxicating perfumes (266-67). Todorov classifies much of Millhauser's subterranean offerings as themes of the fantastic (91-156). Going down represents discovering our own secret desires, but the underground levels are bothersome because they should not exist, especially not in such numbers and with such detail. This brings us back to Freud, who explains that the horror of the uncanny stems from something "that ought to have remained hidden and secret, and yet comes to light" (130).

In entering Martin's buildings, people are entering into his physical and psychological body, a pseudosexual penetration that evokes the fantastic. The women in Martin's life also suffer from this type of bodily effacement, melding into him and into each other. During Martin's first sexual encounter, he cannot distinguish between himself and Mrs. Hamilton: "And Martin entered her fever-dream" (31). Millhauser gives no physical description of the act, except to briefly describe Mrs. Hamilton's skin and Martin's "sinking" (31). Then, in a swift narrative ellipsis, Martin stands in his uniform, water pitcher in hand. There is no clear indication that the two consummated their relationship, which further confuses the body/mind distinction: did Martin penetrate Mrs. Hamilton when he entered her dream?

The women in Martin's life become associated with rooms, as if in being part of himself, they are also part of his architectural body. So it happens that Martin cannot find Caroline without navigating a maze of rooms: "and again it seemed to him that he was passing through many rooms, through all the rooms of the city, in order to reach his wife" (157). Here again the modalizing formula, "it seemed," introduces the fantastic element (Todorov 80). All of the women in Martin's life eventually meld into each other and into Martin's architectural spaces: "Often at night Martin lay thinking of Marie Haskova in her ghostly attic chamber, of Louise Hamilton in her dusky parlor, of Dora and Gerda in the house with rattling windows, of the actresses in the hallway . . ." (162). All of his metaphorical wives are "sliding into one another," just as his hotels seem to be reproducing (182). Like his buildings, his women fragment his body, so that some recall the attic and others the hallway. Marie Haskova represents ascension and the actresses transformation, for Martin must climb to reach Marie and traverse a passage to find the actresses—actions that reinforce the vertical and horizontal yet again: for *Martin Dressler* is always in motion, never arriving anywhere. Not only the multiplication of floors, but also the morphing of the body work toward suspending the reader in fantastic ambiguity.

Martin Dressler capitalizes on the reader's hesitation through its unrelenting conflation of dream and reality, represented by the interior and exterior worlds and real and imaginary protagonists. The world outside the hotels and the one within exist as manifestations of Martin's waking and dream life. Freud states that "effacing the distinction between imagination and reality" often produces "an uncanny effect" (152). Early on, Millhauser establishes the hotels as reverie: when Martin first visits the Vanderlyn, "it was as if he had stepped into someone's dream" (12). Once ensconced there, "his life in the hotel was a dream-life, an interlude, a life from which he would one day wake to his real life" (35). Once Martin equates his dream-life with reality by spending more and more time in his hotels, the repositories of imagination, reality slowly deteriorates, as the hotels begin to vanish. First, "The Bellingham had simply vanished" (254); then, Martin imagines that "the Dressler, the New Dressler, and the Grand Cosmo would melt away" (276). The physical structures disappear, simultaneously obliterating Martin's new reality, which is housed in dreamscape.

But if the hotels begin as representations of Martin's dream life, they result in his reality, so that by the end of the novel, the outside world becomes the facsimile. In the end, the wrecking cranes likely disintegrate Martin's dream reality: outside, Martin spies the Grand Cosmo through a patch of leaves, "which perhaps were moving only to prevent him from attending closely to the crumbling masonry and falling steel behind them" (286). So he is forced to enter the outside world, where the sky is "so blue, so richly and strangely blue, that it seemed the kind of blue you might find in pictures of castles in the books of fairy tales, after you peeled away the crackly thin paper" (285). The real world has become the place of fairy tales, so that when Martin steps outside, "he had passed through a crack in the world, into this place" (286). Reality is then a fissure, a break in Martin's dream. In having been asleep for so long within his creations, when Martin finally awakens to reality, the reality has lost all believability.

Millhauser gives the reader apt preparation for this reversal by repeatedly describing the inorganic as organic. Construction becomes a metaphor for growth, the city imagined as forest: the lobby of the Vanderlyn is a "deep, peaceful forest" (169); buildings grow from a hole "dug into the ground" (185); skyscrapers "throw down deep roots" (191); "a five-room apartment had become a forest" (208); "the avenues had begun to erupt in strange, immense growths: modern flowers with veins of steel" (229). Like a living organism continuously in flux, the Grand Cosmo exhibits limitless variety (261). If the hotel world is natural, then the real world must necessarily become artificial. Todorov explains this phenomenon: "The physical world and the spiritual world interpenetrate; their fundamental categories are modified as a result" (118). In taking on a life of its own, Martin's dream world destroys the natural world, like Hoffman's mechanical doll Olimpia, who replaces her living, breathing counterpart Clara. The double, in both cases, symbolically murders the original who gave it life in the first place. In "The Double as Immortal Self," Otto Rank explores this betrayal: "the killing of the alter-ego invariably leads to the death of the hero himself" (92). Martin's body is doubled in the conflation of his architectural and physical bodies, as his life is doubled, split between reality and dream. One could say that all of Martin's doubling is manifested in his creations, that his hotels are twofold because he himself is a split personality: "The duality of art is a fatal consequence of the duality of man" (Baudelaire 3). By allowing his dreamscape to overshadow his reality—for the Grand Cosmo is meant to replace the world—Martin destroys himself. The dream Martin who resides in the Grand Cosmo replaces the real Martin who created it.

Perhaps this suicide is best seen through *Martin Dressler*'s use of real and false personages, characters and actors. Of course, this duality is further complicated by the fact that characters are always actors. The actors in the novel, however, are impersonating their counterparts to such a degree that everyone loses substance. The false reality of the novel, for which the reader should suspend disbelief, becomes effaced by a doubled falsity in which actors represent actors—this multiplicity echoes the architecture's doubling, because inside Martin's dream world, there exists yet another dream world represented by professional actors playing characters. The presence of actors as hotel guests occurs early in the novel when Martin first visits the Vanderlyn and discovers that "a troupe of actors and actresses had rented a row of rooms" (12). Martin is informed that "They liked to rehearse at strange hours" (12). The reader, like Martin, can never be certain if the actors are acting or simply being. This calls into question whether any guests are ever not acting, for at the very least, they are playing out Millhauser's script.

The separation between characters and actors gets more slippery when Martin hires actors to play hotel guests, so that the Grand

Cosmo will seem more occupied than it actually is. No sooner does Martin hire the professionals than he can no longer differentiate between them and the real guests. This does not bother him, however: "And Martin liked the effect, the rather complicated little effect of false life that, in the acting, became less false, that spilled into the real" (280). The actors begin to overtake the characters, so that there is a trio of women much like the Vernon women (281) and a man much like Martin (283). (Martin's alter ego is appropriately named John Painter, as he becomes the creator of the "real" Martin: in the process, the original Martin loses substance, becoming two-dimensional.) We cannot be sure if the actors are more real than the characters, because as they act, the actors convince themselves that they are what they represent. This "collapse of the limit between matter and mind" is "the first characteristic of madness" (Todorov 115). Millhauser recognizes this and pushes it to the extreme by housing a sanatorium in his hotel:

> a gloomy Asylum for the Insane, with barred windows and shafts of pallid moonlight, in which more than two hundred actors and actresses portrayed patients suffering from more than two hundred delusions of melancholia, including the sensation of being on fire, of having one's legs made of glass, of being possessed by the devil, of having horns on the head, of being a fish, of being strangled, of being eaten by worms, of having the head severed from the body. (262)

If Martin cannot distinguish the real from the imaginary, then how can the actors? Note that all of the types of insanity found in Martin's hotel asylum involve delusion, particularly an inability to separate the body from its environment.

According to Todorov's generic definition, *Martin Dressler* is a fantastic text in the pure state, driven as it is by unrelenting ambiguity—a vagueness characterized by a continual undulation between various polarities: vertical and horizontal, interior and exterior, self and other, dream and reality. Millhauser achieves this liminal state through architecture. This technique of using spatial constructions in literature to intensify the strange is examined by architect Anthony Vidler in his book *The Architectural Uncanny*. Building on the theories of Freud among others, Vidler defines the architectural uncanny as "a representation of a mental state of projection that precisely elides the boundaries of the real and the unreal in order to provoke a disturbing ambiguity, a slippage between waking and dreaming" (11). This is quite similar to Freud's *unheimlich*, though the evocation of eeriness becomes possible through architecture: "the special characteristics of architecture and urbanism as arts of spatial definition allow us to advance the argument into the domain of the tangible" (Vidler 13). *Martin Dressler* provides an ideal example of using the concrete to recall the intangible. Millhauser's architecture in the novel stresses the uncanny, because his hotels erase all of the distinctions that usually put us at ease. In particular, Martin's hotels avoid uniformity and amass ornamentation, thereby constructing spaces that reject order and hospitability, and confounding our expectations about how space should be organized.

In her article "The Use of *Fiction* to Interpret *Architecture* and Urban Space," Katherine Shonfield discusses the desire of modern architecture to create order and thus avoid pollution. She points out that anthropologist Mary Douglas defines dirt as "matter out of place," which establishes pollution as transgression (371). Architecture, then, should establish "the delineation of *boundary*" (372) in order to accomplish "the assertion of *order*" (372). In modernity's desire to organize life, everything must be kept in its proper place. Martin identifies this lust for order, which he reduces to geometry: "all the blocks went repeating themselves, rectangle by rectangle" (56); "he looked down over the railing and saw the sharp-turning stair-flights dropping away in smaller and smaller rectangles" (154); "vast spaces were divided neatly into small, repeated rectangles" (274). But Martin overthrows order by avoiding uniformity: while his hotels do exhibit compartmentalization, they eschew pattern, thereby disorienting the visitor: "Monotonous regularity, he had told Rudolf Arling, was to be avoided like the plague . . ." (191). In order to win "the battle against symmetry," Martin rejects "the reassuring sense of boredom provided by multiple sameness" and insists on infinite variety in the hotels' floor plans (207, 274): "What struck most of the first wave of observers was the overthrow of the conventional apartment. Instead the Grand Cosmo offered a variety of what it called 'living areas,' in carefully designed settings" (259). Martin's quest to abolish regularity creates an architectural world that can only house dream. In order to understand the whole, people must be able to see "the distinction between parts," but Martin's hotels banish delineation in favor of fluidity (Shonfield 383).

Not only do the hotels lack pattern, but also they evince a protean mutability, so that quite like a dreamscape the architectural spaces are perpetually becoming and metamorphosing: "in order to avoid the tedium of a fixed architectural scheme, the Grand Cosmo employed a staff of designers, carpenters, landscape artists, and architectural assistants who roamed through the building and decided on changes. . . . It was therefore possible to say that the Grand Cosmo was never the same from one day to the next, that its variety was, in a sense, limitless" (260-61). This perpetual shape shifting emphasizes the lack of boundary—an erasure that once again stresses transgression: a violation of reality through pollutive encroachment.

One of the most troubling aspects of *Martin Dressler*'s structures concerns the effacement of exterior/interior duality. More than anything else, a building should provide shelter from the elements; this is, after all, the main function of architecture. Ultimately, Martin's hotels fail to distinguish between outside and inside: "The logical extreme of the hotel's expansion, self-sufficiency, and autotelism is that it means to undo the exterior-interior dichotomy altogether" (Saltzman 605). Like the Shorncliffe Barracks that Shonfield discusses, whose emphasis on structural visibility compromised "the role of an outside wall" by letting water in (385), the Dressler's roof also suffers from constructional seeping, so that customers huddle in a corner to avoid the rain (213). Avoiding a clarity of delineation is akin to deception:

> Fundamentally important is the idea that such truth must be *seen*. If there is any fuzziness or bastardization or transgression at the junction between two parts Architecture must visibly reveal how it stands up, and what element supports what. This means that the distinction between parts must be as clearly drawn as possible to avoid any accusation of obfuscation or tinkering with the truth. (Shonfield 383)

Because its boundaries are all fuzzy, the Grand Cosmo is a master of illusion. Like an expert magician, the hotel hides its own structural existence. How it stands remains a mystery, so that all who enter desire nothing more than to discover its underlying form.

Much of the conflation of exterior and interior in *Martin Dressler* results from introducing elements inside that usually belong outside: countryside and gardens, lakes and ponds, lagoons and grottoes, bazaars and alleyways, catacombs and caves. Interestingly enough, the delay for the opening of the Grand Cosmo came from "a flaw in the refrigerated-air system" (258)—the building itself rejects the import of conditioned air as if it were as unnatural as a respirator. Since the building has become a natural space, it requires natural air. All of these contained, orchestrated spaces eliminate the sense that people step inside from outside. Without a boundary, it is impossible to determine where you are going and where you have been, consequently destroying history as progression, so that the Grand Cosmo also conflates time, offering Victorian parlors and Grecian cities side by side. Outside the hotel there exists that bustling turn-of-the-century New York with which the novel began, but inside we find "a dramatic, tragic suspension of time" (Rollo 26)).

The liminal spaces of *Martin Dressler* are confusing not only because of their rejection of uniformity, but also due to their accumulation of decoration. If "The decorative is that which undermines or challenges the firmness of category and delineating boundary," (Shonfield 372) then Martin's hotels grow progressively unsteady.

The ornamentation parallels the multiplication of floors, so that the end effect is an unsteady heaping that is always in danger of toppling, hence foreshadowing the eventual "crumbling" of the Grand Cosmo (286).

In *Eccentric Spaces*, Robert Harbison describes the estrangement resulting from architecture's cumulative drive, which is composed of "images that look like layer cakes" (Harbison 81). Millhauser uses almost identical language to describe the phenomenon, as Martin's "profusion of images" recall "a gigantic wedding cake" (Millhauser 203, 205). This heaping is particularly troublesome in a skyscraper, because it reminds people of its own spectacular verticality, creating a sense of vertigo. Interior compartmentalization, in contrast, achieves an emphasis on the horizontal: "the sense of a series of more or less identical rooms arranged side by side in a rectangle of steel" (260) minimizes that awesome verticality. The result of displacing the vertical is that "the height of city buildings is a purely *exterior* one" (Bachelard 27). But Martin's excessive ornamentation has done away with this false sense of security.

It isn't simply ornamentation ad nauseam that defines Millhauser's architecture; more importantly, it is the juxtaposition of distinct elements. Here *Martin Dressler* defines the "'both-and' spirit of postmodernism" (Saltzman 608)—so that "Martin may be deemed an early practitioner of postmodern pastiche" (Saltzman 597). Martin's hotels exhibit "contradiction" (174), "mingling" and "inclusion" (176), "juxtaposed objects" (177), "hybrid form" and "transitional form" (235). In describing his oneiric house, Bachelard maintains the importance of oppositional simultaneity: "Indeed, everything comes alive when contradictions accumulate" (39). This is, however, a feature of dream. In one moment, there is "the transformation of a cafeteria into an Italian garden" (Millhauser 260). Nothing remains constant in dream, especially architecture.

There is no doubt that the Grand Cosmo is uninhabitable. People cannot live in a space that continually effaces boundary. Inside and outside, structure and ornament, vertical and horizontal, past and present: the line differentiating all of these binaries collapses, giving way to a pollutive seeping. But the beauty and genius of Martin's architecture lies in its very impossibility—a body of fiction within a body of fiction. One of Katherine Shonfield's main points in "The Use of *Fiction* to Interpret *Architecture* and Urban Space" is that architects can learn about their craft by "moving fictional insight to center stage" (387). Fictions work ideally to present baroque reason, "in which the instability of forms in movement opens onto 'the reduplicated and re-duplicable structure of all reality: enchanted illusions and disenchanted world'" (Shonfield 386 quoting Buci-Glucksmann in *Baroque Reason*). *Martin Dressler*'s hotels embody baroque reason: first, the spaces duplicate themselves; second, they duplicate reality; and third, they house dream. The tragic irony that Martin discovers is that people cannot live in their ideal, illusory world: that dreamscape must exist as an alternative to reality. Not even fictional characters can inhabit the Grand Cosmo; they can have no substance if their surroundings have no substance—and, paradoxically, the fictional characters require reality within their constructed world. Their world does not have to present *the* real world as we know it, but it must present *a* real world.

Structurally, *Martin Dressler* presents two distinct movements: its narrative structure is firm, faithfully remaining in the fantastic genre as defined by Todorov; but its architectural structure is fluid, continually transgressing the boundaries as established by modernism. Millhauser's use of architecture enables the fantastic in its pure state; Martin's hotels use doubling and effacement to maintain hesitation. Throughout the novel, the possibility of the hotels is questioned, and the use of modifying expressions intensifies this uncertainty. Millhauser never answers the question regarding the physical reality of his architectures. In fact, he swings back and forth like a pendulum—for every hint that the architecture is indeed possible, there is a clue that it is not. Paradoxically, Millhauser's architecture upholds a generic line by effacing its own structural delineations. At every turn, Martin's hotels destroy the pure edge and opt instead for a fuzzy seeping. The skyscrapers reject compartmentalization, eliminate interior/exterior duality, and amass ornamentation. The end result of all this transgression is a conflation of dream and reality—so much so, that Martin's dream world replaces the real world, turning the real world into illusion. The Grand Cosmo becomes the universe and everything outside becomes unreal. By housing all reality within a structure, Martin destroys reality, because what should be all encompassing cannot be contained.

Steven Millhauser's use of architecture in *Martin Dressler: The Tale of an American Dreamer* parallels the novel's own formal movement: the impossibility of the hotels is analogous to the impossibility of fiction. If fiction exists as an alternative reality, it does so at the expense of a corresponding reality—the "real world," which we all agree we can see, feel, hear. Likewise, if dream exists as an alternative consciousness, it must do so in conjunction with the waking consciousness it works against. In this way, *Martin Dressler* is the story of artistic folly: if we try to convert dream into reality, if we try to transform fiction into fact, we fail. A story can no longer be an escape if we interpret it as an accurate reflection of our known world; herein lies the tragic irony of realism. Similarly, Martin's hotels cannot house dream, because dreamscapes must exist in the realm of intangibles. Both fiction and dream work because they recall an original, which is much like the miniature. Once the miniature—the novel, or the Grand Cosmo—destroys the need for its double—its original correspondent—it destroys itself. This is perhaps the lesson we learn from *Martin Dressler*, though this lesson does not warrant classifying the novel as allegory: "We must insist on the fact that we cannot speak of allegory unless we find explicit indications of it within the text. Otherwise, we shift to what is no more than a reader's interpretation; and at this point every literary text would be allegorical . . ." (Todorov 73-74). The task of the writer, the architect, the miniaturist, lies in developing uncertainty: Is the novel, the Grand Cosmo, the model train possible? Real? The hesitation caused by Martin's hotels recalls the viewer's awe when faced with the sublime and, more importantly, the reader's uncertainty when encountering the fantastic. Steven Millhauser exploits architecture in *Martin Dressler* in order to explore the symbiotic relationships between substance and dream, reality and fiction, original and double, realism and the fantastic. Ultimately, Martin's hotels represent an attempt to metonymize creation; if we apply Shonfield's idea that fictional architecture can instruct, then the lesson of Martin's endeavor is clear: the oneiric house must remain in dream.

Works Cited

Bachelard, Gaston. *The Poetics of Space*. Trans. Maria Jolas. Boston: Beacon Press, 1964.

Baudelaire, Charles. *The Painter of Modern Life and Other Essays*. Trans. Jonathan Mayne. London: Phaidon, 1995.

Chénetier, Marc. *Steven Millhauser: La précision de l'impossible*. Paris : Belin, 2003.

Freud, Sigmund. "The 'Uncanny.'" *On Creativity and the Unconscious*. New York: Harper & Row, 1958. 122-61.

Harbison, Robert. *Eccentric Spaces*. Boston: David R. Godine, 1977.

Hebel, Udo J. "Performing the Spectacle of Technology at the Beginning of the American Century: Steven Millhauser's *Martin Dressler*." *The Holodeck in the Garden: Science and Technology in Contemporary American Fiction*. Ed. Peter Freese and Charles B. Harris. Normal, IL: Dalkey, 2004. 192-211.

Kinzie, Mary. "Succeeding Borges, Escaping Kafka: On the Fiction of Steven Millhauser." *Salmagundi* 92 (1991): 115-44.

Masschelein, Anneleen. "The Concept of Ghost: Conceptualization of the Uncanny in Late Twentieth Century Theory." *Mosaic* 35.1 (2002): 53-68.

Messler, Norbert. "Architecture and Popular Art: The American Skyscraper." *Anglistik & Englischunterricht* 25 (1985): 63-79.

Millhauser, Steven. *Martin Dressler: The Tale of an American Dreamer.* London: Phoenix, 1996.

Nye, David E. *American Technological Sublime.* Cambridge: MIT Press, 1994.

Rank, Otto. "The Double as Immortal Self." *Beyond Psychology.* New York: Dover, 1941. 62-101.

Rollo, Alberto. "Postfazione." *Martin Dressler: Il racconto di un sognatore americano.* Rome: collezione immaginario, 2004.

Saltzman, Arthur. "A Wilderness of Size: Steven Millhauser's *Martin Dressler.*" *Contemporary Literature* 42 (2001): 589-616.

Shepard, Jim. "Steven Millhauser." *Bomb Magazine* Spring 2003: 18 Feb. 2005 <http://bombsite.com>.

Shonfield, Katherine. "The Use of *Fiction* to Interpret *Architecture* and Urban Space." *Journal of Architecture* 5.4 (2000): 369-87.

Todorov, Tzvetan. *The Fantastic: A Structural Approach to a Literary Genre.* Trans. Richard Howard. Ithaca: Cornell UP, 1973.

Vidler, Anthony. *The Architectural Uncanny: Essays in the Modern Unhomely.* Cambridge: MIT Press, 1992.

A Steven Millhauser Checklist

Novels

Edwin Mullhouse: The Life and Death of an American Writer, 1943-1954, by Jeffrey Cartwright. New York: Knopf, 1972; New York: Vintage, 1996.

Portrait of a Romantic. New York: Knopf, 1977; New York: Washington Square Press, 1987.

From the Realm of Morpheus. New York: William Morrow, 1986.

Martin Dressler: The Tale of an American Dreamer. New York: Crown, 1996; New York: Vintage, 1997.

Novellas

Little Kingdoms. New York: Poseidon Press, 1993; New York: Vintage, 1998.

Enchanted Night. New York: Crown, 1999; New York: Vintage, 2000.

The King in the Tree. New York: Knopf, 2003; New York: Vintage, 2004.

Short Stories

In the Penny Arcade. New York: Knopf, 1986; Normal, IL: Dalkey Archive Press, 1998.

The Barnum Museum. New York: Poseidon Press, 1990; Normal, IL: Dalkey Archive Press, 1997.

The Knife Thrower and Other Stories. New York: Crown, 1998; New York: Vintage, 1999.

Acknowledgments

Danielle Alexander thanks Alicita Rodríguez for the original conception for this project and for acting as liaison with Steven Millhauser; Pedro Ponce for compiling the issue's scholarly apparatus; and both for their generous and intelligent collaboration. She also thanks Cheryl Brown and John Paine for their assistance with translations in the novella overview and in "Steven Millhauser: Interpretive Approaches."

Alicita Rodríguez thanks Patrick Muckleroy, Interlibrary Loan Librarian at Western State College of Colorado, who worked quickly and diligently to fulfill all loan requests, and Joseph Starr for extensive and careful proofreading as well as astute suggestions.

Pedro Ponce thanks Danielle Alexander, Alicita Rodríguez, and Sidney L. Sondergard for referring him to several sources relevant to the scope of his critical essay. Sidney L. Sondergard also assisted with translations for the critical essay and the short fiction overview.

Danielle Alexander, Pedro Ponce, and Alicita Rodríguez all thank Steven Millhauser for corresponding with them about this project, commenting on their work, and granting them an interview.

Dear Editor

Dear Editor: I'm very in love with my husband, even though lately I've been involved with another man. That's the way things go in life, I guess. Well, my question is this. When I'm going to see this other man, I always bring our dog with me because it looks like I wouldn't be bringing the dog if I'm going to be making love with this gentleman. But I'm beginning to think that hubby has caught on because he's a very suspicious person who has a real big problem with trust, and I think that's why I've been forced into this situation with the other man in the first place. This is very confusing to me, especially because I feel like I'm cheating on my lover if I have sex with hubby, which really makes me feel guilty about my lover and also upsets him.

Editor: I'd suggest you read Daniel Bowman's *How to Forget Your Guilt and Enjoy Living!* It's among the myriad of books that arrive here daily for review consideration, though why publishers think that we would review such books is beyond my power to imagine. Some brilliant marketing person out there who, like most marketing people, has suffered severe brain damage. In any event, Bowman's thesis seems to be, though the endless grammatical errors make the book nearly unreadable, that any human action is equal in moral value (or lack thereof) to any other one. He compares the modern marriage to getting a new car: "You feel guilty when you get tired of you're old car and go gets a new one? I'd say you doesn't, and you don't waist ten seconds worrying about what became of that old heap, right? Well, what I'm saying is that you should view your husband or wifes this way. Time to move on, get something new, and put the past behind you." You seem quite ready to do this, and so you will probably want to embrace Bowman's advice: "Dont worry about it."

Dear Editor: Last night I had a dream about my ex-wife up in Chicago. I don't know how, but I'm at her house and her new husband, who used to be our neighbor, says hi to me, like we're all sophisticated people who should be getting along with each other, but this is the first time I've seen the guy since he married my wife. Then she comes downstairs and doesn't say a word, but she goes over to the kitchen and starts getting out all the ingredients for making chocolate chip cookies, which is kind of an old story with her. The thing about the chocolate chip cookies is that's what she used to do when we were married and she was having an affair with some guy. Suddenly she'd be baking cookies and say she was bringing them to work with her, but getting laid doesn't count for work in my book. All those cookies flying out the door like she was some kind of machine. Then I wake up, and I'm sweating like a madman, and I start thinking about the dream and I'm wondering why the hell I'm having this dream about her because it's been about ten years since the divorce and when I moved all the way downstate to LeRoi, which is another sick joke.

Now I'm living in a town that's like something right out of a porn movie. I mean these people all seem to be jumping in and out of each other's beds, but they're always talking about religion and asking me if I've been saved. They come up to me on the street and say, "Do you know Jesus?" How the fuck am I supposed to answer that? Even the town's welcome sign has this bullshit on it: "Welcome to Le Roy: Love Jesus or Keep on Truckin'." One woman who used to live down the block from me kept putting a pile of homemade bread and cookies at my front door, but they tasted like things you wouldn't want to give a pig. She'd attached a note that said, "Did you give Jesus a hug today?" Then I heard that she was doing this all over the place, making this crap by the truckload and dumping it on people's doorsteps. Someone said she was shacking up with a lot of the men in the neighborhood and the baked goods were just a front for getting out of the house. Another story was that she was getting ploughed by some guy up in El Paso at the Super 8, but I don't know how this fits into the bread and cookies thing, and besides you had to wonder who would ever want to screw this fat thing. Then one night her husband blows out his brains. People said he'd had it with all the baking, especially since the neighbors started taking the wonderful baked goods and throwing them at his house at night. And they had a daughter who worked at the Dixie truck stop and supposedly was giving free hand-jobs to any trucker who wanted one. I mean, she was like just giving the things away. So, what's the story with my dream?

Editor: You might want to take a look at a book that recently came in here for review called *The Grass Is Always Greener* by Lutecia Mahu ("Distinguished Professor, Illinois State Community College at LeRoy"). Its thesis seems to be that humans are possessed of the need to believe that their lives can change, that the future will be better than the past, and that the past can be forgot or overcome. By one recent estimate she cites, 83% of all books currently published in the United States hold out such hopes to readers. Such views are premised upon the idea that lives move forward, if not in a straight line, then at least in some discernable direction that suggests a purpose to what has gone before. However, there appears, according to Professor Mahu, to be near overwhelming evidence that life does not so move, and that such concepts as "improvement" and "growth" are, though needed, only illusions. In the past three years, she says that no less than 4,769 books were published whose titles promised to make one's life better, and that almost 60% of them claimed that past catastrophes (e.g., deaths of loved ones, childhood abuse, terminal illness, abandonment by a spouse) even improved the chances for future happiness. In another book by Professor Mahu, *No End to Pain* (I should say that both of these books appear to have been self-published), she argues that no one has any real chance at happiness, "nor were we intended to be happy." Instead, she says that the best we can do is make slight adjustments in our lives so as "to lessen the degree of our unhappiness, thus bringing a modicum of relief to our everyday experience. Pain is a natural state for human beings, and through some degree of effort, we might not only alleviate it but even find moments of peace." While "moments of peace" might sound like a real letdown after reading such best-sellers as Annette Levert's *I Found Love with the Handyman* (another title that just arrived for review), which promises to turn one's life around within a month, Professor Mahu would seem to confirm for most people, at least those who write to me, what in fact is their experience: fleeting moments of peace are about all that we can expect.

Dear Editor: I am in the midst of writing a novel that I plan to submit to Dalkeys for consideration. The problem I've run into is that the characters have developed lives of their own, and are now doing and saying things that are, in all reality, quite at odds with what I intend. For instance, there is a woman who has just said to her husband that she told her lover, one of their neighbors, that she would like to have his baby and then goes on to explain to her husband that she isn't saying that she wants the lover's baby or is planning on having his baby, but that she is amazed that she could feel so in love that she would have this feeling. Not only is all of this at odds with how I conceive of this woman, but it doesn't even follow the plot that I carefully outlined. It was supposed to be a happy love story about family values in a small Midwestern town! What I fear is that this behavior comes out of nowhere and stretches the plausibility of what a wife would tell her husband and what a husband would put up with. And yet every time I try rewriting this scene, the characters come right back to square number one and start in on this baby business again.

Editor: Just send it in to Dalkeys Archives, or whatever you choose to call it, when you're finished. It will join, next to where I sit, about 300 other submissions in an ever-growing mountain of what publishers

call "the slush pile." As to your immediate question, I am not sure
what to say. I will direct you to a manuscript that I have just read
by yet another professor from Illinois State Community College at Le
Roi [*sic*?], "Wives and Lovers: Family Values in An Age of Infidelity."
Professor Roberta Latirail, through interviews with 100 married
women who had had affairs, claims that 71% desired to have a child
with their lovers; 23% hoped to have sex on a webcam so that (to
quote) "the whole world would be fucking me at once"; 21% wanted
their lovers to build a deck onto their existing home; 14% wanted
them to install winding brick paths; 19% fantasized a night at a
swappers club and another 12% fantasized about "getting fucked"
(the professor's phrase) on their lover's outboard boat while being
observed by other boaters; and 1% (one woman) wanted her lover
to kill her husband and cut his body into "tiny pieces." First, I realize that the percentages here add up to something well beyond 100,
which is either an outright error on the part of the author, or suggests
that some women wanted more than one of these things. Further,
89% of the 71% desiring the lovers' babies also confided this desire
to their husbands. One, when queried about why she had told her
husband, whom she admitted was speechless after her revelation,
said that she did so because she wanted to share this "wonderful
feeling" with him, but that she was then disappointed that he didn't
respond at all, which she took to mean "that it was just dandy with
him." Astounding as well is the professor's discovery that few of these
desires or fantasies were ever realized except for what she calls "the
boat syndrome." All 12% had their day or days on the boat and all
felt "quite good, quite healthy, a feeling of release and freedom" even
though one woman reported other boaters (mostly families with
children on board) shouted at her such things as "whore," "slut,"
"pig." Which adds up to what the professor calls in her grand conclusion "sure-fire proof that marriage is strange." As to whether these
"statistics" will be of any help to you in relation to your characters,
I've no idea.

Dear Editor: I've been married now for thirteen years, and I always
thought of this as a happy marriage, and still do. But around nine
months ago I fell in love with a neighbor who was fixing various
things at our house. Though some people might say he's not well
educated (including my husband), that has nothing to do with how
intelligent he is or what he could have become, other than a handyman. I think he could have become anything, perhaps the president
of a corporation or even a senator. When I fell in love, I told my
husband because, well, I believe, as the old saying goes, honesty is
the best policy. He just sat there like a bump on a log. Move it ahead
a month or two, and I told the man that I desired to have his baby

and he was the first man I ever felt this way about. He said he'd like to do this for me, which is how he treats me and always puts my needs and desires first, unlike my husband. Then I told my husband about this, following my policy. Well, once again he doesn't say anything, just sits there like he didn't have a tongue. I think the story about my lover and me would make a great romantic movie. But the thing that really irritates me is my husband's reaction. Now the whole cat has kind of gotten out of the bag, and he's started asking a lot of questions, like whether I had ever talked to this man about a possible divorce, which I had but that's none of my husband's business. I don't know what to do, to tell you the truth. My husband is kind of successful and we have a nice house and all of those things. So, I don't want to upset the apple cart too much. It would be quite a change for me because even though my lover is very talented, he doesn't make much money being a handyman. And my husband, who's really filled with bitterness now, keeps pointing out to me that the man has had a lot of affairs in his marriage and I'm just another one and that he'll go on doing the same thing, something that I think is pretty unfair for him to say because he doesn't know the man the way I do. I should add here that the man's wife is a real bitch and drove him to do this. She even accused him of having affairs even when there wasn't any proof of it. Now my husband wants me to make a choice about our marriage, and I feel like I'm not ready to for reasons I explained up above about the house, and not knowing whether the man will marry me. I told my husband that the best thing would be for him to give me some time to figure this out and just allow me the freedom to see where things go. But he's the type that wants an answer to things. I don't know what to do, but I can tell you that I'm not very happy.

Editor: I really don't know what to tell you. These letters are beginning to depress me.

Dear Editor: My wife and I communicate through notes we post on each other's bedroom doors. She quotes from Shakespeare, and I give her Marlowe. Or she gives me Milton and I give her Donne. On the really bad nights, it's a simple "FUCK YOU!" You know, there is a great misconception out there represented in novels and movies, and that is that the well-educated, the sophisticated, the well-bred are any different from trailer-park people who have, as their profession, "handyman," which inevitably means that they know how to do a lot of things quite badly. If you look at one of those trailers, with the American flag waving at the door and a box of geraniums attached to a window, you think that the quality of these people's ethics is qualitatively lower than that of two professors who live in an upscale house on the edge of town and have their faux, motor driven waterfall pond sending sweet trickling sounds through the night air, with wind chimes playing softly in the background. My wife and I are two of those professors, and I can assure you that the quality of our moral and ethical life cannot possibly be beneath that of anyone who has ever stuck a little leprechaun in their 2 x 2 lawn outside their metal trailer, along with their welcome mat that says "God bless you all." Her "FUCK YOU!" to me and mine back to her is filled with as much malice and hatred as anything you will ever read in a Frederick Barthelme or Raymond Carver story about the depraved idiots they show watching "The Dating Game" on their shoddy TVs on Christmas morning. You all must be imbeciles out there to fall for this, or it makes you feel superior to this hopeless couple named Gus and Gertrude and their half-crazed son named, what else, Sonny.

My lovely wife, who can quote you verbatim anything ever written by Shakespeare, as well as anything ever composed by Coley Cibber, has her own porn site where, almost every night, she masturbates on her webcam to every demented male around the world who shoots his load as my dear moans something so Shakespearean as "Yes, yes, fuck me hard, Oh God! Yes, fuck me in the ass!" And, God help me, I stand on the side of her out of camera view (a really cheap camera that we got at a Sam's Club), whacking off. Yes, there we are. Night after night. And then later, leaving notes like, "You fucking whore, I could tell you liked it!" Or her, "You sick bastard, you made me do this!" Yes, just like the professors you see in Hollywood movies or in your putrid novels. And every night I fall asleep fantasizing about bashing her brains out, and now I lock my bedroom door because I know that she is thinking the same thing and will probably do it some night when the webcam isn't working and she doesn't know how else to vent all of that rotten swirl of disgusting desire.

Was it ever so between us? Who in the hell knows? After seventeen years of this hell on earth, I don't think either one of us can remember anything that wasn't at least paving the way to where we are now. If this were a movie, the camera would do a fade-out, and then a hazy vision of the past would appear, showing us in better times, or what look like better times, and then pulling out to reveal some sneer on one or both of our faces. Or if it's a really bad movie that's going to serve up a wholly improbable happy ending, we would be shown as blithering idiots in love, running through fields, staring deeply into each other's narcissistic, love-struck eyes. That would be our "past." Our past? Our past is what we relive almost every fucking moment of our lives, always beginning with, "Yeah, like the time I saw you with her at the You Come Back Inn" (I'm not making up this name, this is the bar we go to here in LeRoy).

The "her" was our babysitter, and I'd taken her there to meet her boyfriend. That was fifteen years ago. No, that was yesterday! There is no past in a marriage. The past is a sword to be pulled out of its sheath, completely disconnected from time. Just try saying, "But that was fifteen years ago and I wasn't doing what you say I was doing!" And she'll say, "I didn't say what you were doing!" And I'll say, "Then *think* what I was doing! Do I have it right this time? The enormous, relevant difference between *say* and *think*. As if that's the fucking point!!" And she'll say, "Always a point, there always have to be a point with you." Then depending upon whose turn it is, one or another throws something on the floor (though we've learned over the years not to throw anything breakable, because even an ashtray, back in the days when we allowed them in our home, costs a few bucks, and a lot of few bucks leads to a lot of big bucks) and icily leaves the room, which then gives us a starting point for the next night, so that one or another can say, "You wouldn't even talk to me last night, you just left the way you always do!" Jesus Christ, I wish I were dead. I am so tired of all this.

Editor: *You're* tired of all this?

Dear Editor: About two years I had to start using Viagra for the usual reasons. Well, I'll tell you, this did nothing to help. While I'm popping the pills, she's off buying all of these strange sex toys. I'll tell you, I couldn't even tell what in the hell someone was supposed to do with these things when I'd find them stuffed in some box in the closet. One of them was so big that all I could think is that if she put it up her it would come out of her mouth or the top of her head. And not all the Viagra in the world was going to make me compete with that big pink thing. Then she starts spending hours and hours on the Internet every night. When I'd ask her what she was doing she'd say "just looking for things." Then she starts going out at night, saying that she's meeting some old friend from high school or some bullshit story like that. One night she springs it on me. She tells me that she's been out "experimenting" and would like me to experiment with her. She starts showing me all these pictures of herself with other men and women, and I don't mean one at a time. So, here I am with this goddamn Viagra that isn't worth a shit to me and my wife telling me about these guys who go for hours with the biggest goddamn hard-ons in the world. I'm confused and feeling very inadequate.

Editor: I don't know what to tell you. Maybe God would. In the meantime, take at look at a new book called *Sexual Infideltiy in Marriage: The Last Refuge*, sent into "The Reviews of Contemporary

Literatures" for review. The author states that "A man and a woman first discover their 'love' through an overwhelming physical attraction that is expressed in the act of love. This attraction, as well as its expression, soon passes, sometimes within a few years, sometimes as if overnight. The bond of this great, overpowering love is replaced by the bond of property, possessions, and, most of all, children. Once the children have matured to the point where they leave home for greater things, the man and the woman stare in disbelief at each other, wondering—to use a common phrase—who is this person who stands before me?" Through "thorough investigations with half the people" in the greater "LeeRoy area [sic, etc.]," the author, Professor John "Buddy" Holly (Dean of Instructional Affairs at Illinois State Community College) has "determined that 87% of these people return to the origins of their relationship—their base sexual desire, which now no longer even has the pretense of 'love,' though for a time at least, they may feel that their newly discovered passion is reuniting them. A rather staggering 97% percent of this 87% percent embark on what they 'innocently' call 'sexual experimentation.' For a time they, once again, feel ever closer to one another as they share their sexual adventure stories, which frequently involve the swapping of each other with couples who are, for lack of a better phrase, 'in the same boat.' They realize after a time that, rather than bringing them to the endless moments of bliss that they encountered when they first met and fell 'in love,' they are in fact using these disturbing adventures as a means of escaping what a few of the interviewees called, in retrospect, 'a living hell.'" The remaining 13% in Professor Holly's study either killed themselves or became "hopeless drunks." Further, 57% of the "hopeless drunks" later committed suicide or were committed to the LeeRoy Institute for the Insane. I am sure that all of this will be of enormous help to you.

Dear Editor: First of all, my wife has had what she calls "a friend" for the past several months. One day she mentioned that she was sexually fed up with me and didn't want to perform her duties anymore, and she did call them "duties." Well, the way things work is that one thing led to another, and suddenly this friend is coming over to our house all the time and I see them giggling with each other and looking at each other the way people aren't really supposed to if they're married. I'm sure you know what I mean. And then one thing led to another, and this guy is suddenly sleeping over at our house on some nights, and even sleeping in my wife's bed, which she moved out of our bedroom into one of the kids' rooms. So, here I am with this man around most of the time, and the more he's around, the more fooling around goes on. I mean that he doesn't keep his hands off my wife, even in front of me. And she even smiles at me while he does this stuff to her, the way that women do in porn movies. I just put up with it because I know that in the sexual department, the plumbing just doesn't work too well. Then one night, out of the blue, she tells me that she told this guy a few nights before that she's in love with him. Wow! This really knocked my socks off. But I thought, Well, this ought to last until he finds her in one of her bad moods. The next week she tells me that he told her that he loved her too when they were out on his crappy little boat fucking their brains out! Well, my socks really got knocked off this time. Then, nothing. She just stops talking about him at all. Not another word. But I just thought about something. One of the things about this guy was that she had him fixing everything around the house. You wouldn't believe all the things that he could fix. If the toaster broke, he'd fix it. The TV not working? He'd fix it. The garage door wouldn't open? Fixed. Roof leaking? He'd put a new roof on! There wasn't anything this guy couldn't do. I don't know if all Italians are this way, but this guy certainly was. He's the Fix-It Man. But the thing is that when I got this bad news from my doctor, I began to think that these two were planning on me not being around too much longer. It occurred to me that it must have occurred to them that I might not make it. And what do you know? The next thing you know the guy rents the house next door about a month ago, and so now we're even neighbors with each other, which makes it very convenient for them because she spends most of her time at his house. She doesn't even make meals for me anymore, but just brings leftovers that taste like something awful. To be honest, they taste like living filth. I'm beginning to think that maybe they're putting something in the food or maybe it's my wife's lousy cooking, which was always lousy. My question is whether this whole thing is normal? Most people don't live like this, do they?

Editor: Apparently your marriage is quite normal (see letters above).

Dear Editor: About a year ago my wife and I under went a separation. To be blunt about it, one weekend when I was away, she packed up the kids and her things and took off, and then about a week later I got served the divorce papers. It's strange because we never talked about any of these things. She just up and left. I wasn't surprised and I certainly wasn't disappointed. One of us had to make the first move, and she's the one who did. Given the fact that we live in a small town, I think everyone knew about this before I did. I mean they probably saw the U-Haul truck outside, asked a few questions, and then they'd be off to the races about what was going on. What was even stranger is that she never even asked me where I was on all those weekends for the past few months when I was going to see the woman I was in love with and doing odd jobs around her house. Not a single word. Which is not how I think a marrage should be. I'm not saying that I was the perfect husband or that I didn't cheat a few times in our marriage the way that most men do. But she never asked about those times either, even though I knew she knew. Why are some women like this? Instead she just gave me the silent treatment, and wouldn't touch me. We had gone for months without any sex by the time she left, but never a word from her on this subject. I had always wanted there to be comunication in our marrage, and I wanted us to be honest with each other. But you can't have a conversation with a block of ice, and that's what she was like, just a big block of ice. Well, to make a long story short, the woman I was seeing left her husband, and then things really heated up between us. For a while it was great. We did a lot of things together, some of which I won't mention here because I don't think you'd understand. Then of course my roving eye started roving again, and one day BANG! Suddenly I'm going to see another woman on weekends that I met on one of those boared housewifes websites, and my wife, my second wife, starts making all these comments to me about what she gave up for me, and now I'm doing the same things, and that she can't even understand me sometimes because of my bad grammar and she is so much smarter than me. As far as I'm conserned, she must have known the way I was and didn't mind it, or at least didn't mind it as long as it was happening to someone else, like that husband of hers who got all broken up when she told him she was in love with me and not him. Some guys really take this news the wrong way. He was one of them. So, here we are. Now she's not talking much to me, and she certainly isn't touching me, except on my birthday she gave me a spin around the world. What do people do in these situations? Is she really being completely fair to me? Should I just dump her for this new woman? I am really in love with this new woman and feel that this is my one chance to make a life for myself and be happy.

Editor: I would like to remind readers that this was supposed to be a column concerning literature, not a lovelorn advice feature. Almost all of your questions concern the unhappy relationships you find yourselves stuck in, but I don't know the first thing about any of this. That is, I have my opinions, but that's all they are. You want expert advice in these matters and the only resource I have are all of these books or manuscripts that arrive here that people keep sending in about anything and everything, even though Dalkey Archive (or however you people choose to spell it) publishes only a certain kind of fiction ("not for everyone," the reviewers usually say). I could pull out a few dozen of these manuscripts and I'm sure that one of them at least would provide information, however useless, for you on this subject. I'd suggest you just read your own letter and figure it out for yourself. You're banging one woman while married to someone else, and then you complain that your wife doesn't understand you! Then you go on to the next woman, get married, and then start banging some other woman. Remarkably, the only thing not in your letter is any reference to these women being your neighbors, which seems to be a recurring pattern in most of the letters sent here. It's like an epidemic sweeping America: Look out for your neighbors, they're all trying to covet your wife or husband! I've no useful advice, and I'm sorry if I sound like I'm judging you (my first warning from the Publisher here was "don't judge the letter-writers"). Off the top of my head, I'll suggest that you take the new gal for a ride on your boat (I assume you have one) and bang the hell out of her in front of the biggest crowd you can find. Or go international and bang the hell out of her on some webcam site. Just keep banging away and to hell with everything else. When I come across statistics in these manuscripts such as 94% of married couples regularly fantasize that their husband or wife will be killed in a fiery car accident and that 99% are either having affairs or wish they could, I think that perhaps we are looking at a whole new day in the history of American marriages. In fact, one of the manuscripts I just finished reading is called "The Big Bang!" and it's not about the origins of the universe but rather the trajectory of marriages based upon this author's two-year series of interviews with married couples in an unnamed Central Illinois town (probably LeRoy, LeRoi, LeeRoy, Le Roy, etc.). He concludes his study (which seems to me not much more than a piece of pornography as he gets into all kinds of heated details about what people do in their illicit sexual practices) by saying, "In lieu of love and fidelity and commitment, which seem to have gone out with the horse and buddy [sic], stop torturing yourselves and go for it! The Biggest Bang ever!!!" Some advice. But better than any I can give you.

Dear Editor: You once said that the heart wants what the heart wants.

Editor: I don't believe I ever said this, it doesn't sound like the kind of thing I'd say. I did say, however, that there was once a time of peace, and I had thought this couldn't last because lovers choose betrayal. You said this wasn't true. I then told you a story about a woman standing in a kitchen who sees her husband coming up the back steps with his arms full of groceries, or children. He sees her crying and knows that she is thinking of her lover. She hates her husband for not being someone else, namely, her lover. And yet she feels guilty that he wouldn't survive if she leaves. They have lived like this for many years. The man in the story says, "But the heart will destroy you," or had wanted to say this. The woman had planned to tell him that she must leave. This, too, has been repeated for many years. One day the man dies, or the lover, or the wife. I forget. This was long ago and I lost interest in all the tragedy that people put themselves through. I said that this is what people do with their lives, they destroy those they say they love, laughing amid the ruins they've created. You complained that I made my stories too complicated. I said, or thought to say, Yes, I know, you would like things simpler, but the truth is in the complications, even if all we can do is look at them, amazed at their patterns. You said, We're different. And I said, But does that have to be so bad, or might we not just say that, yes, we are different, and go on looking, even if all we can do sometimes is stare at the darkness together and be happy that we need not look at it alone? Then, smiling, you left, carrying a banner high, snapping in the chilly wind of an autumn air. I had thought that this looked quite beautiful.

Book Reviews

Witold Gombrowicz. *Cosmos*. Trans. Danuta Borchardt. Yale Univ. Press, 2005. 208 pp. $25.00.

Gombrowicz's last novel in its first English translation directly from the Polish, *Cosmos* takes us on a rather unsettling school holiday with "Witold," a university student of the early 1960s. Following an apparent row in Warsaw with his father, Witold escapes to the country to study for exams, where he unexpectedly meets Fuks, an acquaintance, in Zakopane, a Carpathian resort town. The ill-matched companions decide on the spur of the moment to room together, settling on the Wojtys' modest guesthouse. Beset by a curious lethargy, the young men, while walking in a nearby wood, stumble upon a dead sparrow dangling by a thread. This and further such discoveries impel them to become detectives, working on the sly to piece together incidents pointing to some unaccountable wrong. Each new find suggests a perverse plot of no clear purpose, in which the entire Wojtys family—retired, self-indulgent Leon, an arch paterfamilias; his wife, household martinet "Roly-Poly"; newlywed daughter Lena, whom Witold lusts after, and her bland husband Ludvik; even maidservant Katasia of the deformed lip—become suspect. Still, the results of amateur sleuthing prove mere grist for rumination as Witold puzzles over the fecklessness of language and absurd correspondences, winding significance around quotidian events, imprisoning himself with trivial details. Scorning Fuks's perpetual uneasiness over his boss's disfavor as he probes the Wojtys family's tics and quirks for clues, Witold records the minutiae of his moment-by-moment existence with the scrupulousness of a forensic pathologist. At length, nearly overwhelmed by a panoply of conflicting impressions, he matches wits with father Leon, whose mocking, onanistic wordplay also suggests a darker purpose than he lets on. Stumped by so much misleading evidence, Witold's unwitting exploration of human disingenuousness displays Gombrowicz's art at its most elusive, dissecting life beyond and without reason. [Michael Pinker]

Lydie Salvayre. *La Méthode Mila*. Seuil, 2005. 222 pp. €18.00.

The narrator of Lydie Salvayre's latest novel is a forty-year-old bachelor by the name of Fausto Arjona. He is a solitary, misanthropic man who has withdrawn from the company of his fellows and who spends his days pleasurably enough reading philosophy and watching pornographic films. That idyll comes to an end, however, when his widowed mother comes to live with him. Caring for her, he sees death written all over her aging body, which inspires horror in him. Gradually, he comes to loathe his mother, discovering in that loathing a monstrous side of himself that he never suspected. Quite certain that he is going mad, and seeking some way to make reason prevail, he seeks consolation in Descartes's *Discourse on Method*. Yet he finds none. Descartes has no grasp of the real, Arjona feels, his "pure abstraction and elevated theses" provide no succor to people enmeshed in the problems of daily life. Arjona craves another method entirely, and he will find one in the ministrations of Madame Mila, a seer who enthralls him with visions of his putative ancestry in twelfth-century Andalusia, feeding him a delicious genealogical mulligatawny spiced with Muslims, Christians, and Jews. She provides him thus with a history—and, more importantly perhaps, with a story tailored precisely to fit his needs.

Cast as an unrelenting indictment of Cartesian philosophy, in an apostrophe directed to Descartes himself, Salvayre's novel displays many features that her readers will find familiar. Finely honed irony, scathing invective, and dark humor color these pages, leavened by a deeply humanist understanding of the difficulty of shared lives and the ways in which people make others bear the burden of their own fears, both on the personal and the political level. Arjona plays out that dynamic with his mother, of course; but so too do his fellow-citizens in Moissy demonize Gypsies—until Madame Mila casts her spell upon them as well. Her own discourse on method is offered here as an alternative therapeutic, one that relies on the curative power of fable. In that sense, *La Méthode Mila* puts onstage a wry struggle between philosophy and fiction, and the way that Lydie Salvayre chooses to resolve that agonistic says a great deal about her faith in the novel as a vital cultural form. [Warren Motte]

William H. Gass. *A Temple of Texts: Essays.* Knopf, 2006. 412 pp. $26.95.

Aside from being a great novelist, Gass is arguably the smartest and most stylistically perceptive American essayist alive today. This latest collection includes previously published essays, reviews, introductions, prefaces, forewords, and afterwords. One review even explains why the differences between these forms matter. Complementing these occasional pieces are essays that explore several big topics: the importance of classic texts, psychological and literary influence, the music of prose, the rhetoric and violence of the spectacle, and the factual and philosophical dimensions of evil. Also included are essays on Renaissance classics, and many more on twentieth-century writers like Gertrude Stein, Ernesto Sábato, William Gaddis, Elias Canetti, and of course Rainer Maria Rilke. Brief laments on the state of the world also crop up occasionally. At one point, Gass explains Rabelais's continuing relevance by suggesting that "he welcomes us to his feast on what might be Inflation Sunday during Hypocrites' Holiday in the year of the Warmonger, 2004, or maybe 1532." In a particularly eloquent piece, Gass defends the material importance of printed books during the age of the Internet. He illustrates this defense with a conceit that sums up one of his running themes: "Books are like bicycles: You travel under your own power and proceed at your own pace, your riding is silent and will not pollute, no one is endangered by your journey—not frightened, maimed, or killed—and the exercise is good for you." These essays prove that even the moribund discourse of critical appreciation can still achieve greatness in the hands of a master practitioner. Of Rilke's *Duino Elegies*, for example, Gass writes, "They gave me my innermost thoughts, and then they gave those thoughts an expression I could never have imagined possible for them." Likewise, when you read Gass's accounts of his literary and philosophical influences, you'll want to be influenced by them too. [Thomas Hove]

John Banville. *The Sea*. Knopf, 2005. 208 pp. $23.00.

Max Morden made a vocation out of a remonstration. At seven, preparing for his First Communion, Max was admonished by a zealous priest to eschew the mortal sin of *looking*. Nevertheless, he became an art historian. More than fifty years later, he returns to the seaside site where his penchant for observing people unobserved produced consequences he could not foresee. A year after the death of his wife, Anna, Max takes up residence in the Cedars, the boarding house in seaside Ballyless where he first—and last—encountered the Graces, an affluent family who seemed, in the eyes of an awestruck boy, the very embodiment of their name. His eyes were drawn to Constance Grace's seasoned flesh, while he consorted with her peculiar twins, Chloe and Myles. Max's sinuous narrative keeps circling back to the dramatic summer in which he was initiated into the mysteries of eros and extinction. At present, when he is more likely to tipple than type another page of his monograph on painter Pierre Bonnard, he describes himself as "a person of scant talent and scanter ambition, greyed o'er by the years, uncertain and astray and in need of consolation and the brief respite of drink-induced oblivion." Max's ungainly daughter Claire, who disappointed him by abandoning her studies in art, accuses him of living in the past, and, at least to himself, he admits: "The past beats inside me like a second heart." It is a powerful beat. Claire cannot understand what drives Max to take up residence in an antiquated house whose only permanent inhabitants are a stiff old gent called Colonel Blunden and the lodging's prim manager, Miss Vavasour. Nor does she fathom what draws her widowed father, who does not swim, back to the sea. Until the end of John Banville's novel, neither does the reader.

Max, who dreams he owns a typewriter without the letter "i," longs to vanish in an act of penitential self-effacement. Like Dostoyevsky's Underground Man, he explains: "I am like a man with an agonising toothache who despite the pain takes a vindictive pleasure in prodding the point of his tongue again and again deep into the throbbing cavity." And his last name, Morden, suggests the mordancy of a troubled man who enjoys gnawing on what annoys him (Banville delights in Dickensian onomastics; when he reveals that the physician who diagnoses Anna with terminal cancer is named Todd, we are told: "This can only be considered a joke in bad taste on the part of polyglot fate"). Anna, whose name commemorates the transitory years, photographs unwilling patients in the hospital ward where she is dying. As scopophilic as her husband Max, she says the images she collects are her indictment of everything. An exercise in repetition compulsion, *The Sea* demands a reader willing to chew over its sumptuous but elliptical sentences, in quest of all there is to learn of Max. [Steven G. Kellman]

Kenneth Koch. *The Collected Fiction of Kenneth Koch*. Coffee House Press, 2005. 408 pp. Paper: $18.00.

The bulk of this volume consists of what are typically categorized as a novel, *The Red Robins*, and a collection of eighty-five very short stories, *Hotel Lambosa*, to which are added a handful of additional works both early and late. Separating these texts out as "fiction" is largely a publishing convenience made marginally plausible by their compositional layout in paragraphs, but actually these prose pieces are more usefully read as extensions of Koch's poetry or as writing that freely straddles the distinction. *The Red Robins* (1975), written over a period of fifteen years, nominally concerns the globetrotting adventures of a group of aviator friends, although the real action is in the complex textual surface. Unpredictability and simultaneity characterize writing that intends to create a sense of immediacy and spontaneity, of "fresh air" to evoke one of Koch's best-known poems. Drawing on all the tricks of fiction and poetry, the writing compulsively reframes and transforms itself. Yet for all Koch's well-known playfulness and hilarity, which is in ample evidence here, this work is haunted by those powers of violence and co-optation that his humor and invention are posed to resist. These darker elements assert themselves more pervasively in the later ministories of *Hotel Lambosa* (1993), almost all just a paragraph to a couple of pages in length. While generally more subdued in tone, the collection again demonstrates Koch's impatience with generic or stylistic consistency. Although given their small scale these stories are individually digestible, as a whole the collection exhibits a deliberately eclectic range, from fairly realistic vignettes to fantasy, with abrupt stylistic shifts possible at any moment. This volume appears simultaneously with Koch's *Collected Poems* (which at 800 pages still excludes his longer poems, to be collected separately) and allows us to appreciate the considerable achievement of his creative prose, as well as its place in the larger body of his amazingly diverse and still underappreciated work. [Jeffrey Twitchell-Waas]

Rick Moody. *The Diviners*. Little, Brown, 2005. 567 pp. $25.95.

The Diviners, Rick Moody's big, brilliant new novel, is about a hot miniseries project, a thirteen-part epic stretching from ancient Mongolia to the founding of Las Vegas, held together by divining, the semisupernatural ability to find water in even the driest places. Everyone wants a piece of the miniseries, but there's one problem—it doesn't exist. It's the desperate improvisation of a production company assistant who's lost a film treatment. Moody offers us dozens of quirky and memorable characters whose stories intersect and intertwine: an alcoholic old woman who can hear cell phone conversations in her head and whose daughter, the production company boss, is addicted to Krispy Kreme doughnuts and has an assistant, the one who thinks up the miniseries but who really wants to sell her script about the Marquis de Sade's wife and who has a failed-artist and Manhattan bike-messenger brother who's accused of smashing the skull of an art gallery curator with a brick, and so on, nearly infinitely. This web of narratives is sandwiched between two larger narratives. The first is the plot of the miniseries, divining, which transcends its Hollywood-schlockiness to represent the possibility of peace in the face of war, of resisting the official realities created for us by the mass media, of quenching the thirst that almost all the characters feel for something more than what their vapid consumer culture can give them. The second is the 2000 presidential election: the action of the novel begins on the day after that disputed election and ends the night before the Supreme Court rules in favor of Bush. This suggests an interregnum, a temporary uncertainty that offers the chance to remake reality, a chance the characters miss in their pursuit of the chimerical miniseries.

Moody demonstrates a keen ear for the voices of contemporary America, a sharp eye for the absurdities of our culture, and a rich, versatile, and virtuoso style. He is young and has, I hope, many more books to give us, but for the time being, *The Diviners* is his masterpiece. [Robert L. McLaughlin]

Robert Coover. *A Child Again.* McSweeney's, 2005. 276 pp. $22.00.

Readers of experimentalist Robert Coover will find themselves in familiar territory with his newest story collection, *A Child Again.* Here the author of *Pricksongs & Descants* returns, once again, to satiric and parodic retellings of myths, fables, and children's stories. Coover is well-paired to publisher this go-round. McSweeney's, known for their innovative and intelligent book design, has given us a product in which form is matched perfectly to content: *A Child Again* is made to look like a children's book from the 1950s, muted in color and professionally distressed at its edges. A pocket on the back cover contains an "extra" (or external, depending how one views it) story entitled "Heart Suit," vignettes printed on fifteen oversized cards that may, per instructions, "be shuffled and read in any order." Inside the book proper we encounter reworkings of Aesop, Punch, and Lewis Carroll, some played for a kind of vaudevillian humor, others, such as "The Return of the Dark Children" (a recasting—quite literally—of the Pied Piper story) evoking a nightmare space where the polarities of the folktale are reversed, each blessing a curse, and vice-versa. This proves to be the modus operandi of Coover's latest: the name of *A Child Again*'s game (a book replete with puzzles and brainteasers) is inversion. By overturning conventions of the familiar, Coover allows his readers to view the most recognizable tales with a quality many sophisticates of the literary world have lost: wonder. [Aaron Gwyn]

Julian Barnes. *Arthur & George*. Knopf, 2006. 390 pp. $24.95.

Julian Barnes has long enjoyed creating fictionalized versions of historical personages and events, as early work like *Flaubert's Parrot* or the "Shipwreck" chapter of *A History of the World in 10 1/2 Chapters* attests. In *Arthur & George* he surpasses those efforts with what is likely his finest work thus far. The title's names refer to Arthur Conan Doyle and George Edalji, men from different occupational and social worlds whose paths crossed in the early years of the twentieth century. In a sensational miscarriage of justice, Edalji, a solicitor working in Birmingham, was imprisoned in 1903 for a series of livestock mutilations. After his release from prison Doyle became his champion. This is historically verifiable, but what Barnes so brilliantly adds to this account is the vital and intriguing portraits of its title characters. The text is divided into numerous short third-person sections, each named after its central consciousness. In alternating accounts we come to know Doyle and Edalji from childhood and only leave them years after the period of their acquaintance. Despite its ostensible "true crime" focus, *Arthur & George* becomes very much a meditation on narrative. Larger sections of the novel ("Beginning with an Ending," "Ending with a Beginning") allude to Doyle's composition of the Sherlock Holmes stories, and as the narrative continues we are treated to the abilities of a master of characterization, voice, perspective, pacing, and style. Barnes evokes an entire world, and it is this sense of cultural possibilities and constraints, the freedoms they might make possible and the havoc they can wreak, that makes reading *Arthur & George* such a rewarding experience. Though it did not win, Barnes's book was shortlisted for the 2005 Booker Prize for good reason. This novel is among the very best to arrive from England in recent years. [Stephen Bernstein]

———————

Paul Auster. *The Brooklyn Follies*. Holt, 2006. 306 pp. $24.00.

Like Paul Auster's other recent novels, *The Book of Illusions* and *Oracle Night*, *The Brooklyn Follies* is a postmodern page-turner, drawing us immediately into its narrator's broken world. Nathan Glass, retired, recently divorced, estranged from his family, and recovering from lung cancer, has moved to Brooklyn, looking, as he puts it, "for a quiet place to die." To fill the time, he begins a modest project, *The Book of Human Folly*, for which he draws on his own experiences, experiences of people he knows, and incidents from history to record meaningful slips of the tongue, improbable accidents, serendipitous encounters, and ironic happenstance. This project is the metaphorical model for what follows, a string of incidents governed by chance, incidents that nevertheless have significant consequences for Nathan and those around him. The novel's shaggy-dog-story quality, its lack of motivated narrative cohesiveness—as Nathan meets a long-out-of-touch nephew who lives near him and works in a bookstore for a man who is involved in a scheme to sell the forged manuscript of *The Scarlet Letter*; as the nephew suddenly becomes the guardian for his missing sister's daughter; as a random exit off the interstate leads to a utopian Vermont inn—seems to be the point. Near the end of the novel, Nathan imagines founding a company that would write biographies of deceased people who would otherwise be forgotten, "to rescue the stories and facts and documents before they disappeared—and shape them into a continuous narrative, the narrative of a life." His brainstorm arises from the events related in the novel: ordered, coherent, meaning-providing narratives are possible only in retrospect; immersed in the process of living, we have only randomness, contingency, chance—stories of human follies. Like its narrator, *The Brooklyn Follies* delights in and grieves for everything involved in being human. [Robert L. McLaughlin]

David Albahari. *Götz and Meyer*. Trans. Ellen Elias-Bursać. Harcourt, 2005. 168 pp. $23.00.

Götz and Meyer is, as the press release states, "the extraordinary story of the mass murder of Serbia's Jews in 1942 as told by a teacher whose relatives were among the victims." But the storyline is only one of several rather compelling things about the novel. The novel begins with the lines "Götz and Meyer. Having never seen them, I can only imagine them." As we soon discover, Götz and Meyer are two noncommissioned SS officers whose main job was to transport prisoners from one place to another in a truck, the Belgrade Saurer, ingeniously designed to gas the "passengers" during transport. The narrator, a fictional archeologist of memory, comments on the rather pedestrian lives of Götz and Meyer as they go about their daily task of *transporting* live bodies from the Belgrade fairgrounds to their ultimate destination: a mass grave somewhere across the Sava River. But what makes the novel compelling isn't just the storyline, which is told in a well-controlled lyricism (with kudos to Ellen Elias-Bursać), but the fabric of the fiction reads in a manner not unlike a mixture of Thomas Bernhard and W. G. Sebald. Like Bernhard's structures, Albahari's structure is seamless. No paragraphs. Sentences that move freely from third person to first and back again with the constant repetition that the narrator can only "imagine" Götz and Meyer or Meyer or Götz. As the narrator states, he knows "the real purpose of the Saurer, and the real meaning of the words *transport* and *load*, and the story about the fabled camp in Romania, or Poland. Although when Götz and Meyer are at issue, I must admit I do not know who is who, which makes me, in a sense, more ignorant than those who knew nothing of their names." The brevity of *Götz and Meyer* should not belie the lyrical and dynamic prose of the piece or the impact of its content. [Mark Axelrod]

Magdalena Tulli. *Moving Parts*. Trans. Bill Johnston. Archipelago Books, 2005. 133 pp. $22.00.

The second of Tulli's works published by Archipelago, *Moving Parts* is an invigorating puzzle of grammar and narrative that takes the reader on a fantastic journey through the last hundred years of European history without ever leaving the confines of a hotel. This curious building contains an impossible number of floors, trapdoors, and tunnels that seem to *be* the architecture of the story itself as well as the whole world. We follow here a nameless narrator who "would prefer not to tell about anything at all," and who is not the book's narrator but has been paid to narrate a certain plot, a banal tale involving a love triangle and an argument in a garden. This narrator gets bored, sidetracked, and ultimately lost as he struggles to maintain his hold on a story in which characters mutate or complain about their story line, other narrators of other stories get in the way, and a trapdoor in the hotel's basement leads to the house in which the story he is supposed to tell is unfolding—which leads to a subterranean train, which leads to a bar, which leads to a tunnel, which leads to an apartment building during World War II, which leads to an elevator, which leads to something pretty close to hell on earth. Because he is not a reader or character, our narrator can move behind the scenes of the hotel—which stand in for the constructed realities of narrative and history—with a set of keys that open doors to other places and times; but he is finally as powerless as anyone to understand or affect the nightmare of the world he confronts. In its surprising movements through history, space, and language, *Moving Parts* is an incisive social commentary that suggests how crucial it is we pay attention to dominant structures of narrative in literature and life. [Danielle Dutton]

Nenad Veličković. *Lodgers*. Trans. Celia Hawkesworth. Northwestern Univ. Press, 2005. 200 pp. $16.95.

This seemingly artless tale, the first of Veličkovič's works translated into English, displays the fortitude of the people of Sarajevo while living under the guns of Serbian artillery. As told in the wry witness an endearingly self-conscious narrator stunned by a friend's death from a shrapnel wound, teenaged Maja decides to write a novel-chronicle-diary to express herself amid the daily grind of privation and peril. We watch her inventing a language to convey the antics of her family and their unlikely retainers, two old World War II Partizans, in obtaining food and water, bartering for goods, and coping without utilities and other creature comforts while awaiting the birth of a child to her stepbrother and his wife. Their home in ruins, the family lives in a city museum directed by Maja's father, who is determined to save as many relics in his charge as possible despite looting and threatened destruction. Between trips to the basement during episodes of shelling and adjustment to codes of conduct that change by the hour, clever Maja finds more comic relief than pathos in wartime accommodations, for what must be done gets done, by hook or crook. Her richly colloquial, fugitive impressions display ingenuity under fire as a form of comic entertainment, a disarmingly effective narrative technique. If her paranoid stepbrother resists military service to remove his pregnant wife from the city, Maja's mother remains serene through yoga and macrobiotics; despite her father's struggles to retain his exhibits, the Partizans trade them for articles of daily survival—and Maja does not miss a trick. The hardships of a contemporary tragedy fail to daunt her irrepressible innocence, for, in deploying his curious cast of "lodgers," Veličkovič reveals an artistry that defeats the forces of brutality with wit, indirection, and boundless good humor. [Michael Pinker]

———————————

Gabriel García Márquez. *Memories of My Melancholy Whores*. Trans. Edith Grossman. Knopf, 2005. 101 pp. $20.00.

García Marquez fans will be delighted to see that, after years of nonfiction, he has a new novella out. It contains his trademark sensibility, quirks and extravagant touches. Built into the memoir of a minor columnist who has contemplated writing a book called *Memories of My Melancholy Whores* are disquisitions on mortality—familiar from *Love in the Time of Cholera*—and the shape of a life that has not achieved anything significant. The unnamed narrator says he once thought to write about "the miseries of my misguided life," though such miseries are apparently confined to romance, for he has a modestly paying occupation, a fine house inherited from his parents, and rude good health at the age of ninety. It is on that birthday that the narrative starts. The whores are women who have possessed, fascinated, or confounded him, and it is a sign of the narrator's unreflective nature, sometimes his denseness, that they have little individuality and that he is the melancholic, not them. Aphoristic on occasion—"love is not a condition of the spirit but a sign of the zodiac"—and almost humorless about himself, the narrator is a craftsman when it comes to words, but much less capable in real life. His memoir contains a love story about a particular woman, and as usual with García Marquez, there are mystical events—mysterious writing, visions of the dead, natural phenomena that reek of sulfur—yet those things are not strong enough, in themselves, to rouse the narrator to investigate their root causes. He is self-absorbed about their meaning and insufficiently curious about their occurrence. This habit of thought extends to the women he meets, whom he fills with content often without understanding them. *Memories of My Melancholy Whores* is minor García Marquez, but it is a fine case study of self-regard. [Jeff Bursey]

———————————

Joshua Cohen. *The Quorum*. Twisted Spoon Press, 2005. 193 pp. Paper: $14.00.

Jonathan R. is crossing a tightrope of his own intestines. He has just noted how pleased he is to think that "contrary to Euclid and Spinoza . . . somewhere our parallel intestines, impossibly, meet and run into one." And then he says, "But we have decided to discard the perpetual." This happens in the first sixth of a story called "Six Dreams" from *The Quorum*, Joshua Cohen's remarkable collection of short fiction. Here, in this scene and in these sentiments, we can see, on a very small scale, the fingerprints of a fiction that leaves few other clues as to what, exactly, it is up to. The surreality is always qualified by the possibility—even likelihood—that the speaker (and there is *always* a first-person narrator speaking, or writing, to someone) is unreliable. In the above case, Jonathan R. is dreaming. In "Letter about Hair," the narrator is writing home to his family about the hair-based economy of the country he has moved to, imploring them to come: "Build a hair bridge over to this side and avoid the price of passage. . . ." In "Hessh's Beds," the narrator speaks to her psychiatrist about the death of a lover, a bed salesman who seduced women on the mattresses he sold them and who was the last surviving speaker of a strange language. The reader can never be sure if it's the narrator or the narrator's world that is so strange. This uncertainty creates momentum, prevents the reader from floundering in this dreamscape. That said, it is not the stories themselves that are so compelling, but the writing. Cohen writes with a purpose and clarity that belies his youth, but with all the ferocious energy of inexperience. "And as for your Jews: you wanted them to live inside and out of the world simultaneously," he writes, "like worms on the fruit, surfacing and then again burrowing into the core. . . ." In this collection, Cohen employs the destabilizing irony and complexity of the best innovative writing to reach toward—as Jonathan R. says on his gut-made tightrope—the "perpetual": the idea that some consistent, underlying truth does, or should, exist. This is Cohen's first book. Its ambition and achievement portend that the next ones will only be better. [Theodore Louis McDermott]

———————

Michael Martone. *Michael Martone*. FC2, 2005. 190 pp. Paper: $15.95.

The playful, inventive, and daring Martone gives us a short story collection, but his "stories" are quite odd—they are told as "Contributor's Notes"; they juxtapose "real" facts (Martone was born in Fort Wayne; he taught at Syracuse and currently teaches at the University of Alabama) with fictional characters and plots. To complicate matters, Martone even writes a blurb about his own book: "Michael Martone's *Michael Martone* squares *the facts about his life* with the *stories about his life*. I found I couldn't put the book down, and I never wanted it to *end*" (my italics throughout). The blurb is chilling because it suggests that Martone doesn't want his written life to end—but nor does he want his *non*-writing life to end. The collection has no center, no progression, no *plot*, which, as DeLillo has suggested, demands a death. Perhaps the most intriguing "notes" (which are *fictions*) are those in which *doubling* hit us forcefully. Here, for example, Martone speculates on returning to the scene(s) of his childhood: "If he could find such a hint, he suspects, he would drive out to that very location, a place not that far away, and gather in the *fresh intelligence* of the *spot* he inhabited for a *few minutes* during a *part* of *one spring* years ago." Consider the words "spot," "part," "few"; they are skillfully combined with "years ago" and "fresh intelligence" so that we realize that although we remember special moments, we cannot completely "go home again." Nor can we ever truly remember in any rational way. Memory is an unreal *construction*, a design we cannot *master*. And in the wonderful last line of one note, Martone writes that he "remembers the lights of that evening on the campus and the lights of the other times he has been in front of the camera and how the lights that made it possible for him to be seen also made it impossible to see." The camera light, the "spotlight," confuses the seen and unseen. Perhaps we can never see ourselves as others see us. We are, in truth, ghostly, spectral, shadowy; this pronouncement and this collection claim that we can never grasp the total picture of our lives, our identities. [Irving Malin]

Karel Čapek. *The Absolute at Large*. Intro. Stephen Baxter. Bison Books, 2005. 242 pp. Paper: $16.95.

The industrialist G. H. Bondy faces economic catastrophe in the opening pages of Karel Čapek's satirical novel *The Absolute at Large*. With the coal supply dwindling, the bottom line of his Metallo-Electric Company is threatened by the cost of alternative sources. Desperate for a solution, he stumbles on the Karburator, a machine that can coax seemingly endless energy from small amounts of fuel. But the machine has an unsettling by-product: a vaporous substance known as the Absolute. As explained by its inventor, "What is left behind is pure God. A chemical nullity which acts with monstrous energy." This energy brings religious fervor out of everyone exposed to it. The world embraces the presence of the divine, only to split into violent factions over whose vision of the divine is superior. Late in the novel, Bondy muses, "That's just where the trouble lies. You see, everyone measures off a certain amount of Him and then thinks it is the entire God. Each one appropriates a little fringe or fragment of Him and then thinks he possesses the whole of Him." Čapek's skewering of human greed and faith is all the more impressive given that the novel was originally published in 1922. Čapek, known for his play *RUR: Rossum's Universal Robots*—which introduced audiences to a staple of science fiction—has no illusions about the robot's flesh-and-blood counterparts. As the Absolute takes over more of the world's industries, the world is deluged with fertilizer, shoes, flour, and other products. "Thus there ruled in the world a state of boundless plenty of all that men could need," observes the narrator. "But men need everything, everything but boundless plenty." [Pedro Ponce]

Richard Kalich. *Charlie P.* Green Integer, 2005. 240 pp. Paper: $12.95.

One critic recently condemned a novel for being "familiar," as if somehow novels could be *unfamiliar*. No paragraphs. No language. Heck—no paper or ink or binding. Duchamp's urinal—now *that*'s a novel. However, life *is* familiar. If only allowed to produce work that was not "familiar," we would have no literature at all. I would rather that the "familiar" be embraced and the novel resonate beyond itself and intone the spheres of Plato or Beckett. *Charlie P* is familiar. The antihero of the title is actually a nonhero, for he does absolutely nothing and is an Everyman who, like all of us, is afraid to take risks. Charlie P, by taking none, lives no life at all. He achieves nothing. He thinks himself a great lover, yet never makes love. He fancies himself a great host, yet never invites guests. He imagines himself to be a great novelist, yet he relies heavily on pat phrases (one favorite, "needless to say," precedes the superfluous) and dozens of clichés (e.g. "a deer caught in the headlights" and "apple of his eye"). Even more egregious are incorrectly turned phrases ("suffice to say" rather than "suffice it to say") and misused words ("his pecuniary nature" when he means "penurious"). Although "Charlie P has a novel in him," he also claims "the novel is dead," which explains why he is merely "a dabbler in writing fiction." Charlie P is the Everyman who thinks he can write a novel but can't—a modern day Gordon Comstock, Orwell's famous antihero from *Keep the Aspidistra Flying*, a poet who never finds the time to write. Despite the dabblings of Charlie P, Richard Kalich succeeds in making the story of Everyloser interesting. The work resonates with allusions to other works about losers, including D. H. Lawrence's "Rocking-Horse Winner," Gogol's "The Nose," and Heinrich Mann's "Blue Angel." Under the care of physicians, Charlie dies a hundred deaths—burning, drowning, dismemberment, disease. The doctors he fervently believes in are as incompetent at medicine as he is at fiction: they attribute a case of lockjaw to ptomaine poisoning, for example. They are Everylosers, too. And when Charlie P smiles at the end, buried in his coffin face down, we smile with him because we're fellow losers. [Eckhard Gerdes]

Richard Burgin. *The Identity Club.* Ontario Review Press, 2005. 330 pp. Paper: $24.95.

"Less is more, more or less," says a young writer across the creative-writing desk. No one knows how to respond to this slogan, whose meaninglessness makes it impossible to argue against. Less can be more, but it can also be less; and so it's easy to be cynical about the possibilities of the seemingly straightforward short-story form. But this is a naive bias. Richard Burgin, in *The Identity Club*, a collection of new and previously published stories, shows that writing termed "minimalism" and misnomered "realism" can do much more than its adherents normally attempt. These stories—four of which won the Pushcart Prize and one of which was collected in *Best American Mystery Stories 2005*—manage to expand the possibilities of the short story through prose that, to paraphrase Hemingway, is clear enough to let us see the iceberg of implications and meanings submerged beneath. In the title story, Burgin describes, in exact prose, a club whose members each assume the identity of a famous person. The staff of a New York advertising agency become, variously, Edgar Allan Poe, Thomas Bernhard, Bill Evans, Erik Satie, and a host of other artists and intellectuals. And the protagonist, a tyro in the midst of experts, is considering becoming Nathanael West. As the story progresses, the implications of absolute imitation become, through suggestion and gesture, clear: you are required to reenact not only your chosen person's life, but also their death. With admirable patience, incisive turns, and echoes of the very artists his characters are portraying, Burgin reveals to us the strange potentialities of the seemingly normal. In nearly all of these twenty stories, Burgin shows that "minimalism" need not be slight. For, as John Barth writes in his essay "A Few Words about Minimalism," "There truly are more ways than one to heaven. As between minimalism and its opposite, I pity the reader—or the writer, or the age—too addicted to either to savor the other." [Theodore Louis McDermott]

Elizabeth Block. *A Gesture Through Time*. Spuyten Duyvil, 2005. 280 pp. Paper: $14.00.

"It is impossible to do without love altogether," Marguerite Duras writes in an epigraph Elizabeth Block cites at the beginning of *A Gesture Through Time*, and the novel (if that's what it is) tells of the love of Elizabeth, a teenage heir to a steel factory in Detroit (Block is from Detroit), for Magnitude Hortense Zappa, a worker in the plant who seduces her but leaves abruptly after Elizabeth's father is killed by one of his workers. Twenty years later the lovers meet once again at a San Francisco Film Festival, where Magnitude is now Sarah Ona Broome (Block is a filmmaker).

"Are you the moment upon which the turn of events depends? Are you the point of no return?" Elizabeth asks Magnitude in a letter. "If so, how do I tell my story?" How does one tell the story of love? The love celebrated in popular song, love letters, and anguished sobs into pillows? There is no way to tell it that tells it, except to tell it as one can, in as many ways as one can tell it. "Harmony always fragments the truth of any experience," Elizabeth adds. *A Gesture Through Time* is told through different points of view, interviews, screenplays, notes on film history, projection, and editing, flipbooks, dramatic dialogues (between Pleasure, Humiliation, and Narrator; between Danton and Executioner), notes, more notes, and memories. Memory takes you to one place, geography to another. Elizabeth learns about labor. It becomes her capital—twenty years' absence, twenty years' desire. Kathy Acker is among those Block thanks in her acknowledgments, and, in doing so, Block tells us how we must read her. It places her in a tradition that stretches back through Acker, B. S. Johnson (the pages of his *The Unfortunates* can be read in any order—the life of the wretched is the same no matter how one reads it), William Gass (*Willie Masters' Lonesome Wife*), Ann Quin (*Tripticks*), Abraham Lincoln Gillespie (who practiced automatic writing), and Sterne, if not farther—fucking with the form of fiction to write what needs to be written. [Robert Buckeye]

Donna Seaman. *Writers on the Air: Conversations about Books*. Paul Dry Books. 2005. 467 pp. $24.95. Vendela Vida, ed. *The Believer Book of Writers Talking to Writers*. Believer Books, 2005. 485 pp. Paper: $18.00.

When a writer is interviewed, there's often the risk that he or she will come off like an idiot or inadvertently gut their work of significance. Neither of those things is avoided in the books under review, but the self-embarrassment is minimal.

The first title collects thirty-two interviews ably conducted by Donna Seaman and drawn from her radio program *Open Books*. A gentle and skilled interrogator, she clearly does her own research. Margaret Atwood's self-congratulation leaps off the page, while Peter Carey takes the questions, broadens them, and courteously involves Seaman in the process. Philip Lopate preens, while Diane Ackerman infectiously enthuses. Aleksandar Hemon is unfettered: "Nonfiction is for cowards" puts things clearly, contrasting with Lee Gutkind making a case for creative nonfiction and Ward Just arguing that journalism is the best way to "get into the way of life." Such contrasts enrich the book. T. C. Boyle's views on the decline of the environment are counterbalanced by Wade Davis and Sy Montgomery. First-time novelists understandably speak on more narrow topics, but Seaman respects each guest's contribution. Such is the power of radio that it can throw a veil over all disfigurements, despite its apparent intimacy. Unfortunately, the editing methodology behind the transposition of the spoken word to the page so as to "conform to print conventions" and make the interviews easier reading is not revealed.

The mediums in Vendela Vida's *Believer* book include regular mail, e-mail, telephone, fax, and in-person interviews. Each subject was chosen because someone said, "I'd like to have a conversation with ____." The results show that a national broadcast can cow those who are intrepid in print. Edward P. Jones opens up to Z. Z. Packer more than he did with Seaman. Since interrogator and subject know each other, the interplay between Zadie Smith and Ian McEwan, Adam Thirlwell and Tom Stoppard, Dave Eggers and Joan Didion, or, especially, Ben Marcus and George Saunders, display humor and a performance aspect which are often missing from pronouncements on what the role of the artist is in today's world. Jonathan Lethem and Thisbe Nissen ask questions that are more insightful than the answers Paul Auster and Siri Hustvedt supply. When Janet Malcolm gets " all huffy" over a vexing topic, she analyses her reaction for the benefit of Daphne Beal, and concludes: "even journalists are not immune to the vanity and self-deception that interviews bring out in their subjects and that journalists, like novelists, lie in wait for." Readers of these books will come to their own conclusions on how the subjects accidentally reveal or hide themselves. Vida and Seaman have compiled entertaining and valuable sources for further examination of new and familiar authors. [Jeff Bursey]

Books Received

Ardizzone, Tony, ed. *The Habit of Arts*. Indiana Univ. Press, 2005. $50.00. (F)

Arvio, Sarah. *Sono*. Knopf, 2006. $23.00. (P)

Balina, Marina, Helena Goscilo, and Mark Lipovetsky, eds. *Politicizing Magic*. Northwestern Univ. Press, 2005. $24.95. (NF)

Barone, Dennis. *Precise Machine*. Quale Press, 2006. Paper: $14.00. (F)

Bell, Sam Hanna. *December Bride*. Dufour Editions, 2006. Paper: $17.95. (F)

Bellmer, Hans. *The Doll*. Trans. Malcolm Green. Atlas, 2005. £ 20.00. (F)

Broderick, John. *The Pilgrimage*. Dufour Editions, 2006. Paper: $19.95. (F)

—. *The Waking of Willie Ryan*. Dufour Editions, 2006. Paper: $19.95. (F)

Bykov, Vasil, and Boris Yamplsky. *The Sacred Generation: Two Novels*. Trans. Rachel Polonsky and John Dewey. Glas, 2005. Paper: $15.95.

Close, Helena. *Pinhead Duffy*. Dufour Editions, 2006. Paper: $16.95. (F)

Costello, Brian. *The Enchanters vs. Sprawlburg Springs*. Featherproof Books, 2005. Paper: $12.95. (F)

Cravan, Arthur, Jacques Rigaut, Julien Torma, and Jaucques Vache. *4 Dada Suicides*. Trans. Terry Hale, Paul Lenti, and Iain White. Atlas, 2005. £20.00. (F)

Curran, Colleen. *Guests of Chance*. Goose Lane Editions, 2005. $22.95. (F)

Davis, Kathryn. *The Thin Place*. Little, Brown, 2006. $23.95. (F)

Dobychin, Leonid. *Encounters With Lise*. Trans. Richard C. Borden with Natalia Belova. Northwestern Univ. Press, 2005. Paper: $16.95. (F)

Domingues, Carlos Maria. *The House of Paper*. Harcourt, 2005. $18.00. (F)

Dorner, Francoise. *The Woman in the Row Behind*. Trans. Adriana Hunter. Other Press, 2006. Paper: $14.00. (F)

Evslin, Tom. *Hackoff.com*. dotHill Press, 2006. $24.95. (F)

Foster, Edward. *What He Ought to Know: New and Selected Poems*. Marsh Hawk Press, 2006. Paper: $10.00. (P)

Franco, Jorge. *Rosario Tijeras*. Trans. Gregory Rabassa. Seven Stories Press, 2004. Paper: $13.95. (F)

Gaitskill, Mary. *Veronica.* Pantheon, 2005. $23.00. (F)

Garber, Eugene K. *Vienna ØØ.* Spuyten Duyvil, 2006. Paper: $14.95. (F)

Gordon, Bill. *Mary After All.* Dial Press, 2006. Paper: $14.00. (F)

Grimes, Christopher. *Public Works.* FC2, 2005. Paper: $15.95. (F)

Groot, Tracy. *Madman.* Moody Publishers, 2006. Paper: $12.99. (F)

Harper, Rachel. *Brass Ankle Blues.* Touchstone, 2006. $23.00. (F)

Harrigan, Stephen. *Challenger Park.* Knopf, 2006. $24.95. (F)

Hastings, Max. *Warriors.* Knopf, 2006. $27.50. (NF)

Herrin, Lamar. *House of the Deaf.* Unbridled Books, 2005. $23.95. (F)

Hirshfield, Jane. *After.* HarperCollins, 2006. $23.95. (P)

James, P. D. *The Lighthouse.* Knopf, 2005. $25.95. (F)

Janko, James. *Buffalo Boy and Geronimo.* Curbstone Press, 2006. Paper: $15.00. (F)

Jenson, Kim. *The Woman I Left Behind.* Curbstone Press, 2006. Paper: $15.00. (F)

Katz, Steve. *Antonello's Lion.* Green Integer, 2005. Paper: $14.95. (F)

Kelly, Adrian Michael. *Down Sterling Road.* Coach House Books, 2005. Paper: $16.95. (F)

Kingston, Madelin. *Something in the Head: The Life and Work of John Broderick.* Dufour Editions, 2006. Paper: $22.95. (NF)

Knight, Arthur Winfield. *Blue Skies Falling.* Forge, 2001. $22.95. (F)

Koethe, John. *Sally's Hair.* HarperCollins, 2006. $24.95. (P)

Lasker-Schuler, Else. *Three Plays.* Trans. Jane Curtis. Northwestern Univ. Press, 2005. $74.95. (F)

Lebert, Benjamin. *The Bird Is a Raven.* Knopf, 2006. $16.95. (F)

Lenz, Millicent and Carole Scott eds. *His Dark Materials Illuminated.* Wayne State Univ. Press, 2005. Paper: $25.95. (NF)

Maharaj, Rabindranath. *A Perfect Pledge.* Farrar, Straus & Giroux, 2005. $25.00. (F)

Manrique-Hyland, Lory. *Revolutions.* Dufour Editions, 2006. Paper: $18.95. (F)

Martin, David Lozell. *Facing Rushmore.* Simon & Schuster, 2005. $23.00. (F)

Mathews, Harry, and Alastair Brotchie, eds. *Oulipo Compendium.* Atlas, 2005. Paper: $19.99. (NF)

McGahern, John. *All Will Be Well.* Knopf, 2006. $25.00. (NF)

McInerney, Jay. *The Good Life.* Knopf, 2006. $25.00. (F)

Meras, Icchokas. *Stalemate.* Other Press, 2005. Paper: $13.95. (F)

Mesler, Corey. *We Are Billion Year Old Carbon.* Livingston Press, 2006. Paper: $14.95. (F)

Mozetic, Brane. *Passion.* Talisman House, 2005. Paper: $14.95. (F)

Nicaud, Edgar. *Tremble + Ennui.* Coat Pocket Press, 2006. Paper: $8.95. (F)

Nielsen, Francis W. *The Witness of St. Ansgar's.* Steerforth Press, 2006. $23.95. (F)

Olsen, Lance. *Nietzsche's Kisses.* FC2, 2006. Paper: $15.95. (F)

Pearcy, Lee T. *The Grammar of Our Civility.* Baylor Univ. Press, 2005. Paper: $24.95. (NF)

Pettet, Simon. *More Winnowed Fragments.* Talisman House Publishers, 2005. Paper: $10.95. (P)

Place, Vanessa, Jennifer Calkins, Pam Ore, and Teresa Carmody. *TrenchArt Material.* Les Figues Press, 2005. Paper: $13.00. (F)

Rees, Ellen. *On the Margins.* Dufour Editions, 2006. Paper: $38.95. (F)

Rezenikoff, Charles. *The Poems of Charles Rezenikoff.* Black Sparrow Books, 2005. $45.00. (P)

Rice, Anne. *Christ the Lord: Out of Egypt.* Knopf, 2005. $25.95. (F)

Rodriguez, Ralph E. *Brown Gumshooes.* Univ. of Texas Press, 2005. $40.00. (NF)

Savage, Sam. *Firmin.* Coffee House Press, 2006. Paper: $14.95. (F)

Schaffert, Timothy. *The Singing and Dancing Daughters of God.* Unbridled Books, 2005. Paper: $14.95. (F)

Schwarts, Leonard. *Ear and Ethos.* Talisman House Publishers, 2005. Paper: $13.95. (P)

Shapiro, Susan. *Lighting Up.* Delta, 2006. Paper: $10.00. (NF)

Shelton, Richard W. *Children of the Fire.* Xlibris, 2005 $26.96. (F)

Shepherd, Paul. *More Like Not Running Away.* Sarabande Books, 2005. Paper: $14.95. (F)

Shumaker, Peggy, and Kesler E. Woodward. *Blaze.* Red Hen Press, 2005. $39.95. (P)

Smith, Patti. *Auguries of Innocence.* HarperCollins, 2005. $22.95. (P)

Snyder, Jason, ed. *New Standards: The First Decade of Fiction at Fourteen Hills.* Fourteen Hills Press, 2005. Paper: $15.00. (F)

Sobin, Gustaf. *The Places as Preludes.* Talisman House Publishers, 2005. Paper: $14.95. (P)

Sternburg, Janet. *Optic Nerve: Poems and Photographs.* Red Hen Press, 2005. Paper: 16.95. (P)

Thilleman, Todd. *Gowanus Canal, Hans Knudsen.* Spuyten Duyvil, 2006. Paper: $14.00. (F)

Thomas, Edward. *The Ship of Swallows.* Dufour Editions, 2006. $39.95. (F)

Umrigar, Thrity. *The Space between Us.* William Morrow, 2005. $24.95. (F)

Wasserstein, Wendy. *Elements of Style.* Knopf, 2006. $24.95. (F)

Wineberg, Ronna. *Second Language.* New Rivers Press, 2005. Paper: $14.95. (F)

Winthrop, Elizabeth Hartley. *Fireworks.* Knopf, 2006. $23.95. (F)
Wright, Franz. *God's Silence.* Knopf, 2006. $24.00. (P)
Young, David. *Black Lab.* Knopf, 2006. $23.00. (P)

Contributors

DANIELLE ALEXANDER teaches creative writing, writing, and literature at Belmont University. She has published work in a variety of national literary and nonfiction periodicals.

PEDRO PONCE teaches fiction writing and twentieth-century American literature at St. Lawrence University. His fiction has appeared previously in *Ploughshares*, *The Beacon Best of 2001*, *3rd bed*, *DIAGRAM*, and other publications.

ALICITA RODRÍGUEZ teaches creative writing and literature at Western State College in Colorado. Her fiction has appeared or is forthcoming in *TriQuarterly*, *New Letters*, and the anthology *Coloring Book*. Additionally, she serves as fiction editor for the literary magazine *Marginalia*.

Robert Creeley • Gertrude Stein
dous Huxley • Robert Coover • Jo
rth • David Markson • Flann O'Bri

www.dalkeyarchive.com

uis-Ferdinand Céli • Marguer
ung • Ishmael Reed • Camilo José C
Gilbert Sorrentino • Ann Quin
icholas Mosley • Douglas Woolf
ymond Queneau • Harry Mathews
kki Ducornet • José Lezama Lima
dan Higgins • Ben Marcus • Colem
owell • Jacques Roubaud • Dju
rnes • Felipe Alfau • Osman Lins
avid Antin • Susan Daitch • Vikt
klovsky • Henry Green • Curtis Wh
Anne Carson • John Hawkes • Fo
adox Ford • Janice Galloway • Mich

Your connection to literature.
DALKEY ARCHIVE PRESS

Bard   FICTION PRIZE

Bard College invites submissions for its annual Fiction Prize for young writers.

The Bard Fiction Prize is awarded annually to a promising, emerging writer who is a United States citizen aged 39 years or younger at the time of application. In addition to a monetary award of $30,000, the winner receives an appointment as writer-in-residence at Bard College for one semester without the expectation that he or she teach traditional courses. The recipient will give at least one public lecture and will meet informally with students.

To apply, candidates should write a cover letter describing the project they plan to work on while at Bard and submit a C.V., along with three copies of the published book they feel best represents their work. No manuscripts will be accepted.

Applications for the 2007 prize must be received by July 15, 2006. For further information about the Bard Fiction Prize, call 845-758-7087, send an e-mail to bfp@bard.edu, or visit www.bard.edu/bfp. Applicants may also request information by writing to the Bard Fiction Prize, Bard College, Annandale-on-Hudson, NY 12504-5000.

Bard College
PO Box 5000, Annandale-on-Hudson, NY 12504-5000

Golden Handcuffs Review

NEW WORK BY:

Rachel Tzvia Back	Tim Keane	Joe Ashby Porter
Daniel Borzutsky	Stacey Levine	Matthew Roberson
Laynie Browne	Catherine A.F.	Jerome Rothenberg
Bill Dorn	Macgillivray	Jacques Roubaud
Emily Grosholz	Harry Mathews	Lou Rowan
Anna Maria Hong	Douglas Messerli	Alan Singer
Jeanne Heuving	Robert Mittenthal	Dionysius Solomos
Leslie Kaplan	Toby Olson	Bruce Stater
David Karp	Michael Palmer	James Tierney

SUBSCRIPTIONS, $12/ ANNUM BOX 20158, SEATTLE, WA 98102

www.goldenhandcuffsreview.com

DISTRIBUTORS: INGRAM 800-627-6247; DEBOER, 973-667-9300, UBIQUITY 718-875-5491

DELILLO FIEDLER GASS PYNCHON
University of Delaware Press
Collections on Contemporary Masters

UNDERWORDS
Perspectives on Don
DeLillo's *Underworld*

**Edited by Joseph Dewey, Steven
G. Kellman, and Irving Malin**

Essays by Jackson R. Bryer,
David Cowart, Kathleen
Fitzpatrick, Joanne Gass, Paul
Gleason, Donald J. Greiner,
Robert McMinn, Thomas Myers,
Ira Nadel, Carl Ostrowski,
Timothy L. Parrish, Marc Singer,
and David Yetter

$39.50

LESLIE FIEDLER
AND AMERICAN
CULTURE

**Edited by Steven G. Kellman
and Irving Malin**

Essays by John Barth, Robert
Boyers, James M. Cox, Joseph
Dewey, R.H.W. Dillard, Geoffrey
Green, Irving Feldman, Leslie
Fiedler, Susan Gubar, Jay L.
Halio, Brooke Horvath, David
Ketterer, R.W.B. Lewis, Sanford
Pinsker, Harold Schechter, Daniel
Schwarz, David R. Slavitt, Daniel
Walden, and Mark Royden
Winchell

$36.50

INTO *THE TUNNEL*
Readings of Gass's
Novel

**Edited by Steven G. Kellman
and Irving Malin**

Essays by Rebecca Goldstein,
Donald J. Greiner, Brooke
Horvath, Marcus Klein, Jerome
Klinkowitz, Paul Maliszewski,
James McCourt, Arthur Saltzman,
Susan Stewart, and Heide Ziegler

$35.00

PYNCHON AND
MASON & DIXON

**Edited by Brooke Horvath and
Irving Malin**

Essays by Jeff Baker, Joseph
Dewey, Bernard Duyfhuizen,
David Foreman, Donald J.
Greiner, Brian McHale, Clifford
S. Mead, Arthur Saltzman,
Thomas H. Schaub, David Seed,
and Victor Strandberg

$39.50

ORDER FROM ASSOCIATED UNIVERSITY PRESSES
2010 Eastpark Blvd., Cranbury, New Jersey 08512
PH 609-655-4770   FAX 609-655-8366   E-mail AUP440@ aol.com

NOON

A LITERARY ANNUAL

1369 MADISON AVENUE   PMB 298
NEW YORK   NEW YORK   10128-0711

EDITION PRICE $9 DOMESTIC $14 FOREIGN

Visions of Alterity
Representation in the Works of John Banville

Elke D'hoker

Amsterdam/New York, NY 2004. VII, 243 pp.
(Costerus NS 151)

ISBN: 90-420-1671-X   € 50,-/US$ 63.-

Visions of Alterity: Representation in the Works of John Banville offers detailed and original readings of the work of the Irish author John Banville, one of the foremost figures in contemporary European literature. It investigates one of the fundamental concerns of Banville's novels: mediating the gap between subject and object or self and world in representation. By drawing on the rich history of the problem of representation in literature, philosophy and literary theory, this study provides a thorough insight into the rich philosophical and intertextual dimension of Banville's fiction. In close textual analyses of Banville's most important novels, it maps out a thematic development that moves from an interest in the epistemological and aesthetic representation of the world in scientific theories, over a concern with the ethical dimension of representations, to an exploration of self-representation and identity. What remains constant throughout these different perspectives is the disruption of representations by brief but haunting glimpses of otherness. In tracing these different visions of alterity in Banville's solipsistic literary world, this study offers a better understanding of his insistent and thought-provoking exploration of what it means to be human.

USA/Canada: 906 Madison Avenue, UNION, NJ 07083, USA
Call toll-free (USA only)1-800-225-3998, Tel. 908 206 1166, Fax 908-206-0820
All other countries: Tijnmuiden 7, 1046 AK Amsterdam, The Netherlands.
Tel. ++ 31 (0)20 611 48 21, Fax ++ 31 (0)20 447 29 79
Orders-queries@rodopi.nl   www.rodopi.nl
Please note that the exchange rate is subject to fluctuations

the minnesota review

*a journal
of committed writing*

www.theminnesotareview.org

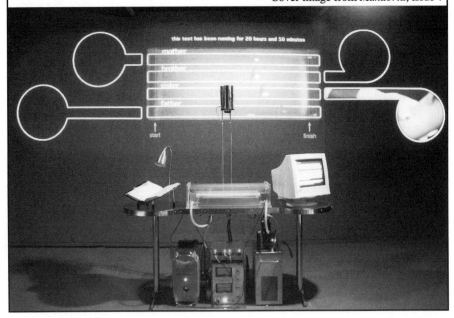

Dalkey Archive Press

NEW RELEASES

Look at the Dark
NICHOLAS MOSLEY

The King
DONALD BARTHELME

In Night's City
DOROTHY NELSON

Distant Relations
CARLOS FUENTES

Realm of the Dead
UCHIDA HYAKKEN

Voices from Chernobyl
SVETLANA ALEXIEVICH

A retired academic and writer becomes a media celebrity, appearing on talk shows to voice his controversial views on human nature and the state of the world ("Of course the FBI do not want to discover actual bombers!"). While in New York, he is the victim of a hit-and-run and ends up confined to a hospital bed. This forced inactivity allows him time to reflect. Dredging up long-buried memories while trying to make sense of the here and now, the narrator begins to see his provocative ideas about fidelity, sin, and grace play themselves out in his own life.

Look at the Dark

NICHOLAS MOSLEY

Coleman Dowell British Literature Series
A Novel
$13.95 / paper
ISBN: 1-56478-407-X

"Mosley's latest offers a phantasmagoric journey through the darkness of memory and the human psyche, with the narrator probing the shortcomings of love, the anxieties of relationships, the inadequacy of language, the ambivalence of family life, and the absurdities of political life."

—*Library Journal*

"Rife with erotic, political, metaphysical, and moral implications, his piquant musings unobtrusively explicate the tragedies of war, the divides between men and women and humans and animals, the threat of chaos, and the struggle to do right."

—*Booklist*

On the night of a father's death, Esther, the wife denied, and
Sara, her corrupted daughter, look back at the father's overwhelming cruelty and ahead to their freedom from him. Liber-
ated from his terrible physical and emotional abuse, they must
decide whether they will accept new possibilities or conform
to old values. The darkness, no matter how black, is not complete: "I don't hate being a woman," Sara tells herself. "I don't."
Beautifully written and remarkably powerful, *In Night's City*
extends the tradition of the lyrical, impressionistic Irish novel.

In Night's City

Dorothy Nelson

Irish Literature Series
A Novel
$11.95 / paper
ISBN: 1-56478-418-5

"It is both impressive and utterly compelling."
—*Image Magazine*

"For women who have experienced the intimidation of a
city at night, and learned where the power in society rests,
this book will find a friend."
—*Workers Life*

Distant Relations begins in the elegant Automobile Club de France, as an elderly Count tells a rambling story to a much younger friend—but the book doesn't remain there. As the Count speaks, the novel moves across time and space, from Latin America to Europe, from generation to generation. It is a story of lost memories and failed promises, a story about the past's unyielding influence on the present. In *Distant Relations*, a tale of confused familial relationships explodes into one about the conflict between the Old World and the New.

Distant Relations

CARLOS FUENTES
TRANSLATION BY
MARGARET SAYERS PEDEN

A LANNAN SELECTION
Latin American Literature Series
A Novel
$13.50 / paper
ISBN: 1-56478-345-6

"Carlos Fuentes in all his books draws tight a tense conjunction of opposites. . . . In *Distant Relations* . . . these tensions operate in a cat's cradle of plot, crisscrossing each other to make a puzzle worthy of Poe or Borges."
—Guy Davenport, *New York Times*

"*Distant Relations* is a ghostly poem, a vexing puzzle, an amazingly constructed argument on the relatedness of human spirits, past and present."
—William Kennedy, *Washington Post Book World*

With a series of disconnected dreams and images that fade into one another without logic, these stories describe the worlds of both the living and the dead. In one story, the narrator watches footage from the Russo-Japanese War, but then, moving across the screen, finds himself fighting in the war. In another, the narrator goes to a freak show with a woman, only to find the woman herself has become a freak. One of the foremost innovators of Japanese modernism, Hyakken incorporates a non-Western set of myths that opens doors into another world.

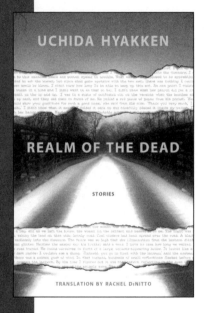

Realm of the Dead

Uchida Hyakken
Translation by Rachel DiNitto

Japanese Literature Series
Stories
$22.95 / cloth
ISBN: 1-56478-447-9

from *Realm of the Dead*:

"As to whether this all really happened, or whether improbable delusions have crept into my already hazy memories, I no longer know myself."

"I picked up my pace and caught up with the girl. I tried to pull her sleeve. She rejected me a second time with a tearful gaze and hurried after the old woman. Right there I resolved to kill the old woman."

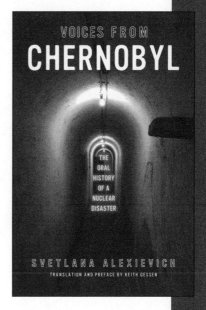

ORDER FORM

Individuals may use this form to subscribe to the *Review of Contemporary Fiction* or to order back issues of the *Review* and Dalkey Archive titles at a discount (see below for details).

Title	ISBN	Quantity	Price

Subtotal _____

Less Discount _____
(10% for one book, 20% for two or more books)

Subtotal _____

Plus Postage _____
(domestic: $3 + $1 per book / foreign: $5 + $3 per book)

1 Year Individual Subscription to the **Review** _____
($17 domestic, $20.50 foreign)

Total _____

Mailing Address _____

_____

_____

_____

xxvi/1

Credit card payment ☐ Visa ☐ Mastercard

Acct # _____ Exp. Date _____

Name on card _____ Phone # _____

Please make checks (in U.S. dollars only) payable to *Dalkey Archive Press*

mail or fax this form to: Dalkey Archive Press, ISU Campus Box 8905, Normal, IL 61790-8905; *fax:* 309.438.7422; *tel:* 309.438.7555